Where
the
Waters
Divide

W h e r e
t h e
W a t e r s
D i v i d e

A 3,000-Mile Trek Along
America's Continental Divide

by Karen Berger
and
Daniel R. Smith

The Countryman Press / Woodstock, Vermont

Library of Congress Cataloging-in-Publication Data

Berger, Karen, 1959–
    Where the waters divide : a 3,000-mile trek along America's Continental Divide / by Karen Berger and Daniel R. Smith. — 1st pbk. ed.
        p.   cm.
    Originally published: New York : Harmony Books, 1993.
    Includes index.
    ISBN 1-88150-403-3 (alk. paper)
    1. Continental Divide National Scenic Trail. 2. Hiking—Continental Divide National Scenic Trail. I. Smith, Daniel R. (Daniel Richard), 1946–. II. Title.
F721.B47   1997
917.3—dc21
                                                                97-23823
                                                                    CIP

Published by The Countryman Press, Inc., a division of W. W. Norton & Co., P.O. Box 748, Woodstock, VT 05091

Distributed by W. W. Norton & Co., 500 Fifth Avenue, New York, NY 10110

Printed in the United States of America
10 9 8 7 6 5 4 3 2 1

To those who walked with us:

Gordon Smith, Sue Lockwood, Karl Haupt, Dave Plum, Sandy Borthick, Deb Bornemeier, Mardell Gunn, Anne Emry, Steve Emry, and Tom Carlin.

"There are none happy in the world but beings who enjoy freely a vast horizon."
—*Thoreau*

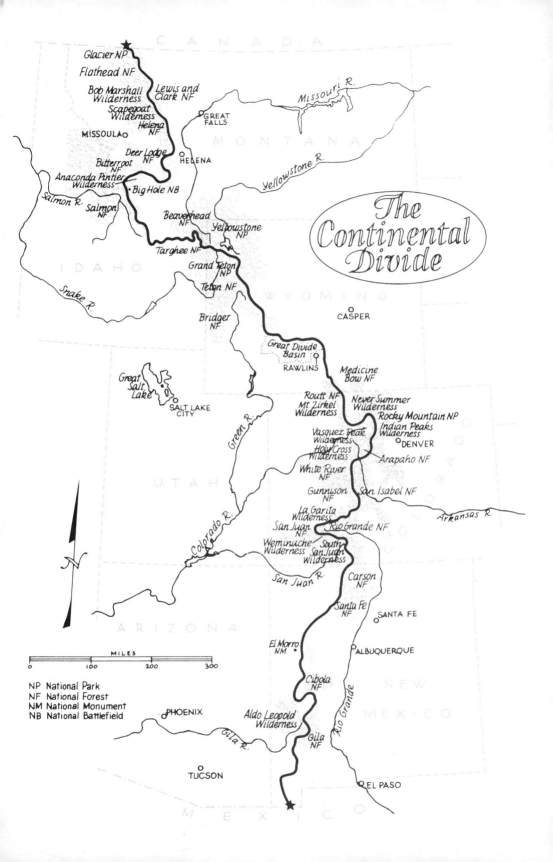

Contents

Acknowledgments

Perhaps the most rewarding part of this project is to be able to thank the many, many people who helped us on our way. It would have been impossible to attempt—let alone complete—both our walk and this book without their help and support.

We are grateful to all of our friends who took our dream into their hearts, each in his or her own way: by following our progress, sending us care packages, joining us for part of our journey, or helping us out with everything from passing on messages to ordering library books to packing boxes of food and gear. Particularly, we extend our heartfelt thanks to Tony Verrelli, Brian Nickerson, Mike Halloran, and Ralph Johnson, for their countless favors—before, during, and after our journey. Without them on hand to order maps, move furniture, drive us to airports, make travel arrangements, and handle a host of other such chores, we might never have even gotten on the plane west. Thanks to Linda Soldatos for managing the homefront during our extended absences. To Pat Lisella, for mailing us 80 boxes of food and gear, giving us a place to stay when we visited New York, and stepping in when we needed help. To Karl Haupt and John Graham, for contributing both their expertise and time to mapping out our route. To Sandy Borthick and John Bentz, for carting, storing, and mailing various boxes of gear. To Dan Cooper, for smoothing our way through Montana. And to Gordon Smith and Sue Lockwood, whose encouragement, help, and friendship meant so much to us throughout the trip.

Thanks are also due to our literary agent, Susan Levin, who represented us with enthusiasm, energy, and encouragement; and to our editor, John Michel, whose deft touch and incisive comments made this book a joy to work on and, undoubtedly, a much better book to read.

We are grateful to Iona College, which provided funds to support Dan's participation in this project as part of its faculty fellowship program. We also thank the professionals at the Iona College library, secretarial services, and computer center for their much appreciated assistance during our research and writing. And we thank Dan's colleagues in the history department, who dealt with his impossible schedule and frequent traveling with flexibility and understanding.

We also thank the many people who took the time to talk to us about their areas of expertise, particularly the recreation and trail managers of the National Forest Service and the National Park Service, and the local historians, environmental activists, ranchers, loggers, and community leaders who shared their love of the West with us when we barged into their lives asking for "a few minutes of their time."

We are grateful to the countless strangers who smoothed our way, offering us water, food, encouragement, shelter, rides, and help. We thank them not only for what they did for us, but also for what they taught us: that America is full of kindnesses, big hearts, and open doors. In such ways do strangers become friends. In particular, we thank Steve and Barbara Green, Charlotte Trego, and Donna and Ken McMurry, who not only helped us while we were walking, but who also assisted us when we returned to do research for this book.

Finally, we would like to thank Jim Wolf, director of the Continental Divide Trail Society. We owe Jim a debt of gratitude, not only for generously taking the time to share his expertise with us, but also for the vision and years of hard work that he has put into making the Continental Divide Trail a reality.

Readers interested in more information about the Continental Divide National Scenic Trail are urged to write to the Continental Divide Trail Society, P.O. Box 30002, Bethesda, Maryland 20824.

Where
the
Waters
Divide

〜〜〜〜〜〜〜

INTRODUCTION

≈≈≈≈≈

The woods are quiet and the stream innocuous, no more than a few feet wide, not even knee-deep. It barely seems to merit its grand name: Two Ocean Creek.

It's warm this late September morning in northern Wyoming, but not warm enough to conceal that the seasons are changing. There's been a cold snap to the air at night and by morning ice clogs our water bottles. The sun, too, hints at winter sluggishness, rising later each day and retiring earlier. At higher elevations, the aspen have already turned, and their delicate branches quake with a treasury of gold leaf coins.

We are walking north into winter. We've been walking for 136 days now, almost 2,000 miles since we left the Mexican border, heading for Canada at 2.5 miles per hour. The deserts of New

Mexico, the Colorado Rockies, Wyoming's Great Divide Basin are all behind us. In front of us is another 900 miles.

Our pace is steady, as it has to be—15 miles a day, sometimes more. But at the moment we're standing still, staring down at the creek.

There is but one remarkable thing about this creek: On its way downhill it hits a geographical feature called the Continental Divide. We are at a place called "Parting of the Waters," which explains the name of the little creek. Here, in this remote spot in the Teton Wilderness, you can watch as the Divide goes about its business of defining America's watersheds. The waters of Two Ocean Creek are indeed headed to opposite ends of the continent.

Half of the stream turns east and becomes Atlantic Creek. This water will end up—if it is not used first—in the Gulf of Mexico via the Yellowstone, Missouri, and Mississippi rivers. Pacific Creek casts its lot with the Snake and Columbia rivers on its journey to the northwest coast. On the way—whichever way they go—the waters from Two Ocean Creek will be imprisoned in dams, trapped in irrigation ditches, drunk by cattle, siphoned off for industry, funneled through dishwashers and bathtubs, and enjoyed by windsurfers, boaters, and fishermen before they finally break free in the salty surf of their final destinations.

We have been following the Continental Divide north all the way from the Mexican border—over mesas and mountains, through deserts and plateaus, and over some of the highest peaks in the Rocky Mountains. Yet this is the first time we have actually seen the Divide at work.

I throw a leaf into the water and it floats along uncertainly, snags against a rotting log, stops. I try again, this time with a twig.

Dan looks puzzled. "What are you doing?"

"Which way do you think it will go?" I ask, watching the stick as it begins to drift downstream. There's a long journey ahead for this twig. A small wooden Forest Service sign, with arrows pointing east and west, tells us the distances to salt water: "ATLANTIC OCEAN, 3488 MILES; PACIFIC OCEAN, 1353 MILES." Our little stick might not last that long: It might be used in a bird's nest, or entangled in streamside brush, or washed ashore. But it could end up in an ocean. Which one will it be?

The Blackfoot Indians of northern Montana call the Continental

Divide the "Center of the World." On maps, the Divide is an irrefutable line running from the tip of Patagonia to the Bering Sea, a landmark as incontrovertible as the Great Wall of China.

In practice, it is not as simple as all that. Contrary to our image of it, the Divide is not a single, discrete ridge, but rather a collection of mountain chains. It did not form all at once, the product of some mammoth geological upheaval, but rather evolved, over time, as the waters that fell in its mountains found their way downhill to the faraway seas.

In one sense, there is nothing special about the Continental Divide. Every river system on earth is separated from every other river system by a "divide." Divides are merely the boundaries of watersheds; they define drainages by sending runoff into trickles, trickles into streams, streams into tributaries, tributaries into rivers. Functionally, the Continental Divide is no different from the divides that separate the Rhine from the Danube, or the Nile from the Congo, or the Ganges from the Indus.

What is special about the Continental Divide is the way it goes about its business. No other divide presumes to split the river systems of not only one continent but two, from southernmost Patagonia to the Bering Strait, from a latitude of 55 degrees south to a latitude of 65 degrees north. No other divide separates drainages in such continental proportions, sending rivers not only in different directions but to different oceans. And no other divide follows so dramatic, rugged, and diverse a topography as the divide that runs through the great mountain chains of North and South America.

The Continental Divide is a dominant feature—perhaps *the* dominant feature—in the landscape of the American West; everyone can tell you where it is, and when highways cross its crest there is invariably a sign. Yet despite this dominance, the Continental Divide is not always obvious. It stays on neither the highest peaks nor the most conspicuous crests; sometimes it veers off a perfectly obvious ridge to head down the flank of a mountain and then back up quite a different slope. It hides itself among waves of parallel ridges; it masquerades as just another unimportant bump in the flatlands of New Mexico and southern Wyoming. Sometimes it goes on long detours, making 100-mile curves to the east or the west.

But here, in this quiet place in the Teton Wilderness, perhaps as nowhere else, the Continental Divide reveals itself and its job as clearly as the line on the map. There is no doubt at all where it is or what it does: It is under our feet, and it parts America's water.

For a moment, the twig floats, and then it drifts aimlessly downstream. It picks up speed, swirling around a few times as it rides the eddies like a pinball trapped in a maze of hazards. Ricocheting off rocks, it stumbles along, now bouncing to the right, then to the left. Finally, it swivels around one last time, pauses, and catches a last decisive current. And then it is gone—on a 3,500-mile journey to the Atlantic Ocean.

We go on, too, walking north. To Canada.

〰〰〰

Dan and I had first talked about the trip three years earlier, standing in front of a huge physical relief map of the United States. We were in Shenandoah National Park—we had just finished a hike and were taking a break in one of the park lodges. I was half watching a football game on television; Dan's attention was snared by the map, his hand caught in the bumpy ridges of Colorado.

"This would be a great hike," he said.

"Colorado?" I asked.

But Dan's reach extended to include nothing less than the length of the United States—the Continental Divide, from Mexico to Canada. "It would be a great hike," he repeated.

As simple as that: Let's go on a hike. No matter that it was 3,000 or so miles and could take anywhere from six to eight months. No matter that my longest hike to date had barely hit the 50-mile mark. No matter—although this didn't quite occur to me at the time—that Dan had just proposed to walk up the length of the entire country.

"It would," I said absently, absorbed in a touchdown pass.

"We could do it," Dan said.

I don't remember exactly how I responded—something about jobs, money, schedules.

Dan went home to New York and started collecting information. I went home to Virginia and almost forgot about the conversation. Almost. In the back of my mind, the idea took hold.

〰〰〰

The Continental Divide. The Backbone of America. America's Rooftop. The Great Divide. Whatever you call it, it is a grand idea—a mountain ridge that divides a continent. A formidable reality, too, as every early American trapper, explorer, mountain man, railroad baron, miner, or settler well knew. The Divide was an obstacle, a barrier to every historical movement west. Littered along its landscapes are the ruins of ancient Indian civilizations, the settlements of early Spanish missionaries, the ghost towns of miners, and the trails of pioneers and explorers. Back then, the goal was simply to cross it: climb over it, find an easy way around it, tunnel through it. But walk alongside of it?

In 1968, Congress passed the National Trails System Act and designated the Appalachian Trail (AT) and the Pacific Crest Trail (PCT) as the first two national scenic trails. It appointed a team to study other trails for inclusion in the system, and specifically recommended evaluation of the possibility of building a trail along the Continental Divide. In 1978, the Continental Divide Trail was approved, and work on it began.

As the nineteenth-century settlers would have been able to tell you, constructing a trail along the Divide is no simple matter. A trail of this length is a quixotic thing. When completed, the CDT will stretch for 3,000 miles, give or take a hundred or two, through three national parks, twenty-four national forests, and three Indian reservations, as well as wilderness areas, private lands, Bureau of Land Management (BLM) acrcage, lands managed for grazing or timber, lands too close to cities to offer a genuine wilderness experience, lands so remote and barren that no one would ever hike them unless they were part of something grand. The amount of red tape is mind-boggling, and the clephantine machinery of government work has only begun to grind out its abundance of plans, reports, assessments, and analyses of how to put a trail along this impossible terrain of rock and sand and ice. It is a herculean task. Seventy years of work went into assuring the Appalachian Trail its current, protected corridor; the Continental Divide Trail will probably not be completely finished—constructed, marked, and secured through land acquisition and easement—until well into the twenty-first century.

The sheer audacity of a long-distance trail captures the imagination. It fuels dreams of adventure. And if adventure is what you are looking for, the Continental Divide may be the best place left to find it in the contiguous United States—now, before it is marked from one end to another, before it has been tamed. Now, before the footsteps of other hikers have smoothed the trail before you. Now, when the route is still so incomplete that every person who walks on it takes a different path—his or her own.

The Continental Divide crosses six of the seven ecological zones found in North America, from the harsh sands of the New Mexican desert to the arctic-alpine tundra of Colorado's highest peaks. It is remote—there are times when the nearest town or settlement is days away, times when you can look out from a mountaintop and see no sign of human habitation. And it is beautiful, with a beauty that spans the range from stark to sublime. There are peaks of indomitable granite, challenging the heavens with their bulk; there are carpets of delicate purple columbine and crimson Indian paintbrush. There are shifting sand dunes that catch the evening light in a play of shadow and contrast. And there are ice fields that dare the hiker to cross them, but then yield to the warmth of summer by melting into green glacial tarns. And always, there is the sky: cool, endless blue in the desert, angry brown in the Colorado afternoons, snow-laden gray in the north country—and at night, a field of black ink filled with more stars than the mind can comprehend.

But only part of the Divide is a wilderness. This is, after all, the late twentieth century. As a society, we have managed, in the process of consuming goods and making money, to destroy a good part of our natural heritage. There are pressures on this land. Ranchers graze their cattle on it, loggers cut down its trees, miners explore it for mineral wealth—not only gold, copper, and silver, but minerals, like molybdenum, uranium, and oil, that meet more modern needs. Recreationists camp and ski and cycle and drive and hunt and fish on the land. Power companies dam its waters; Native Americans demand their share of reserved water rights; anglers and rafters try to keep wild rivers flowing free. And then there are the government agencies charged with managing the land, and the politicians, environmentalists, and grass-roots groups claiming to represent everything from a single prize trout-fishing stream to nothing less than the entire region.

The Continental Divide bisects the American West: its cultures, its history, its environment, its conflicts. This grand idea, this formidable obstacle, was once the most remote, uninhabited part of America. Even now, it crosses the only two regions in the contiguous United States wild enough and large enough to provide a home for that wildest and largest symbol of the American wilderness—the grizzly bear.

The Divide has been used, crossed, inhabited, cursed, logged, grazed, and climbed. Has it been conquered?

≈≈≈≈≈

Perhaps there was a certain inevitability to this walk. Dan had already hiked the 2,200-mile Appalachian Trail and the 2,600-mile Pacific Crest Trail. Now he was looking for other hikes, other challenges. I, too, had spent a good part of my life in the outdoors, most recently teaching outdoor education and leading weekend trips for a variety of organizations. It was our shared love for the outdoors that had brought us together. Our first date had been a day-hike up Old Rag Mountain in Virginia; from there our relationship progressed to weekend backpacking on the Appalachian Trail and canoe trips on the Potomac River. We both had shelves of books on outdoor adventure, and dreams to match.

My dreams, at least lately, had been kept in check by the demands of urban life and the ceaseless routine of work, rent, and the pittance of two-week vacations. Dan had done a better job of assembling his world—he was a college professor with the luxury of real vacation time—but he was going to need more than that to walk the Divide. In the next year or so, he would be eligible to apply for a sabbatical. The more we thought about it, the more inevitable the trip became. We stopped saying "if" and started saying "when."

Through the winter, we talked about getting married and buying a house—normal things for a young couple. And hiking the Continental Divide. Not so normal. But the adventure bug had bit. Dan went to Washington to climb Mount Rainier and Alaska to climb Denali. We found ourselves sneaking away for mini adventures: Thanksgiving in a tent in Pennsylvania, Christmas week camping in the Tetons, President's Day skiing in Washington, and Easter in Machu Picchu in Peru. In between, we commuted between my job as a book editor in Washington, D.C., and Dan's job as a college professor in New York. We had bitten off too much; we couldn't, we finally realized, squeeze planning a 3,000-mile hike into lives already crowded with working, commuting, and traveling. We pushed the trip back a year, got married, and went to the High Sierra for our honeymoon.

It was an inauspicious start to my long-distance hiking career. We walked 200 miles. I got blisters.

When Dan's sabbatical was approved, the planning began for real. Instead of spending weekends in the woods, we had to content ourselves with maps that conjured images of wild and remote lands: Red Desert, Wind River Range, Gila Wilderness. And also: Starvation Gulch, Dead Horse Creek, Massacre Peak, Calamity Pass. Not to mention: Bad Marriage Mountain.

The prospect of walking 3,000 miles was daunting, but it was the planning that was truly overwhelming: We needed to choose a route, purchase maps, figure out where we could resupply, estimate how long it would take us to reach each successive resupply point, and pack the food we would need for each of these stretches. There was also the question of seasons: We could expect to walk through all four of them, from the blistering heat of New Mexico's deserts to the snow fields on Colorado's highest peaks. What seasonal clothes and equipment would we need? And when? Although we each already owned a complete set of backpacking gear—tents, sleeping bags, boots, rain gear, stoves, and backpacks, we needed what amounted to shopping carts loaded with supplies we were likely to use up or wear out: dozens of pairs of socks, bug repellent, suntan lotion, potscrubbers, film, notepads, soap, toothpaste, and first aid items. But by far, the biggest job was packing our food. One day, Dan returned from a trip to the grocery store with a dozen bags filled with nothing but instant soup and Ramen noodles. Another day, he filled two shopping carts with snacks. For the previous three years, I had stuck to a largely vegetarian and health food diet. Now, looking at the piles of chocolate, nuts, and sugared snacks, I suddenly realized that in the months ahead I would consume more junk food than I had previously eaten in my entire life.

But first things first. Before we could start packing, we had to resolve the most basic of issues: whether to go north to south, or south to north. Even this straightforward question became complicated. Walking south from the Alberta-Montana border would require that we wait until June to start; Glacier National Park's late-season snow-pack would make travel impossible any earlier, even with snowshoes. Between Glacier's snow-covered passes and the swollen rivers of the Bob Marshall Wilderness, a southbound hike guaranteed that we would be miserable for the first couple of hundred miles—and this before we were broken in to the trail. There would be a reward: a virtual romp through southern Montana and Wyoming. But any romp would come to an abrupt halt in Colorado, where the average elevation of the trail is more than 11,000 feet. It takes somewhere between six and eight weeks to cross Colorado, depending on your route and your strength. That would put us in the remote, high mountains of the South San Juan Wilderness in late October, just in time for winter blizzards. After that, New Mexico would be an easy finish—if we could get there.

A northbound hike had its own problems, and they were much the same. Starting in May would put us at the Colorado border in late June, before the snow that blocks the San Juans' high passes would have had time to melt. Once through southern Colorado, we would be free of winter until it caught up with us again somewhere in Montana. Whether we would be able to finish or not would be an open question until the very last.

Of course, all that assumed that nothing else stopped us first. Physical strength. Emotional strength. Blisters. Illness. *Giardia.* Navigation. Our ability to work together as a team.

Back and forth went the debate, and finally it came down to a preference for dry feet and postponed misery. We decided to start at the international border just south of Columbus, New Mexico.

Route selection was the next task.

The Continental Divide National Scenic Trail may one day exist to the same standard as its more famous cousins, the Appalachian and Pacific Crest trails. But at this point, much of it exists only on paper or in the most preliminary stages of planning and construction.

On the Appalachian Trail white blazes lead you from Georgia to Maine. You're hardly ever out of sight of a marker, and you don't even have to know how to read a topographic map. The Pacific Crest

Trail isn't marked as frequently, but it is sufficiently well blazed to allow even a novice hiker to manage with the aid of a guidebook and not much else. If you get lost on the Appalachian Trail or on the Pacific Crest Trail, and if you are lucky enough to run into a ranger, you can ask "Where is the trail?" and the ranger will know what you are talking about.

In contrast, on the Continental Divide Trail, the hiker has one small problem: Most of the trail's route has yet to be determined. There are a few published guidebooks that describe recommended routes, and sometimes government agencies, particularly in Montana, provide information about sections of trail that have been designated or completed. But in its entirety, the Continental Divide Trail exists only as a hodgepodge of plans, alternate routes, jeep tracks, cross-country bushwhacks—and yes, sometimes, cut footway. Through most of its length, if you were to get lost and ask a ranger "Where is the Continental Divide Trail?" the response would most likely be a blank stare.

For us, the fact that the trail is not yet a hiking highway was one of its attractions. An unfinished trail promised adventure and discovery; it promised that our journey would be unique. But it also added an unbelievable amount of frustration and confusion to the planning process. We decided to enlist the help of Jim Wolf, director of the Continental Divide Trail Society (CDTS) and author of the society's series of guidebooks to the trail. A lawyer based in the Washington, D.C., area, Jim is, more than any other individual, responsible for the inclusion of the CDT in the National Trails System Act. His work on behalf of the trail can only be called a labor of love, and he is knowledgeable not only about hiking concerns, such as trail conditions, but also about the Continental Divide's environment, botany, zoology, and history.

Jim agreed to help us identify a route. In some regions, like parts of Colorado, several viable alternatives exist. In Montana, the Forest Service has officially designated a preferred route but has not finished construction. In New Mexico and Wyoming, very little work has been done beyond the preliminary planning stages.

On most established hiking trails, route selection is a matter of buying the guidebooks: long-distance hikers on something as well traveled as the Appalachian Trail need only concern themselves with whether to hike solely on the official, white-blazed trail, or whether to sometimes take one of many alternate, blue-blazed trails. Debate over the status of a hiker who has taken blue-blazed detours for part of his hike—is he, or is he not, a true thru-hiker?—can fill many hours of discussion on a rainy night in an AT shelter.

On the Continental Divide, such issues are moot. Since there is no official trail to follow, there is no trail to deviate from. Perhaps a half dozen or so hikers attempt the entire trek each year, and each group must decide its own route, based on the interests and goals and abilities of its members.

Selecting a route thus becomes a process of balancing issues of practicality—is there a trail or a jeep road or a cross-country stretch that is navigable?—with the goals of a trek. It was a process intrinsically connected with the question of why we were doing this in the first place. We wanted our route to take us through the spectacular scenery of high mountain passes, and through the places that were most representative of the Divide's environment, culture, and history. And although we wanted to stay as close to the Divide as possible, we decided that we would be willing to stray somewhat away from the Divide if another route promised to be more interesting or more scenic.

There was also the issue of shortcuts. As the crow flies, the distance from Mexico to Canada is 1,200 miles; as the Divide meanders, it is 3,100. We intended to follow the Divide's serpentine wanderings, although we knew that meant more miles of walking and a greater chance of snow up north. Later, we would learn that other factors would also enter into the equation, chief among them the availability of water and the fact that many trails that are marked on Forest Service and BLM maps are so badly maintained that they have, for all practical purposes, ceased to exist. Trails deteriorate with neglect and time, as well as with more dramatic events like forest fires, timber clear cuts, new reservoirs, rock slides, and sand dunes. We were to learn that the route we intended to follow was not always possible—or even identifiable.

But that was still far in the future.

For the present, we had Jim's description of his proposed route through New Mexico, guidebooks for the other states, and a list of maps. We turned our attention to the next task: corresponding with the Geologic Survey (USGS), the Forest Service, BLM, the Park Service, state highway departments, and various county offices. Our 3,000-mile trek was going to take us beyond telephones, bureaucracies, fax machines, order forms in triplicate, and all the other annoyances of everyday life, but first we were going to have one last waltz with "the system." We were going to have to collect maps and information from the government.

The correspondence for our journey fills an entire file drawer. Dan wrote literally hundreds of letters to Forest Service ranger stations, supervisors' offices, and regional headquarters, receiving in return reams of information—a good deal of which was useless. While many individuals in the Forest Service have worked unceasingly on the Continental Divide National Scenic Trail—particularly in Montana—the system has not yet figured out a way to make the necessary information available to hikers. Especially needed is some way of communicating the current condition of the trail. Where is the trail marked well enough that the hiker can follow it without constant reference to maps and compasses? When a section is referred to as cross-country, does that mean that it goes through pleasant open uplands and requires basic map and compass skills, or does it mean bushwacking through thick forests for three hours to cover a distance of 2 miles? When the Forest Service writes that a section of trail is marked from Muddy Spring to Swampy Gap, what happens at Swampy Gap? Does the trail continue unmarked? Must the hiker refer to maps to figure out which way to turn on a Forest Service road? Or does the trail lure the hiker to the edge of the swamp— and leave him there?

Obtaining the necessary maps was no easier. Dan had begun ordering the maps in October. In March, we were still receiving maps, and Dan was still writing letters.

Some of the maps were out of print, out of stock, or otherwise not available. We called the Forest Service headquarters in Washington, D.C., and learned that no, we could not order copies of maps for national forests from the Forest Service headquarters, we would have to write twenty-four letters and send twenty-four checks (usually for three dollars) to each of twenty-four national forests. Tubes of maps began arriving with dizzying frequency. Maps of Colorado, of New Mexico—of Kansas? Someone had mixed up our order.

And then there were the orthophotoquads.

You may not know what an orthophotoquad is. We didn't either, when we received an order form from the USGS telling us that orthophotoquads were the only maps available for some of the remote areas we planned to visit. The clerk at the USGS explained to Dan that the orthophotoquads were "just like topographical maps, except we have to copy them one by one each time they are ordered."

The maps arrived, and when Dan opened the cardboard tube he unrolled something that looked like a science-fiction alien's vision of Earth. That was how he described it to me, and he wasn't far wrong: Orthophotoquads are aerial images.

They could—I'm guessing about this—be used by an archaeologist, a geologist, or a pilot. Or you could throw some paint on them and sell them as art in a New York City gallery. What you cannot do is use them to plan a hike. It would be like asking an architect to work off an impressionist painting instead of a blueprint.

The USGS had sent us seven hundred dollars' worth of orthophotoquads.

There were more letters and more phone calls. Replacement maps dribbled in. Finally, we had the information we needed to put together a route: the guidebooks, the maps, information from the Forest Service, and information from other hikers who had done parts of the trail. Dan did the initial route planning, thanks to a friend who had hiked the northern 280 miles of Montana with Dan back in 1987. John's job for the U.S. Army used to be figuring out how to move NATO tanks around Germany; now he applied his cartographic skills to figuring out how to move a group of hikers up the Continental Divide. About three nights a week after work, Dan would drive 30-some miles to John's house, and the two of them would try to transfer directions from the guidebooks and information from the Forest Service to the maps.

Inch by inch, they moved north to Canada.

Once we had a route, we could begin to figure out how and where to resupply. On the Appalachian Trail, hikers don't generally carry

more than five days' worth of food at a time, and often they carry
far less. On the Continental Divide, towns are much farther apart,
and getting to them is more difficult. Distances are bigger in the
West, and the nearest town to the trail might be 30 miles away—or
more. Our resupplies would have to last anywhere from five to thirteen days.

Fortunately for us, no one has yet managed to convince the post-
masters in small western towns that they are government bureaucrats.
We wrote to every post office within hitchhiking distance of our
route, and all agreed to our request that they hold packages for longer
than the ten-day period required by the U.S. Post Office's general
delivery system. A few sent back notes wishing us luck, or, with
what we would learn was typical western hospitality, offering help.
"If we're closed when you arrive," one wrote, "just come up the
road to the white house, knock on the door, and we'll get your
package out for you."

When there were no post offices near our route (which was the
case in almost the entire state of Wyoming), we wrote to businesses
near our route, places with names like Benchmark Wilderness Ranch,
Sweetwater General Store, and Big Sandy Lodge, to ask if they
would hold our supplies for us. We were complete strangers, but
even so, the West proved its legendary hospitality. Near the tiny
hamlet of Muddy Gap, Wyoming, the owner of a gas station wrote
back to us: He was going out of business, he said, so he wouldn't
be able to help us. But he gave us the address of another store 3
miles down the road that might hold our boxes. We wrote to them,
and sure enough, they agreed to act as Food Drop Number 19.

Finally, we were ready. We had identified thirty resupply points:
To each one, we would send between one and three boxes, depending
on how many days' worth of supplies we needed. The boxes—there
were about eighty of them in all—needed to be packed with the
appropriate maps, food, and anything else we thought we might
need. Our living room looked like the warehouse of an outdoor gear
store. Boxes were lined against the walls and the floor was covered
with marginally identifiable piles of food: 400 freeze-dried dinners,
400 coffee bags, 70 boxes of crackers, 400 packages of instant soups,
and thousands of snacks: candy bars, granola, packages of dried

fruit, and cans of nuts. Also: dozens of jars of sun cream and bug repellent, extra socks, winter gear for the northern part of the hike, and an assortment of other necessities, real or imagined.

Slowly, the packages came together. One at a time, we tied up the remaining loose ends. We rented our houses. Our books and clothes went into boxes, our furniture into storage. Dan gave his last exam; I left my job. The first boxes were sent on their way.

Finally, so were we.

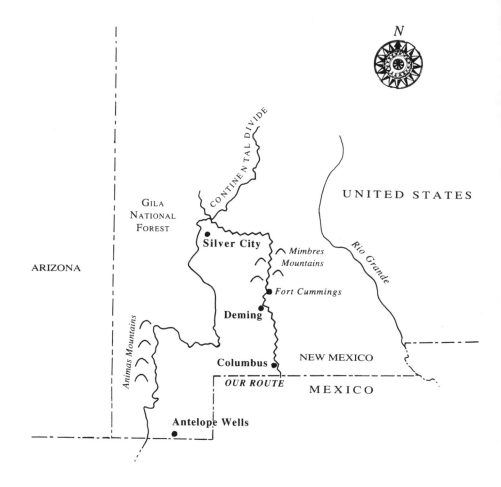

1

≈≈≈≈≈≈≈≈≈≈

THE THIRSTY DESERT

≈≈≈≈≈≈≈≈≈≈

The land looked like a movie stage set. The sand was flat and compact, able to support only a skimpy assortment of creosote and cactus. Surrounding us was an exactly circular horizon of brown-and-gold ridges, their colors muted by the late afternoon sun. In contrast, the sky was a dazzling, saturated blue. Thousands of feet above us, an airplane flashed silver, its contrail a bright streak in the dry desert sky.

We had arrived at the international border between Columbus, New Mexico, and Palomas, Mexico, in an old white van that caught the attention of the border guard. It might have been the canoe that aroused his curiosity. In the entire state of New Mexico there are only five rivers big enough to actually carry something somewhere, and from where we were standing, the nearest running water deep enough to paddle in was at least a hundred miles away. In this parched barren wasteland, a canoe was admittedly an odd thing to be carrying around. But there it sat, conveniently lashed on top of the vehicle, ready to be set afloat in the unlikely event of a flood.

We piled out of the van with our backpacks, and the border guard's expression became doubly perplexed. Looking around us, we could see why. The brown grasses, the heat, the vast emptiness: This was not, to put it mildly, a backpacker's mecca.

"We just want to go through the border and then come back," we explained, far too excited to be making much sense. "We're going to Canada and we want to make it official—a border-to-border trip."

"You're driving to Canada?" he asked. "That's a long way."

We grinned. Such immediate gratification, to be able to answer that question. "No, not driving. Walking—along the Continental Divide."

Walking to Canada. It was the first time we said it, sort of trying it out to see what it sounded like. It sounded hollow. Later—with a few hundred miles behind us, an entire state, the Colorado Rockies— it would become more natural; then, it would mean something. But standing there on the Mexican border, we didn't yet own the trip.

We did, however, relish the guard's disbelieving stare as he waved us through to the barbed-wire-capped, chain-link fence.

The preparation was over now. And the waiting. The planning, the exercising, the packing—all of it behind us. In the end, the only way to really get ready to walk across the country is to start walking across the country. And the act of actually starting—of declaring our intentions to the bemused border guard—made the trip suddenly real, with all its attendant doubts and uncertainties.

And there were plenty of uncertainties. The longest distance I'd ever walked before was the 200 miles Dan and I hiked during our honeymoon in California's High Sierra. On recent, shorter hikes I'd been plagued by blisters and sore muscles. Despite all of our preparation—and all of Dan's reassurances—I was jittery and nervous.

On the other hand, Dan's excitement was transparent. With more than 10,000 miles of hiking behind him, Dan regarded the Continental Divide as merely another romp through the backcountry. An experienced mountaineer and a superb athlete, Dan was already at home in extreme conditions, having walked across the Mojave Desert and snowshoed through 650 miles of a New England winter. He exuded all the energy and confidence of a thoroughbred in a starting gate; I half expected him to start running at the border and disappear into the horizon.

We were to have company for the first few hundred miles. Karl Haupt, who had hiked with Dan for a good chunk of the PCT, had joined us at the El Paso airport. Now he was fitting his skinny, six-foot-four-inch frame into his new North Face pack, and we could hear him muttering about his feet. An officer on leave from the U.S. Merchant Marine, Karl hadn't been able to do much onboard ship to get ready. A veteran of the PCT and the AT, he had enough experience to know that his new boots would give him a rough time for the first few days.

And then there were Sue and Gordon, owners of the van—as well as the canoe. There was nothing that Sue would rather have done than hike the trail with us, but that was impossible. A diabetic, Sue undergoes a daily regime of dialysis and medication, and she can't venture farther than a half day's walk from the van, where her medical gear is. So the backcountry is off-limits. Nor can the van be taken on dirt roads; she can't take the risk of getting dust in the dialysis machine.

Sue's disease has claimed her eyesight, her kidney function, and her strength; it has not claimed her spirit of adventure. With the help of her seeing-eye dog, Mac, Sue walks at least 1,000 miles a summer, ignoring the advice of doctors who tell her she should be confined to bed. A few years ago, while on a trip along the Appalachian Trail, she had to have two toes amputated; two weeks later, she was back on the trail. To put it simply, Sue has guts.

Sue's brother Gordon is the driver of the van, navigator par excellence. An unlikely companion for a wilderness adventure, Gordon is prone to light up a cigarette while wheezing his way up a hill, and his favorite nightcap is a cup of coffee. As often as not, his hiking companion is a tiny, excitable mutt named Muggsie, who, to complete the picture, is blind.

Sue and Gordon couldn't hike the Continental Divide themselves, but they could take part in our journey. They planned to meet us on the rare occasions when our route crossed a paved road, hiking in to welcome us with encouragement, goodies, and a thousand questions about what we had seen since our last encounter.

This, then, was the entourage that stood in the Chihuahuan desert on New Mexico's southern border and declared itself headed for Canada: three backpackers, a blind woman, a leader dog, a blind dog, and the driver of a van with out-of-state plates and a canoe on top. It is safe to say that we did not escape notice as we headed up the highway, aiming to walk the 3 miles from the border station to the town of Columbus on this first and easiest day of our hike.

We fell into relaxed patter. Everyone but me—including the dogs—had hiked together before; the others met on the PCT in 1986. I suppose I could have been more worried about getting to know so many new people, but I was busily worrying about other things. How well would I do on the hike? Would I be able to avoid blisters? How would we deal with the navigation problems we knew lay ahead? Would we find water when we needed it?

An Immigration and Naturalization Service vehicle passed us and stopped, more out of curiosity than of suspicion. Most illegal aliens come through the border in vehicles, and if they were on foot, they wouldn't be walking the main highway carrying brightly colored high-tech American camping gear. When we told the immigration official what we were doing, he drove off shaking his head. A few minutes later he was back.

"You said you were hiking up the Divide?" he asked. We nodded. "Well, this isn't the Divide. The Divide is fifty miles that way." The driver pointed west, across the flat plains toward the Animas Mountains. It was clear that he thought our chances were limited if we were so badly lost so early in the trip.

"We know," we told him. The official route for the Continental Divide Trail had not yet been designated in New Mexico, and there were two different proposals for the southern terminus of the trail. Jim Wolf had recommended that we start in Columbus because the route there passes through dramatic desert mountains as well as areas of important historical interest. The Forest Service recommends a route starting at the border station at Antelope Wells, which is actually closer to the Divide. But at present, land access there is a problem and hikers are not welcome. We didn't want to arouse the ire of gun-toting, cowboy-hat-wearing, private-land-defending ranchers who were, we were sure, just waiting for an opportunity to throw us off their land. After all, this was the West, and a man's ranch is his castle.

As we were to learn, the more a person looked like he was part of the cast of a B-movie western, the more likely he was to invite us in for water, a meal, or a place to stay the night. But we didn't know that yet. As for getting kicked off private land, it never happened to us. Two other hikers who started at Antelope Wells that year were unceremoniously escorted off the Gray Ranch, which straddles the Animas Mountains just north of the Antelope Wells border station. But—just to keep the story straight—the Gray Ranch is not owned by a rancher. It's owned by the Nature Conservancy.

We decided to follow Jim's advice and start at the border station just south of Columbus. Unlike the post at Antelope Wells, it was on a paved road, which meant Sue and Gordon could share the beginning of the trip with us. From Columbus, the route stayed pretty much on BLM land. The downside was that we wouldn't actually be on the Divide for a few days.

"Well, good luck," the INS man said doubtfully. "And watch out for rattlesnakes."

We didn't see any rattlesnakes between the border and Columbus, a one-street town that, with its adobe buildings and white-washed walls, looks more Mexican than American. It's got a three-aisle bodega, where we bought a head of doubtful lettuce and a few chili peppers; one bar, which can't tell you its closing time because closing time depends on who's there; a biblioteca, a museum, an abandoned building with BUDDY'S TRAIDING POST painted on the front in long skinny letters, and the optimistically named Columbus Industrial Park, consisting of a big sign on a cleared lot.

We checked into the Pancho Villa Motel, located across the road from Pancho Villa State Park. It doesn't take much imagination to figure out the town's claim to fame. On March 9, 1916, a Mexican bandit (or, if you prefer, a revolutionary) named Pancho Villa led a 1,000-man invasion of Columbus that came precariously close to causing war between the United States and Mexico.

It is hard, now, to imagine that this sleepy little town could ever have been the subject of an international incident. To give it its due, in 1916 Columbus was a much larger and livelier community, supporting a school with seventeen teachers, three hotels, a bank, three drugstores, two general stores, two groceries, a Coca-Cola bottling plant, a theater, two furniture stores, a blacksmith shop, and a laundry. It also boasted Camp Furlong, one of a series of military bases that the United States had built along the Mexican-American border.

Camp Furlong was the target of Pancho Villa's raid. Curiously, the raid had nothing to do with American territory, or American incursions, or American anything; it was a Mexican response to a Mexican issue, designed to provoke, ultimately, a Mexican reaction. At stake was nothing less than the question of who was going to run Mexico. Pancho Villa was one of the contenders: a legendary cattle rustler, a bank robber, a military general, and a man obsessed with gaining control of the Mexican government. With a bona fide pedigree from the impoverished peasantry, Villa was popular with the American press, and he became popular, as well, among key advisers to the American president—so popular, in fact, that he was finally rewarded with the endorsement of the Wilson administration.

Then he made his mistake: Villa launched a preemptory attack upon his adversary's forces, only to lose not only the military campaign but also any chance of the Mexican presidency and American support. When the Wilson administration granted recognition to the rival Carranza regime, Villa began to plot his revenge.

His plan was to provoke the United States into armed intervention on Mexican soil. A populist uprising, he was convinced, would follow, and the peasants would rally around him and carry him straight to the presidential palace in Mexico City. So, in January 1916, he removed seventeen Americans from a Mexican train and had sixteen of them shot.

To his surprise, there was no American attack on Mexico, no opportunity to mount a heroic defense, and no upswell of support from the peasantry. The Americans had not responded according to plan, leaving Villa to develop another, grander, scheme. If the Americans would not come to Villa, he would go to the Americans. And so, at 4:15 A.M. on March 9, a ragtag army of 1,000 men raided Camp Furlong, looted the town of Columbus, killed ten civilians and eight soldiers, and burned down the Commercial Hotel and several adjacent buildings. The 73rd American Cavalry, with some 300 men stationed at the fort, drove Villa back to the border.

The raid was costly: Villa left 142 dead in Columbus, and lost between 75 and 100 more men on the retreat. But the attack on American soil produced exactly the response that Villa had anticipated. On March 10 President Wilson ordered General John Pershing to launch a "punitive expedition" to capture Pancho Villa. And this was no token response; for its day, it was a major military engagement, ultimately involving 11,635 U.S. troops, ten months of searching and skirmishes, and, for the first time ever, the use of both motorized vehicles and aircraft in a military campaign.

The expedition did not go smoothly. As it penetrated farther and farther into Mexico, the lack of fuel, roads, and supply lines undermined the value of the mechanized equipment; ultimately, the U.S. Army found itself in the ridiculous position of using mules to bring fuel to its trucks and biplanes. More seriously, the peasantry did indeed—as Villa had predicted—view the American presence as an invasion. Popular opinion forced even the Carranza regime, which wanted Villa caught as much as the United States did, to demand a U.S. withdrawal. When the United States not only refused, but entered into several violent skirmishes with Mexican federal troops, war with Mexico appeared imminent. Perhaps it would have been, but in January 1917, World War I was looming on the American horizon. Wilson ordered Pershing to return home.

Pancho Villa had been chased for almost a year by the United States military, and he had managed to escape unscathed. But although he had so correctly estimated the U.S. response to his raid, Villa had been unable to accurately predict the end of the story: He remained an outlaw until 1920, when the Mexican government bribed him into retirement. Three years later he was assassinated. Today, as a gesture of goodwill between the United States and Mexico, a New Mexican state park bears his name.

≋≋≋

At the Pancho Villa Motel, the proprietress said that the three of us—Karl, and Dan, and me—could have one room or two—she didn't care what went on; it was none of her business. What went on was a massive gear-sorting effort. Dan and I had already pared down our gear to what we thought was the bare minimum. But some of what had seemed essential in our suburban living room became quite superfluous now that we were faced with the prospect of carrying it on our backs. We also wanted to check our gear against Karl's to make sure we weren't carrying duplicate communal supplies. No item was too small to escape scrutiny: Did we really need three pocketknives? How many water filters? Extra shoelaces? What's in your first aid kit? Karl cut the handle off his toothbrush and the tags off his stuff sacks. More significantly, we decided to stow our tents in Sue and Gordon's van. Southern New Mexico gets nine inches of rain a year, and less than one inch of that comes in the month of May. Any rain that did fall was unlikely to last for long; our rain jackets and ground cloths would be enough to get us through any surprises.

When we finished, we had a surprisingly big—and pleasingly heavy—pile of unnecessary gear. We headed over to the campground where Sue and Gordon were ensconced. Their campsite was easy to find; it was the only one occupied. Surrounding it on all sides was a gargantuan cactus garden. An ocotillo rose eight feet tall; an absurd plant, consisting of long skinny stalks, each one capped with an extravagant crimson flower. The prickly pears were thick and succulent, with delicate, waxy blooms—either lemon yellow or ballerina pink. And the tiny red flowers of the barrel cactus seemed to mock us from the safety of the surrounding thorns.

With the sun gone, it was a surprisingly cool evening. We fixed dinner: salad, spaghetti with tomato sauce, and Parmesan cheese. Such simple luxuries would become more and more precious in the weeks ahead. So we sat, quietly, and savored a lazy night, getting used to the feel of the wind and the desert air. Already we were divorced from the city. The lives we had left only a day earlier seemed to belong to someone else—some other person with a lot of senseless headaches. The frenetic activity, the endless list of chores, the last-minute crises that had consumed our time and attention— even the memory of them was gone, whisked away by the desert breeze, put to rest in the sand.

At 6:45 the next morning, the walking began for real. We turned off the paved road and headed toward the rocky, angry Tres Hermanas Mountains—three sisters who looked like Amazons armed for battle, so brown and dry it made us thirsty to look at them. It was impossible to tell how far away they were; they could have been a few minutes or a few miles. The light, the scale, and the distances of the West all take some getting used to; to the newcomer, they have the effect of a subtle sort of funhouse mirror.

You can tell whether a person belongs here or not by the way his eyes look out at this harsh, open landscape. A person who is at home in the desert has a way of looking beyond you to the far horizon. He has eyes at ease with the bigness of the country, eyes that effortlessly focus on the subtleties of brown antelope on brown hills and acres of sagebrushed emptiness. In contrast, our eyes were used to clutter, to horizons blocked by buildings and walls, to air blurred by smog. They shifted quickly, rushing to keep up with the constant movement of fast cars, blinking lights, and hurried people. Our eyes would need time before they would settle in to this country, before they could see the antelope, or answer a simple question: How far away are the mountains?

At the same time that we were learning to interpret the big spaces of the Southwest, we were engaged in a more immediate pursuit: combing the ground for rattlesnakes. There's a southwestern locust that makes a noise that sounds like a rattler's rattle—at least to someone who had never heard one. (That would be me; Dan has encountered scores, and Karl has not only seen and heard them, but once ate a Mojave rattlesnake for dinner.) So with every buzz of a locust and every rustle of a dead plant, I stopped, searching the ground for the dreaded diamondbacks, peering into the shade underneath yucca plants and creosote bushes. It took time before we realized that what is true for the rest of the country is true for the Southwest: People exaggerate the dangers. There weren't nearly as many snakes as we had been promised.

There weren't, in fact, nearly as many of any of the dangers about which we had been warned. At home, friends and relatives worried about us getting lost, falling down mountain slopes, being attacked by strangers or fierce wild animals. "Aren't you afraid?" they asked, or "Will you be carrying a gun?" We had been warned about the dangers of flash floods and lightning and grizzly bears and river fords. We had been warned about people, too: ranchers who would take us for interfering, trespassing, East Coast environmentalists; Indians who would block our passage through reservation land; Mexican-Americans who, we were assured, hated Anglos.

There were, it seemed, so many threats that we had to be selective about which ones we were going to worry about. We simply couldn't fret about all of them, so we picked two that seemed particularly terrifying.

The first was blisters.

They start innocently enough. A pucker in a sock, a grain of sand, something so small as to almost escape notice. You feel a slight rubbing; you assume it will go away. A mile later, it's still there, so you tug on your sock and hope that will solve the problem. You promise yourself that at the next break, a half hour away, you'll take off your boots and check things out.

But a few minutes later, the slight rubbing has turned into unbearable pain, and you are already too late. Your innocuous little hot spot has become a swollen, raw blister, and now you have all kinds of things to worry about: infection, bleeding, continued rubbing, and, most of all, pain with every step.

With 3,000 miles to walk—six million steps, as we figured the distance—a blister was a far more terrifying prospect than a rattlesnake. And a much more likely one. Our defensive tactics began with protective armor: pads of moleskin pasted to our feet on skin likely to blister. During our daily breaks—one for lunch and two for snacks—hiking boots, socks, and liners came off, anything wet was hung on a cactus to dry, and feet were examined for telltale hot spots. We solemnly pledged that if one of us so much as sensed the slightest tinge of a possible potential blister-to-be, he or she would declare all-out war. No walking just another quarter mile because we were going to stop anyway for lunch. No thinking it would go away. No hoping that the sock would rearrange itself. Blisters were to be fought on all fronts.

Our second problem was water. More to the point, our second problem was lack of water.

First, some facts: New Mexico is the third driest state in the country. Most of the state's water use is dependent on underground aquifers, because there simply isn't enough surface water to go around. Of the rain that does fall, 97 percent is lost to evaporation. Approximately 65 percent of the state's vertebrates depend on wetlands, but wetlands cover only a meager 2 percent of the state.

It's one thing to know all that, quite another to stand in the New Mexican desert and see what it means. What it means is this: For miles around you, in any direction, there are no streams, no ponds, no pools of rainwater. The dominant color is brown, not green. And when you do find water—usually from windmills that pump groundwater for agricultural use—you have to share it with whatever other animals inhabit the desert.

Unfortunately, other animals have something to share with you: *Giardia lamblia*, a microscopic protozoan that spends part of its life cycle in water and the rest in mammalian intestines. It doesn't respond to the antibiotics commonly used to treat other intestinal disorders. Contracting *Giardia* is not life-threatening, but it is debilitating and miserable, and it can put an end to a long-distance walk. Among hikers, *Giardia* is the bogeyman, the ogre, the devil incarnate; it is something to be avoided at all costs.

But avoiding it can be difficult. The cyst is sort of a superman of waterborne infections. It's small enough to sneak through some water filters, too hardy to succumb to many chemical treatments, and tough enough to withstand the lower temperature of water boiled at high altitudes. To add a further twist: The *Giardia* cyst thrives in cold running water—just the kind you'd think would be most safe.

In recent years, reported *Giardia* cases have increased throughout the country to the point that most guidebooks warn hikers and other backcountry users to treat all their water. Figuring out who to blame for the infestation depends on who you talk to. The ranchers call it beaver fever, hikers blame the cattle, and most resource managers we talked to turned the tables and put the blame on backpackers.

Looking around at the terrain, we could safely rule out backpackers—hiking was not what you would call a high-volume local activity. And we could rule out beavers, too. That left cattle, and there are thousands of them in southern New Mexico. But regardless of whose fault it was, one thing was certain: We'd have to take care to make sure we not only had enough water, but that the water we did find was suitable for drinking.

≋≋≋≋≋≋≋

Four miles into our first day, we saw a flicker of silver blades twirling in the sky—a windmill, reassuringly located exactly where our map said it would be.

Rancon Windmill was shaded by a grove of cottonwood trees, as sure a sign of water as nature has ever invented. It was a pretty spot; the thick, overhanging foliage of the trees seemed almost exotic in contrast to the dusty gray slopes of the Three Sisters Mountains, rising abruptly to the northwest. Under the shade of the cottonwoods, the temperature was a good ten degrees cooler than out in the sun, and the sensation of moving from sun to shade was as shocking as a splash of cold mountain water.

The windmill itself was a simple contraption: a tall steel derrick with a fan, a pump, and some pipes. When the wind blew, the blades spun the fan around, which activated the pump, which, within a few seconds, pulled water out of the ground from 200 or so feet below the surface. Pipes carried the water to a holding tank a few yards away, and from there, water could be diverted to nearby cattle troughs. The fresh cattle dung surrounding the windmill suggested that that had been done in the recent past. When the tank overflowed, water trickled back into the ground and fed the thirsty cottonwood trees. In addition to the cattle and the cottonwoods, we shared the windmill with a horde of bees, attracted here by the water and lured to stay by the wooden boxes of local beekeepers.

The water in the tank was covered by a thin film of green algae, and that led to an earnest discussion of windmill water. We decided that this would be a good time to get to know our brand-new portable water filter. We had tested it at home, and it seemed to do what it was supposed to; namely, it had produced an eight-ounce glass of clear, tasteless water out of a sink full of dirty, soapy dishes.

The filter has four basic parts. There's an intake tube, a pump, a canister containing a charcoal filter, and an outflow tube. One person holds the canister and tubes in place and the other pushes and pulls on the pump. (The ads say it's a one-person operation, but in practice, it doesn't work smoothly if you have less than three hands.) With each thrust of the pump, a couple of tablespoons of water pass through the system and spurt into your water container. You do it again and—voilà—a couple more. The first liter was magic, but the novelty quickly wore off. By the time we'd filled the second bottle, we were bored with our new toy. By the seventh liter, we decided that, in general, it was probably safe to drink windmill water without filtering it.

We didn't need to worry about surface water; there wasn't any. Dozens of dotted blue lines on the maps told us that water did, sometimes, flow here. Deep, scourged arroyos confirmed that there was occasionally a lot of it. But in May, the only water came from deep under the ground, pumped up for cattle or irrigation.

We skirted around the base of the Three Sisters and headed into the much lower Greasewood Hills, named after their dominant plant, the spindly greasewood bush. We were planning to look for a campsite on the north side of the hills, having chosen the site for a simple reason: According to the maps, there were several possible sources of water nearby, and none anywhere else. The fact that the map dated from 1965 did not escape our notice. While not much had changed in southern New Mexico in twenty-five years—at least not where we were walking—there was no guarantee that the wells would be working. One of them wasn't. The other, behind a barbed-wire fence posted with a No Trespassing sign, was actually an irrigation pump, and we could hear it chugging away as it methodically pumped water into cement culverts that fed into acres of dead brown dirt. The earth had been turned over and plowed into straight lines. Within weeks, the water would work its magic, and this place would briefly be a green oasis.

More than any other issue, water—or the lack of it—dominates the West. Diverting it, channeling it, damming it, storing it, most of all, using it. In the West, wasting water is defined as not using it, and to waste this precious resource is a sin of the highest order. It hardly matters what it is used for: grazing cattle, growing hay, harnessing energy—even watering suburban lawns or making artificial snow for ski slopes is preferable to letting water run "wasted" in a stream. There is a preoccupation with water in the West that makes it an object of almost religious reverence. It is a preoccupation that no easterner can fully understand—unless he is standing, thirsty, in the desert looking at someone else's irrigation ditch.

This obsession with water is a matter of simple economics, a basic demonstration of the relationship between scarcity and value. In the East, water is abundant. A farm in Connecticut or North Carolina gets some forty-five inches of water a year, much of it conveniently in the spring planting season. It only takes one acre of good Georgia farmland to support a cow and her calf. An eastern farmer thinks of three weeks without rain as drought, and even if there is a drought, the long growing season is forgiving.

West of the 100th meridian, the picture changes. Precipitation drops to less than twenty inches: seventeen inches in western Oklahoma, ten inches in western Texas. The higher elevation shortens the growing season, and an unpredictable portion of precipitation comes in the form of marble-sized hailstones that can flatten a field of crops in an afternoon. Gone are the rich, dark greens of the well-watered East; the land is painted with the colors of drought: burnt brown, the yellowish hue of a diseased lawn, or, most commonly, the gray-green of the ubiquitous sagebrush. The average rainfall in the state of New Mexico is a paltry 14.3 inches a year, and on southern New Mexico's Deming Plain, where we were standing, it drops even more, to nine inches—in other words, desert. About the only thing you can do with the land is run cattle on it, and it takes fifty or more acres to support one cow and her calf.

Think of it: fifty acres for a cow and a calf! It's an incredible requirement, especially if you hail from the East Coast, where a quarter-acre suburban lot can go for $100,000 or more. Fifty acres? For a cow? But in the West, while there may not be much water, there is no shortage of land. Despite the near-desert conditions in most of the West, despite the lack of water, despite the pathetic clumps of grasses that pass for forage, cattle are almost as common as cactus.

The old-time ranchers were quick studies when it came to the arithmetic of cattle and land. A modest family ranch needs to run at least 100 cows to be profitable; simple multiplication tells you that you need roughly 5,000 acres on land like this. Trouble was, the

Congress of 1862, which voted on the Homestead Act, was over-whelmingly made up of easterners, who had no comprehension of this monolith called the West. They thought 160 acres would be a nice-sized homestead, and they wrote it into law.

But there were ways to get more cheap land, and the ranchers found them. If the law said they needed to erect a residence to file a claim, they built a birdhouse and set it on the ground. If the law required irrigation, they dumped a bucket of water in front of a witness. If the law limited the number of acres they could buy, they filed claim to the rich bottomlands that ran along the streams, and because they then controlled access to the water, they controlled the surrounding land as well.

It was inevitable that someone would start thinking how much more valuable his property would be if he could only get a little more water to it. And so it began: the age of western water projects, conceived to convert the arid West into an agricultural Eden. Water could be stored, diverted, moved, and controlled. It could run uphill, if the need (and money) were sufficient, or flow in tunnels from one drainage to another.

But water projects are expensive, and the profit margins of cattle ranching and irrigation farming can't pay for them. So the federal government pays, sometimes to the tune of ninety cents on the dollar. An example, which would be humorous if it wasn't true, is the federal water subsidy that helps western farmers grow cotton—a crop that the same federal government, at the very same time, subsidizes southern farmers not to grow. Even with the subsidies, western agri-culture is inefficient at best: In New Mexico, for instance, 90 percent of the state's water goes to agriculture, which generates only 20 percent of the state's income.

Regardless of their efficiency—or inefficiency—water projects enjoy the support of western politicians and representatives in Congress. Even those representatives who are solidly aligned with the environmental movement fall into step when the issue is western water. They know that in the eyes of their constituents, there is no such thing as a bad water project, and they know that, in the party of politics, you dance with the guy who brung you. To do otherwise is to write your own walking papers.

Today, the age of big water developments may be coming to an end, not because they are being stopped in the courts—although some of them are—but because the West is running out of water to develop. Most of its rivers are already dammed, and the aquifers are losing water faster than they can be replenished.

But the demand for water is still growing, not only from agriculture, but from cities, which seem to need more and more—always more—water. Yesterday's battles over water rights were part and parcel of the Old West's lore of gunslinging drama. Today's battles—among ranchers, farmers, Indian tribes, environmentalists, rafting outfitters, fishermen, electric companies, city councils, and a host of others—may have moved to the courts, but they have lost none of their high stakes.

If the water supply continues to dwindle, the dying age of water developments may be supplanted by a new age of water wars, as competing users try to establish their claims in the courts. Where will the growing cities get the water they need? Who has the right to the water from an underground aquifer? Will a farmer or a rancher always be able to drill a hole in the earth and mine water from the communal groundwater supply? And once the aquifer is depleted—what will happen then?

We listened to the *bang-chunk-bang-chunk* of the machinery, pulling water from deep beneath the ground. A No Trespassing sign and a fence separated us from the irrigation ditch, where water was flowing from the ground into the culverts. The sign, the pump, and the brown dry field explained water in the West more clearly than any textbook. We were quick learners. In the spirit that has characterized the region since the earliest days of its settlement, we climbed the fence and appropriated some of the water for ourselves.

～～～～

Our campsite was an anticlimactic place for the beginning of the big trip: a bleak spot just in from a dirt road, a hundred yards or so from an abandoned farm-turned-garbage-dump. We rolled out our sleeping pads in the wide flat spaces between creosote bushes. Sitting, eye-level with the desert plants, we could only marvel at the ingenuity with which they approach the challenges of their inhospitable environment.

The creosote, for instance, behaves like the plant kingdom's equivalent of an old-time cattle baron: spreading its roots out over a wide, shallow area and snatching up any water that falls before it can sink into the ground, evaporate—or be claimed by competing users. Other desert plants have different strategies, but they all have a water project mentality. In contrast to the creosote's opportunistic surface roots, the mesquite prefers to depend on the more reliable supply of groundwater, which it finds under the washout areas of hillsides and arroyos. To get to the water is the challenge, requiring tough, thick taproots that bore as much as seventy-five feet into the ground to bring up water from beneath the surface.

And then there are the cacti: those thick, fleshy water hoarders that behave as though every rain could be the last. Having dispensed even with leaves in order to reduce transpiration, cacti are but thick, water-storing stems, protected by needles in an impressive array of shapes, sizes, and clusters. In an emergency, you can cut them open and raid their cache of moisture; mules, in fact, chew on them with tough lips that are unaffected by the plant's sharp spikes. The size of the prickly pear depends on rainfall and sunlight; the specimens around our campsite were sort of spindly-looking. And that wasn't because there was any lack of sunlight.

The daily life of a cactus is a pretty dull affair—unless it rains. Then, the plant comes alive, its sole concern being to capture and use all the water it can. So it sucks it up with an elaborate root system, hordes the water in thorn-protected fleshy stems, and uses any extra energy to produce flowers. There is an urgent efficiency to the cactus's activity; this is a plant that plans for the future.

We are, it seems, kin to the cactus. For with all our technology and intellect, once in the desert, we humans adapt the strategies of our prickle-covered cousins. We become opportunists, changing our route whenever we see the silver blades of windmills flickering in the sky. We become gluttons, drinking our fill, and then more, at every water source, whether we are thirsty or not. We become hoarders, carrying as much as we can with us, hoping it is enough to take us through the next dry spell. We behave as though each windmill might be our last.

We are also kin to the animals of the desert. The desert teaches us to take advantage of the cooler hours of the early mornings and late evenings. We learn that in the dry air, even the spare, spindly, half shade of a waist-high creosote bush can drop the temperature a good ten degrees. And, like our animal cousins, we seek refuge from the heat of the midday sun, squeezing ourselves under whatever shade is available. We clothe ourselves in the colors of the desert: light browns and beige clothing that reflects the light back at the sun and protects our skin. And when it is too hot, we join the snakes and the coyotes in their time-honored tradition of siesta.

≋≋≋

Now, in the early evening, Karl was doing just that, having parked as much of himself as possible under a bush. Dan and I finished setting up camp and sat down to survey our transient home in the desert—in a very real sense, the first home that we would ever share with each other. Although we had been married for two years before we set out on the Divide, we had never lived together. To save money for the trip, we had undertaken a commuter marriage, with Dan living in New York and me in Virginia. After two years of living apart, we were finally beginning our lives together. Here among the creosote, Dan and I would undergo the process that is familiar to every couple: the merging of lives and habits. The Continental Divide would be our home.

There were, however, two aspects that made our experience unique. First was the setting in which we resolved the time-honored questions: What side of the ground cloth do you sleep on? Who does the cooking? The laundry? Where do the spoons go? The second was the total immersion of our new togetherness—twenty-four hours a day from now until we had walked from one edge of the country to the other. And that was going to bring up a whole other slate of issues—about our moods, our expectations, our ability to compromise, our approach to conflicts, and about things inside us that we never even knew were there.

But for now, we concentrated on more modest issues. Dan recorded the data for the day into his diary: 14.5 miles for the day; 18 in all. I started dinner: instant mashed potatoes with canned salmon, instant mushroom soup, dehydrated peas, and onion flakes, all mixed together and served in a plastic Tupperware bowl. It tastes better than it sounds when you eat under the desert stars.

And later, we fell asleep to the sound of the irrigation pump chugging at its task. The only other sign of humanity was the abandoned farm with its heap of sloppily piled garbage. We could easily imagine that we were the only people left after a nuclear holocaust: the bleak, brown landscape; the silent, crumbling home; and the *bang-chunk* of the machinery, on and off, on and off.

Sometime after midnight, I was nudged awake by a bright beam of light piercing my eyes.

"Stop shining the light in my face," I demanded, and squirmed around to get out of its glare. As I slowly emerged from semiconsciousness, I realized that Dan was asleep next to me. There were no lights anywhere to be seen. Except the moon, waxing. You could have read by it.

Walking into Deming three days and 36 miles later, we were tough. Swaggering a little, in fact—at least I was. Dan and Karl had far too much experience with this sort of thing to be self-impressed at this early stage. Even so, they were happy enough to answer questions about our trip, and an opportunity soon presented itself in the form of a van decorated with huge bold-colored letters that proclaimed "Cowboys for Christ."

It pulled up to us just as we were passing Deming's supermarket, trying to get oriented to this small town, which all of a sudden looked to us as big and bustling as a metropolis. A few days on the trail had shifted our perspective, attacked our sense of scale. After four days of sand, rock, cactus, and creosote, the colors and motion of Deming were startling. We felt like rabbits caught in the headlights of an oncoming car. And here was "Cowboys for Christ," at our service.

The driver was all western: cowboy boots, hat, and belt buckle, with that country drawl and an open, howdy-stranger face. He took in our backpacks and our sentinel plant walking sticks.

"You folks need a ride somewhere?"

We loved that question.

"No, thanks. We're walking."

Please ask. Please, please, please ask where we're going.

The cowboy was an obliging sort. "Where ya headed?"

"We're walking to Canada." Not quite, really, nonchalant. For one thing, all three of us answered at once.

" 'S that so?"

The five-minute conversation followed a pattern that would repeat itself countless times in the months ahead. What do you do about food? How many pairs of boots do you go through? How many miles do you walk a day? We explained about our food drops, and got directions to the post office.

"Well, I'll let you folks go on," he said. "If you're sure you don't need anything . . ."

We shook our heads.

"You just take this then." He handed us a business card. "I know lots of people—got friends all over the state. You get in trouble, you need anything at all, you just give me a call. I mean that."

He drove off, and we looked at the card. "Cowboys for Christ," it said, and we tucked it away. You never know.

We walked on through streets named after metals—gold, silver, copper, and others—a reminder of the role of mining in this part of the West. Several campgrounds offered hookups for RVs; a few of them advertised that they had trees. We passed by small, neat houses, some with bright green lawns, and others with cactus and rock gardens. Most of the houses were fiercely guarded by dogs that followed us, barking, along the perimeter of their assigned property, and then deferred to the next dog, who took on the job and guarded the next house. The people, however, were friendly; motorists stopped to let us cross the street, something that took us by such surprise that we didn't quite know what to do. Pickup trucks far outnumbered cars, more people wore boots than shoes, and everyone boasted ten-gallon hats.

We found the Deming Post Office, a standard-issue government building, identified by the flag waving out front. If the postal system worked properly, there would be three boxes waiting for us with enough maps and food to get us to Silver City, seven days and 110 trail miles away. We stood on line and, surrounded by the cotton dresses and leisure shorts of retirees, we suddenly felt the outdoors on us. We did not look as though we belonged in a building. We looked, I imagine, like bums—sunburned, unkempt, with dirty clothes and windblown hair.

We waited our turn, a little nervous. Post office mail drops work fine in theory. In practice, if only one out of the eighty boxes we had packaged got lost somewhere, we could be in trouble. Some of the towns we were passing through weren't even big enough to have grocery stores, let alone map distributors. But there was no need to worry in Deming; the clerk handed us our packages and a handful of letters from home, and we headed off to find a motel.

Town stops are the punctuation of a long-distance hike. They give you a moment to breathe, so to speak: to resupply, rest, get clean; to send postcards to long lists of friends, relatives, and colleagues; to reconnect to the world back home. On the trail, preoccupations with route finding and water push the real world into distant recesses of consciousness. But in town, the almost hypnotic trance of the wilderness is interrupted just long enough to partially reestablish the links to families and friends.

More practical needs come into play, too. Cleanliness, for instance, which is something that seems to fall by the wayside about five minutes after the beginning of a hike. Out on the trail, it's easy to forget about the dirt altogether—it's not until you see yourself in comparison to town folk that you realize exactly what you look like. Laundry and a bath become the most urgent of needs, the only question being which to do first.

Our town stops developed into a sort of ritual. Dan did the laundry while I attacked the cook gear, cleaned the boots, and aired out the sleeping bags. None of the fussy high-tech fabrics could tolerate being machine dried, so our hotel rooms took on the appearance of a flooded outdoor equipment warehouse as we draped soaking-wet gear over doors and curtain rods and chairs and anything else we could find.

The next job was to repackage the food so it would fit into our stuff sacks. We dumped the contents of the food boxes on top of the beds: cereal, nuts, Parmesan cheese, spaghetti, dried milk, instant soups, hot cocoa, coffee bags, freeze-dried dinners, instant mashed potatoes, macaroni and cheese, chocolate bars, crackers, drink mixes, granola bars, and a host of other items. Order emerged from the chaos: neat piles of breakfasts, lunches, dinners, snacks, and drinks, counted and double-checked to make sure we had the right number of each. And then came the repackaging itself. If we needed evidence that the packaging industry contributes to the excess of solid waste produced in America, we had it here in front of us. By the time we had transferred the various items of food from their original packaging to Ziploc bags, our room was strewn with colored cardboard, Styrofoam cups, aluminum-lined paper, plastic jars, metal cans, and plastic wrap. When we were finished, the discarded packaging took up almost as much space as our piles of food, and our stuff sacks were not only easier to pack, they weighed a few pounds less.

Looking over our food for the next few days was enough to set us off on the next item of business: finding a restaurant where we could bolster ourselves against the culinary indignities ahead. The only requirement was that whatever we were eating be the type of food that couldn't possibly be carried in a backpack, the spicier the better.

In Deming, that requirement was easily met by the Mexican restaurant near our motel. Inside, we felt oddly out of place. The other customers all sported rough-and-tumble western wear; in contrast to the standard local uniform, our colorful nylon hiking shorts looked strangely effeminate.

If our hiking clothes contradicted traditional western stereotypes, our dietary habits branded us not only as outsiders, but as outsiders worthy of extreme suspicion. Neither Dan nor I had eaten meat for more than three years. That, however, was about to change. Maintaining a vegetarian-and-seafood diet in the small towns of the American West meant being condemned to a diet of iceberg lettuce and processed cheese, unless there was a trout-fishing stream nearby. In addition, we had decided that we didn't want to make an issue of our purely personal preferences if we were invited into someone's home for a meal. Our solution was to stick with our no-meat regime on the trail and allow ourselves to eat whatever looked best while in town. In Deming, that was a Mexican chicken-and-tortilla dinner, served extra spicy with all the trimmings, washed down with a pitcher of beer. This, now, was living!

Our stop in Deming was short enough. In the morning, we took one last opportunity to shore up our stomachs at a small three-table cantina, and then we headed out toward the forbidding and rugged

Cookes Range, accompanied, for the first few miles, by Sue, Gordon, and, of course, the dogs.

Even early in the morning, the sun shone intensely hot. We tied shirts to the back of our packs so that they would hang down and shade the back of our legs, and on our heads we wore light-colored hats to deflect the sun's heat. Of all of us, Mac suffered the most— his thick dark coat was almost too hot to touch. A jet-black Labrador retriever, Mac was miserable in the sun and he expressed his opinion of the situation by crawling under anything that held out the possibility of shade. Sue stopped every half mile or so to pour cold water on him and to offer him a drink and a rest. Mac was not, however, too hot or too miserable to forgo inciting trouble among other dogs. As we passed by a series of rural homes, he seemed to take a perverse pleasure in irritating as many of them as possible, and Muggsie brought the racket to new decibel levels by running around in circles and barking at the top of his lungs. Clearly, this was the most fun he had had in days. I could hear Dan muttering, "It's going to be a long day," as he stood his ground against a series of dogs that ventured out to show us just what they thought of our trespass on their road.

Sue and Gordon waved good-bye when the road turned to an ill-defined jeep track, and we walked on, through a flat field of sage-brush, toward the mountain range ahead. A dry wind blew waves of hot air into our faces and spun dust devils, miniature dirt tornadoes that pirouette across the desert with madcap abandon. "Thirty miles an hour," Karl told us, when I asked how hard the wind was blowing. "If a dust devil comes at you, close your eyes and mouth," Dan advised.

The wind may have seemed a malediction, but it was, in fact, a blessing. The same gusts that blew off our hats and threw sand in our eyes sent windmill blades spinning, so that plungers pumped and cold water gushed from metal pipes. The retaining tanks were so full that water slopped over the rims and immediately disappeared into the ground. We stopped at each windmill, resting in the lee side and drinking as much as we could. Ahead of us, we knew, was a long, dry stretch where we would leave ranching country, and its windmills, for mountains filled with old prospect holes and the remains of abandoned mines. What, we wondered, had the prospectors done for water?

And what, for that matter, did contemporary travelers across this expanse do for water? For there are other people who try to cross the Deming Plain on foot—not backpackers, but illegal aliens attempting to make their way to new lives and jobs farther north.

Far away, we picked out a pinpoint that moved slowly along a ridge, stopping every once in while. Through our binoculars, we could see that it was a van—the same type of vehicle as those used by the Immigration and Naturalization Service. For a moment, we could put ourselves in the position of an illegal alien crossing this land on foot. We looked around searching for a place in which a person could take shelter and hide, but the landscape was completely open, completely exposed. Our sympathies, now, were with any person trying to cross this sunburned waterless plain while someone with a gun and binoculars tracked him from the comfort of an air-conditioned van. It occurred to us that whoever was in the van was probably tracking our movements as well, and we half expected an INS vehicle to come lurching over the rutted roads to check us out up close. But they must have figured out that we weren't who they were looking for; a half hour later, the van moved off the ridge, and was gone.

≈≈≈≈≈

In the desert, it seems that you can see forever; with all of the land laid out before you, it is only logical to believe that you can see what there is. Logical, but an illusion, another trick of the scale and the space. Heat waves do, indeed, create mirages as patches of shade become imaginary pools of water. And just as the desert creates images of things that aren't there, it does the opposite, too, by hiding things that are there.

Roads, for instance. There are plenty of roads in the desert—a surprising number, considering that about the only traffic is the occasional rancher, driving out to check his herds. But the roads exist not because they are needed or even used today, but because they were needed or have been used in the past. It doesn't take much to make a permanent path through this terrain: The soil is dry and, once disturbed, the vegetation grows back slowly. A jeep road last used fifty years ago is likely to still exist as a discernible cut. Discernible, that is, once you find it. The deceptively flat and even landscape is surprisingly effective at hiding deep arroyos and old jeep tracks—and perfectly good new jeep roads, too.

We quickly learned, once we set out cross-country, that we could be twenty feet away from a road and not see it among the bushes, even though the land is open and the vegetation sparse. And when we did stumble upon the parallel tracks of an old jeep path, we didn't necessarily know that it was headed in the same direction that we were. Most of the roads weren't even on the maps.

This was the way we were walking, then: checking the maps and the topographical features, climbing fences that proclaimed that we were on private property, and, more than once, going the wrong way down the wrong road. We tried to avoid ranch houses, while being certain not to bypass their windmills. We hadn't figured out yet that we were unlikely to run into a landowner in the middle of a ranch in the middle of nowhere, nor that most folks didn't mind someone walking across their land.

By late afternoon we had left the windmills behind and were approaching our targeted campsite. The campsite was next to what the topo map referred to as a detention dam, which is nothing more than an earthen embankment that collects rainwater. The topographical maps colored the dam in dotted blue, indicating a seasonal water source. The name, however, was forbidding: Starvation Draw. As we approached it, we looked at the brown earth and the dusty, dry arroyos, and wondered exactly what water the dam could have collected.

Our suspicions were justified when we finally reached a bone-dry, sagebrush-choked depression in the dusty earth: the so-called dam. We barely even slowed down as we passed it. We had a little water—just enough to get us through the night—but if we wanted more, we would have to go on. Our maps identified the next source as a spring in the ominously named Fryingpan Canyon, a mile or so farther, and we picked up our pace, anxious to end the day with full canteens. But the canyon didn't look promising, either: It greeted us with a streambed that held water perhaps once a year; the rest of the time—

specifically, now—it was a dry gully. We slogged through its soft, ankle-deep sand, which was relieved only by cactus and recently deposited cow manure. We were actually delighted to see the latter—it indicated that there was indeed water in the vicinity. At the dead end of the canyon we found the spring: three inches deep, several feet wide, covered with scum and insects, and surrounded by cattle dung. We sent up a shout of celebration and set up our camp.

Fryingpan Spring lies 1 mile northeast of Massacre Peak, in the middle of the Cookes Range, about 3 miles south of Rattlesnake Ridge. And if you think it sounds inhospitable now, just think what it would have been like 130 years ago, when it became part of the route of the first transcontinental stage line from the Mississippi River to the West Coast.

The terrain looks now about as it did then, as dry and nasty and harsh and stark. It is reasonable, indeed, to ask why anyone would put a stage route through such hostile country. Wasn't there somewhere else to go? And as if the dust and the cactus and the sun and the sand aren't bad enough, imagine it back in Wild West days: Indian country, and not only that—Apache country, smack in the middle of a war party's travel route to and from Old Mexico.

The likes of Geronimo and Mangas Colorado were at home in this rugged terrain. They had learned its secrets as young boys; they knew how to climb the peaks to look for the green, telltale sign of a spring, and to travel at night to avoid detection. They would have known of Fryingpan Spring, and they would have known of Cookes Canyon, a 4-mile narrow defile with high rocky walls: an ambush site that was an invitation to trouble.

The man who built the overland stage route through this hellish expanse of New Mexican desert was a New York–born entrepreneur, but despite his big-city background, he was no stranger to such ventures. John Butterfield had already installed the first telegraph line between New York City and Buffalo, had constructed the first steam railroad in his adopted hometown of Utica, New York, and had operated a number of other stagecoach lines throughout the country. In 1857, he received a $600,000 contract from the federal government to open up the first transcontinental stage line from the Mississippi to the West Coast, and he soon learned of the new and unique challenges that confronted this particular venture.

The route through Cookes Canyon—considered to be one of the most dangerous sites along the entire stage route—was one of them. The surrounding mountains provided hiding places for Indians—and later, for warring Confederate soldiers and southern sympathizers. The flat, open country to the south was far safer; it offered no hiding places for marauding Apaches—but no water, either. The mountains were far more dangerous, but the mountains had water: seep springs that collected rainfall among the canyons and the peaks. Cookes Spring was the only reliable water between the Rio Grande and the Mimbres River. The stage would have to pass through the mountains. Despite the danger, Butterfield's stage company never failed to meet its timetable for the twice-a-week mail and passenger service between Saint Louis and San Francisco, a distance of 2,800 miles, which was traversed within a period of twenty-five days.

Largely because of the presence of Cookes Spring Station, the U.S. Army decided to construct adjacent Fort Cummings in 1863 to protect the stage line and the westward-bound immigrants on the treacherous journey through the canyon. The fort was a serious business. The adobe walls were twelve feet high, with windows that faced only into the interior courtyard. The interior complex included a hospital, commissary, and quartermaster's supply depot as well as quarters for officers and enlisted men. But officers and enlisted men alike had to tolerate the ants, scorpions, centipedes, and tarantulas that overran the fort's dirt floors, and the rattlesnakes that frequently nested indoors—often in an unsuspecting soldier's clothing. When the men consigned to this dismal outpost were not worrying about desert animals, they were worrying about Indians. Even the interior of the fort was not safe: It was not uncommon for Apaches to cut through the walls at night and steal horses. As for outside, the soldiers soon began to refer to passage through the canyon as the "Journey of Death."

Today, little remains of the fort. There are a few crumbling adobe walls, and a cement cap covers once-bubbling Cookes Spring. The Bureau of Land Management administers the area as a historic site, but the only signs of management are a locked mobile home, a trash can, and a box containing a notebook in which visitors can leave their names. The register told us that it had been many months since anyone else had been there; the last visitors had arrived riding on an off-road vehicle.

As we continued north, the terrain slowly changed. We were climbing slightly, which meant that piñon and juniper joined our scanty list of vegetation. Even the cacti responded to the change: The ubiquitous prickly pears were huge and fat, their "ears" sometimes as much as a foot long. And the trees were big enough to offer real shade when we stopped for our daily breaks.

We were approaching the Gila National Forest. The higher elevations just ahead assured us of more trees, and the maps told us that we would soon leave the jeep roads for marked hiking trails. But most important, in the mountains and forests of the Gila, there was the promise of water. From the sparse, stingy desert, we would ascend into rich stands of timber, to Douglas fir and ponderosa pine, with its thick bark that smells like butterscotch pudding. We would walk among the high peaks of the Gila, some of which are more than 10,000 feet in elevation. But to get there, we would have to climb, and that was going to be a problem.

I was getting tired. We had been walking for twelve days now, 158 miles, and we hadn't yet taken a complete day off. My legs were starting to complain, and when we began to climb for real, they staged an out-and-out rebellion. Unfortunately, they picked our first crossing of the Continental Divide to make their opinions known about hiking and climbing in general, and this trip in particular. As a result, what I remember most about that first ceremonial crossing of the Divide—10:57 A.M. on May 13, from the Atlantic to the Pacific watershed—is the pain in my legs. It didn't help that the footway was rough and nasty, filled with rocks that chose the exact moment I stepped on them to slide downhill. Karl dug out some protein powder soy drink and vitamins, which I obediently swallowed, secretly wondering whether this first crossing of the Divide would also be my last crossing of the Divide. Even with Dan and

Karl taking most of my pack weight, it took me quite a bit longer than they to slog to the top of the fire tower, where the warden looked at me and commented, "You guys don't do such a good job of staying together, do you?"

If he had been able to see us trooping downhill, he might have revised his opinion. The three of us almost raced down the mountain, exhaustion forgotten. But the easy jeep trail wasn't the only reason we were rushing off the mountain. At the bottom, Sue and Gordon would be waiting for us with some cold drinks and a ride into Silver City. It was time for a full day off in town—and this time, we had earned it.

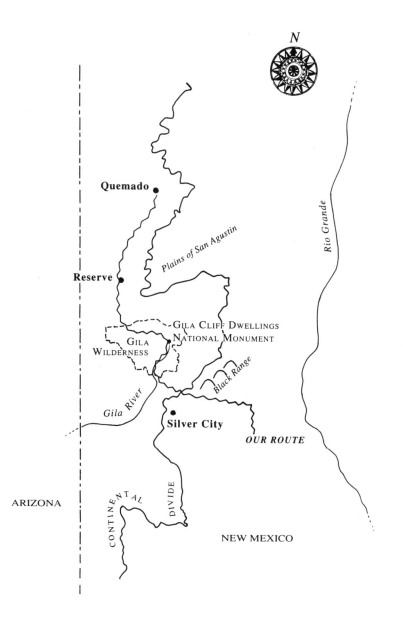

2

≈≈≈≈≈

THE GILA

≈≈≈≈≈

The Gila River is nothing if not serene. Meandering, snakelike—in no great rush to go anywhere—the river makes its lazy way through deep canyons, flowing west, toward Arizona and beyond, to the Pacific Ocean. Cliffs line its edges—steep walls of rock that tower far above the water, 1,000 feet or more. It is the cliffs that give the river its stunning drama; it is the cliffs that isolate the river and defend its solitude. It is the cliffs—brilliantly colored, precipitously vertical—that create a canyon so wild and primitive that one can imagine that he has traveled backwards through geological time.

But the cliffs only seem to dominate the landscape; they are themselves dominated by the river, sculpted by waters that have twisted and turned in an eons-old search for the path of least resistance through the rock. In the end, the river and the rock have come to grudging compromise; the water is allowed to pass, but the cliffs determine its route. Hence the river's circuitous path through the red-and-gold canyons.

The Gila ("Hee-la," you say it), a Spanish derivation so shortened and changed from the original Yuma words that one could be excused for thinking that lexicographers write fiction. Or else how do you get *Gila* from *Hah-quah-sa-eel*?

Spanish and Anglo travelers have given the river many names in the region's 400 years of European settlement. There were other derivations—the Hila, the Helay, or the Xila—and there were grand ecclesiastical names that could only be Spanish—the River of the Name of Jesus or the River of the Apostles. Sometimes, the names are editorial comments: neutral descriptions (the Blue), or happy ones (River of the Sun); and sometimes the opposite: the River of Despair, the Fresh Water Abomination, the Poison. The Yuma name paid tribute to this last aspect of the river's character: It translates to "Running Water Which Is Salty." Farther downstream, in Arizona, the water is indeed saline, but here, near the river's headwaters, the more flattering adjectives applied. The river was blue and sunny.

Today, one might well rename the Gila "the River that Never Reaches the Sea." In the wilderness, the Gila is left to run unfettered, but for most of its 600 miles this is a working river, a thin thread of blue whose job is to transform the surrounding Arizona desert into lush green fields. It is a big job, and the Gila is exhausted by the time it joins the Colorado River in a desert confluence near Yuma, where most of the water that remains in the Colorado River System is siphoned off to California's Imperial Valley. The rest—a pathetic saline trickle—flows downstream to the Morelos Dam, to be used to irrigate Mexican farms.

If not using water is the equivalent of wasting it, and if wasting water is a sin, then the people who inhabit the Colorado River drainage are a community of saints. For water is not wasted here—all of it, every drop, is used long before it reaches the ocean. And even though we think of the Continental Divide as America's giant watershed, sending rainfall to opposite seas, the ironic reality is that, except in a year of exceptionally heavy rainfall, not one drop of water from the Gila—nor from the Green, the San Juan, or any other tributary of the Colorado River—will ever reach the ocean. The Colorado River and its tributaries drain the western slope of the Great

Divide from New Mexico to Wyoming; they carry the waters of tens of thousands of streams and creeks rushing down steep mountain slopes; they drain the winter's accumulation of snow from the highest peaks of the Rocky Mountains. But by the time the Colorado riverbed meets the Gulf of California, it is as dry and dusty as the desert itself.

≈≈≈≈≈≈

We chose our campsite on a sandy spit at the confluence of the Gila River and Sapillo Creek. The site had been used before—we could tell by the initials carved into a few old trees, the rusting cans, half buried in the sand, the fire pits dotting the ground. It was nonetheless a beautiful site, with a breathtaking view of the river. We sat on the spit, admiring the isolated, almost prehistoric landscape that might look today exactly as it did 20,000 years ago, before man ever came to the American Southwest.

The next morning, we awoke to a breakfast flavored by sunrise-colored bluffs and a clear blue sky that promised fine weather. It was easy to be in good humor. The map told us that there would be no big climbs and no route-finding challenges, and although we were heading upstream, the elevation gain would be minuscule—a mere thirty or so feet per mile. The water, of course, was the biggest luxury of all.

On a map, walking along a river looks easy and logical. A river is identifiable; it sets an irrefutable course: There! Right there, it cuts a clear path through the land, a ribbon of blue, edged by green. In practice, a river can be a source of tedious obstacles and diabolical surprises; it can test the traveler's stamina and patience; it can demonstrate precisely why the word *travel* derives from *travail*.

It might, for instance, play hide-and-seek with you, as you walk along one bank and it disappears up the other, leaving you to follow an unwanted tributary. It can twist and turn, forcing you to crawl over flood-eroded banks or to bushwack through riparian vegetation: thorny horsetail, poison ivy, or thick willow, depending on where you are. And then there are the rocks and the driftwood littered in your path, as well as fallen trees ripped from the riverbank. There are boulders to climb over and cottonwood branches to crawl under, and there is the not insignificant problem of getting from one side to the other.

A river can also be deadly; it can run too fast or too deep or too cold. The bottom can be muddy, or rocky, or slippery. Rivers—following them, crossing them, using them—have defined the travel routes of the West. But they have not always been willing collaborators in exploration and conquest. Explorer John Wesley Powell almost died, trapped in rapids of the raging Colorado. Migrants on the Oregon Trail "saw the elephant" as they hauled and pushed and cursed their wagons across the loamy-bottomed North Platte. And the journals of Lewis and Clark describe the power of an undammed and untamed Columbia.

If the gentle, shallow Gila is hardly a monster of life-threatening intentions, neither is it a cooperative traveling companion. It has the personality of a jealous younger sibling who, if he can't be as strong, can at least cause as much trouble.

The cliffs had made it difficult for the water to pass through them; and the water had had all the time in the world to carve its way. It might have occurred to us that the cliffs would put obstacles in our path, too. If we had read the account of the first Anglo-American ever to voyage along the banks of the Gila, we would have known precisely what was in store for us.

"We made but little advance this day," recorded explorer and mountain man James Ohio Pattie, visiting the upper Gila in 1825, "as bluffs came in so close to the river, as to compel us to cross it thirty-six times, sometimes upon our hands and knees, through a thick tangle of grape-vines and under-brush. Added to the unpleasantness of this mode of getting along in itself, we did not know, but the next moment would bring us face to face with a bear, which might accost us suddenly."

Twenty-one years later, the Gila presented the same obstacles to the Army of the West. Led by the indefatigable Kit Carson, the army joined the river downstream from where we were walking and followed it west toward California. In the party was John S. Griffin, M.D., the first licensed doctor to settle in California and a conscientious diarist. "We had two difficulties presented to us," wrote Griffin: "We took [the canyon of the river] as the lesser evil. . . . In following the course of the river, we were obliged to cross it every half mile or so, the mountain jutting down to the very edge of the stream, making a very picturesque affair of it . . . the fact is that we have so much of the grand and sublime I am tired of it."

More than a hundred and fifty years later, the region is much unchanged, and so is the reaction of the traveler. Dr. Griffin and I would both have traded the grand and sublime for a decent stretch of trail.

Later in the hike, we'd have simply walked the whole thing in waterlogged boots, which is what most people would have done in the first place. James Pattie, for instance, wouldn't have bothered with keeping his feet dry. But I was still pampering mine, worried about blisters and unwilling to let wet boots jinx the good luck I'd enjoyed so far. So the ritual began at each of our forty or more crossings: packs off, boots and socks off, cross the river, dry the feet, socks and boots back on, hoist the pack, walk a few minutes, do it again, do it again, do it again.

In between fords, there was the vegetation to climb around, most notably, the bright green triads of poison ivy. It's a beautiful plant, I've always thought: shiny, vibrant, strong. Early immigrants to America thought so too, and tried to use it as decorative shrubbery in their gardens, with predictable results. As for me, I am so allergic to it that touching a piece of clothing that has touched the plant can send me, running, to a doctor. I covered myself with rain gear, trading the future misery of a rash for the present misery of hiking in 90-degree direct sun wearing a full outfit of foul-weather Gore-Tex.

By lunchtime we had walked for four hours, and had barely covered 4.5 miles. We decided to try sloshing through the river crossings in sneakers, which worked for Karl and Dan. For me, the blisters came immediately, and bandages didn't help: They simply fell off in the water. I went back to taking my boots off and putting them back on at every crossing, while Dan and Karl waited in the sun.

There were other folk scattered along the Gila: horse packers, mostly, a few fishermen, and a group of college students headed downstream on rafts. The students were, they told us, doing a field study of the Gila's ecology. But their attention seemed entirely taken up with floating, which is more a problem of physics. For it is no easier to float down the river than it is to walk.

Pattie had camped at the hot springs, near the confluence with the West Fork, but we didn't make it that far. And the next day we took the easy way out: climbing 1,000 feet up a steep path to escape the river bottom. Pattie, the trailblazer, had not had the option of taking a U.S. Forest Service trail.

≈≈≈≈≈≈

This part of the Gila National Forest has some of the most remote country in the United States. It also contains the first officially designated wilderness in America, set aside by the Forest Service in 1924, a full forty years before Congress passed a national wilderness act. It was an important marker, this decision to designate the Gila as wilderness—"a region which contains no permanent inhabitants, possesses no means of mechanical conveyance, and is sufficiently spacious that a person may spend at least a week or two of travel without crossing his own tracks." It marks the point when man realized that it was wilderness that needed protection from him, and not the other way around.

Just a generation before, the wildernesses of the West had been invincible, endless, overwhelming. It would have been preposterous to protect them. Settlers flooded across the plains and over the mountains, miners worked their claims, loggers cut down forests, and still there was no end to the trees and the ore and the animals and the grasses. And then, suddenly, the wilderness was not endless anymore. Old-timers looked at the grasses and said "the range ain't what it used to be." They stopped seeing game where their daddies had once taken them to hunt. And the rivers they used to fish— gone, now, perhaps swallowed by a hydro development that channeled water to some faraway farm.

By the 1920s, the frontier had been declared closed for twenty years. In the far West, Hetch Hetchy Valley was long under water; John Muir was already dead. In Washington, Gifford Pinchot was developing conservation theories that would dominate resource use for the rest of the century.

It was Aldo Leopold, midwestern farm boy and New Mexican Forest Service supervisor, who posed the idea of wilderness in the *Journal of Forestry* in 1920. Two years later, he visited the Gila, and proposed setting aside some 500,000 acres. Leopold was a curious mixture: both a product of his time and a prophet for the future. He hunted elk and mountain lions, and was committed to the government's predator-control program and its single-minded campaign to exterminate every last wolf from the American West. He changed his mind on that, though, letting himself listen to the wilderness's side of the story as he watched the green fire fade in a dying she-wolf's eyes. It was an issue he would struggle with for some years, and one he flip-flopped on more than his late-twentieth-century admirers would like to remember. But in the end, he came down solidly on the side of wilderness and the value of wild things. His legacy to us is the best land ethics statement ever written; he taught us to think like a mountain. We could use him today: a man whose love of the land encompasses using it and preserving it and living with it—not apart from it, and not in violation of it. One of the units of the Gila's three wilderness areas bears his name.

Since 1924, the concept of wilderness—what it is, why we have it, how it is managed—has been refined, developed, and finally, in 1964, written into federal law. Laws mean rules: rules about what can and can't be done if this, that, or the other thing happens. By the time the Forest Service, the industry lobbyists, the politicians, and the environmentalists got done with it, the Wilderness Act was filled with rules and compromises, and an odd conglomeration they were.

Man is supposed to be a visitor, that's simple enough. You won't find any houses, or hotels, or airstrips, or parking lots in the Gila wilderness. So far so good. But the restrictions don't apply to livestock. In a compromise necessary to the bill's passage, Congress permitted grazing in wilderness areas where grazing allotments already existed. They already existed in the Gila, so when you imagine yourself walking in the footsteps of James Pattie, you are more likely to come upon a herd of cattle than upon the bears that worried the old-time explorers.

Natural processes, including naturally caused fires, are supposed to be let alone to play their roles in wilderness. However, just watch what happens if a fire starts near a forest border on the other side of which is a stand of commercially harvestable timber. Then, natural processes be damned and save the timber! Power tools are not permitted in the wilderness, but trail building is, which means that in the late twentieth century, trail crews eschew chain saws for clippers and axes. There are some exceptions about power tools, though: mining for instance. Yes, some mining is permitted in wilderness areas, and it's a fair guess that they don't use picks and shovels.

Still, there are a lot of things you can't do in wilderness: You can't clear-cut timber, you can't roar in on a three-wheeler, you can't open a concession stand, and you can't build a ski lift; and for that, we have to be grateful. In a nation that once seriously considered damming the Colorado River near the Grand Canyon, and still regularly comes up with such environmental insanities as Colorado's Two Forks Dam, hunting Montana's grizzly bears, and logging old-growth forests, our great places need all the help they can get. The Wilderness Act has been a powerful ally.

The contemporary definition of wilderness requires that man's status be relegated to that of a visitor. But man has, in fact, inhabited the remote Gila for many centuries—10,000 years, as far as archaeologists have been able to figure. A hundred years ago this was miners' country; the hills are dotted with old claims and dilapidated cabins. Before gold and silver and copper fed the appetites of early settlers and booming mining towns, this was the land of the Apaches, the hunting and fighting grounds of Cochise and Geronimo and Mangas Colorado. Spanish colonists lived here, too, farming the valleys. And even further back in time, the Gila was home to a vanished culture of people who farmed on the mesas and constructed complex stone pueblos perched high in volcanic cliffs.

It is because of these centuries-old pueblos that our climb out of the canyon led us to a paved road. The road links Silver City to the Gila Cliff Dwellings National Monument. Before 1966, tourists to the cliff dwellings had to trudge in on horseback or four-wheel-drive jeeps. Today, the monument is more accessible than it used to be; all it takes is a tortuous round trip of 88 miles. Once at the monument, you can enjoy all the amenities of developed camping: a nearby general store, a visitors' center, a campground, and livery stables.

Fortunately, the development has not penetrated the backcountry. Visitors to the monument stay pretty much in the campground and on the paths leading up to the cliff dwellings. If you take any trail a mile into the forest, out of earshot from the road, you are back among the mountains and the trees and the wind and the elk and the deer and the bears—and the cows, of course. You can, if you like, go back to the pretty illusion that yours are the first eyes to see this wilderness—except for the work crews who built the trails and the ranchers who must occasionally ride in to move their stock. And except for the occasional shadows from the past: a settler's cabin, roof bowed by rain and time, or a faint petroglyph scratched into a rock wall, whispering to you across the distance of a millennium or more.

※※※※※

At the Gila cliff dwellings, the past speaks in a louder voice. Here, in a series of five caves, are the ruins of one of the earliest apartment dwellings in America, built by Mogollon people of the thirteenth century.

The pueblo is an airy, high-ceilinged place, a cool refuge from the desert heat. In the winter, one imagines that it would be cold, but the caves face southeast, to the sun, and heat-loving prickly pear cactus, yucca, and agave grow in the sand outside. The cave ceilings are smudged with dark layers of ash from countless cook fires, and there are charcoal-stained fire pits in the rooms. The construction is simple and uncluttered; a distant precursor of the Anglicized and sanitized Santa Fe style: hand-hewn stones held together with mortar, wooden vigas, T-shaped doorways, and ladders on which one would descend into the rooms. The interlocking complex blends into the cliff until you must look carefully to see where the man-made structure ends and the cave beings.

There are forty small rooms in this complex, nestled into the cliffs of the Gila conglomerate 180 feet above the valley floor. From the pueblo, you can look across to a mesa on the other side of the canyon; this is where the ten or fifteen families who lived in the cliffs would have planted and tended their crops of squash, corn, and beans. It seems a remarkably sensible existence. The cliff dwellers had shelter, a good source of water, and arable land. In the woods were nuts, berries, seeds, and game. They must have intended to remain in their vertiginous homes for some time; clearly, the pueblo was built to last. But sometime in the 1320s, the people simply vanished.

There is a sense of timelessness here, as though they left only yesterday. They could return, one thinks, and reclaim their cliff. After all, their homes have remained very much intact; in short order, they could repair the roofs and a few collapsed walls and carry on with their peaceful existence.

We know little about this existence, about its day-to-day routines and rituals. The cliff dwellers left clues, but not many: Archaeologists have found bits of clothing, stone tools, bone awls, arrow shafts, jewelry, manos and metates for grinding grain, storage bins filled with corncobs, even a child's skeleton, all preserved by the desert aridity. One thing they have not found is pottery: Almost all of it was stolen before the monument came under protection.

The people of the upper Gila were among the first potters in the region, and among them were the Mimbreños, the most famous artisans of southwestern pre-Columbian earthenware. A few days after we left the cliff dwellings, we would see our first Mogollon ceramics, and we would learn what all the fuss was about.

Our lesson about southwestern artifacts came about courtesy of a Mexican-American rancher on whose land we were trespassing. It was a national forest inholding, a wide open field surrounded by timbered ridges. Three generations of the ranch family live here, in two houses separated by a quarter mile of dirt road. The rancher's home was a half mile or so past the gate, where he intercepted us, stopping to check us out. He chuckled when he heard what we were doing. "I always wanted to try and walk up here from the border myself," he said. "I wanted to see what would happen if a Mexican-American tried walking through that country. I figured I'd get a couple of miles from the border before one of the INS guys came around. Maybe. You want to come in for some iced tea?"

His home was a modest wood structure from outside; inside, it looked as though it could have been designed for a magazine on southwestern style. Except that this home lacked the cloying designer cuteness that seems to infect regional motifs. Perhaps that was because the rancher had built the house himself: cut the wood, chosen the site, dug the foundation. There was something honest in this house that you can't buy from a catalog.

It was while he was digging the foundation that the rancher learned that he was not the first human to be attracted by the possibilities of the gentle valley. For when he turned up the earth, he found that he had dug straight into the garbage heap of the previous residents.

Archaeologists call such a trash heap a kitchen midden, and they flock to the detritus of these old dumps as though yesterday's garbage is today's rare treasure. Sometimes it is; this was one of those times. Among the debris were dozens of ancient ceramic vessels, many of them unbroken. After excavation—by an invited team of archaeologists—the rancher sold most of the pots. A few of them, however, sit in a small collection in a glass case, and every once in a while, he says, as he's walking around the ranch, he kicks up another shard or two.

It's not difficult to understand the attraction of the ancient bowls. Adorned with unique black-on-white designs, Mimbres classic pottery is known for its meticulous decorations. Humans dance across the pots in joyful ritual; animals, fish, and birds—some in shapes and positions strange to our modern eyes—cavort through time. There are abstract designs, too: elegant, vibrant geometric patterns that would not be out of place in a supermodern steel-and-glass office.

We do not know how the Mogollon people first acquired the skill of mixing clay, shaping a bowl, and firing it so that it hardened into a permanent, waterproof vessel. We do not know how they learned to paint with brushes made of yucca fibers dipped into the extracts of mustard or guaco, nor how they mastered the use of heat and fire to stain the vessels in different colors.

What we do know is that these pots dramatically changed the daily lives of the southwestern people. It seems difficult, in our century of material excess, to understand how the possession of a single pot could be so important. But it is only difficult until you look at what the precious pots replaced: baskets, which had been used throughout the Southwest for the preceding 9,000 years. Making the old baskets was labor-intensive: First, fibers were carefully twisted, plaited, and coiled; then they were woven together as tightly as possible to make a good strong basket, one that would last a long time. The baskets were used for carrying, preparing, and storing food—and for cooking, too. Lined with wet clay and left to dry, the baskets could hold water, temporarily, at least, but they were still flammable. Cooking was therefore a tedious process of taking heated, ash-covered stones from the fire and dropping them into the newly waterproofed vessel.

The new pots were an improvement all around: They were permanently waterproof, they could sit right on the fire, and perhaps most important, they could protect food stores from animals. By safeguarding next season's seeds and by holding excess food against an uncertain future, these new pots gave the Mogollon people something they had never had: control over their food supply.

It is not surprising, then, that the pots held spiritual significance.

When a person died, his pot was symbolically killed, with a hole cut into its middle. Thus rendered useless in this life, perhaps its soul was free to accompany its owner to the hereafter. Many of the pots that have been found in the Southwest have been excavated from burial sites, and even those that are intact have a small hole chipped into the bottom. Whether the souls of these pots are in heaven may be up for argument, but their corporeal remains are found throughout southwestern museums. Or in the homes of collectors.

In the Gila National Forest, the value and popularity of these pots is cause for concern. In recent years, the crafts of southwestern Indians have enjoyed a dizzying rise in both popularity and price. The Santa Fe style, with its sleek juxtaposition of native arts, natural building materials, and Anglo sheen, depends on them. You can buy yourself a piece of New Mexico's clear air and sandy land in the tony plaza galleries of Santa Fe and Taos, as well as in the pawnshops and trading posts near the reservations: $8,000 for a first-rate Navajo rug, $1,000 for a Zuñi pot, $300 for a kachina doll, $20,000 for a nineteenth-century Navajo chief's blanket.

But if you are going to collect southwestern art, a pre-Columbian pot is the prize. And a good pot, whole, with a unique design, can set you back $40,000 or more—if you can find it. Which is why, in addition to being wealthy, it helps if you are not overly concerned about where the pot came from.

If you were to concern yourself with such things as provenance, you would know that it is illegal to remove artifacts from federal land. Nonetheless, almost all of the prehistoric sites along the upper Gila have been vandalized. Pot hunters typically excavate with bulldozers and backhoes. If motorized transport is a problem, they use picks and shovels. In either case, by the time archaeologists arrive, armed with dental tools and fine-haired brushes, most of what they could have learned has been altered or stolen.

To an archaeologist, the value of an undisturbed site lies not so much in the artifacts it contains but in the information to be gleaned from these artifacts. Selective stealing leaves behind an altered record. Think about excavating a contemporary landfill. Last year's newspaper lies under today's video game, and the archaeologists of the future will have no trouble at all in finding a time frame for

Teenage Mutant Ninja Turtles. The same happens in middens, where the placement of artifacts in relation to each other and to the layers of habitation puts them in time and context. This bowl was found next to that tool; this piece of cloth lay near that necklace. This tool was contemporaneous with that activity, and so on and so on. This is information that cannot be discerned from any single artifact alone, and it certainly cannot be gleaned from a site that has been disturbed.

Although the penalties on the books are severe, including heavy fines and jail sentences, illegal excavation and theft are difficult to prosecute. Judges and juries aren't disposed to treat pot hunting the same way they would treat other crimes. Despite efforts by the Forest Service, the rewards often outweigh the risks. One or two pots can put a nice chunk of cash in your pocket; a midden can make you rich.

So pot hunters continue to prowl the woods, looking for ancient ollas to sell. And the insatiably curious twentieth-century archaeologists continue to search for sites to excavate, seeking answers to the mysteries left by a vanished culture. They poke around the homes of the long-dead Mogollon, digging in their sacred kivas, their sleeping rooms, their kitchen cabinets, and their garbage dumps, trying to uncover information about the most mundane aspects of their daily existence: What did they wear? Why did they build T-shaped doors? What is the meaning of the figures on their pottery? Why did they construct the elaborate cliff dwellings—a structure so permanent that it survives to this day—and abandon it after only a generation of use? And finally, where did they go?

The cliff dwellings stand silent; they are not telling.

———

We fell asleep, lulled by the timeless sounds of the forest. The breeze whispered its secrets to the pines; these would have been familiar, soothing sounds to the Mogollon people, as they were to the small group of us camped near the base of their abandoned homes. The noises that woke us up would have been familiar to the cliff dwellers, too. The furtive rustling of an animal helping itself to your food is easily recognized, even if you are half asleep and dreaming of another century. We had left our food on the picnic table. The Mogollon, with their ceramic ollas, would have known better.

Rangers usually recommend that backpackers hang their food in trees to keep animals away. In the desert, we hadn't worried about animals coming into our camp, and even if we had wanted to hang our food, we couldn't have: There weren't any trees. By the time we reached the Gila, we were spoiled and lazy, and it didn't even occur to us to think about animals.

It should have. In our drive-in campsite, the birds were so tame that they thought nothing of landing on our arms and helping themselves to pieces of bread. Even some novice car-campers, a teenage couple whose tent-erecting exercise had provided an hour's amusement for us, had had enough sense to stow their food in their car. But here we were, experienced hikers with 20,000 miles under our collective belts, and an animal was dining on its choice of sweet-and-sour shrimp, granola bars, and leftover baked beans at two o'clock in the morning.

And not just any animal, as Dan saw when he approached the picnic table armed with a flashlight. Our nocturnal dinner guest was instantly recognizable, with the raised black-and-white stripes of a tail cocked for action. Obviously, the skunk's instinct to defend its food—stolen or not—was every bit as strong as ours. Dan froze; so did the skunk, and the standoff ended with mutual retreat.

The decision we made next could only have been made by people who were sleepwalking, although the fact that we both remember it quite well makes short shrift of that excuse. Once the skunk was safely out of sight, we retrieved the food and put it near our heads, assuring each other that a wild animal wouldn't come that close.

And then we went back to sleep.

Ten minutes later, I was awakened by a short, urgent whisper.

"Karen . . . are . . . you . . . awake? Don't talk— Don't move."

I didn't have to hear any more. The skunk had chosen the most direct route between the bushes and the food—and that route went directly across the sleeping bag I had pulled over my head. I could feel delicate paws sinking through the down sleeping bag onto my nose. If you've ever had a cat, you know what it feels like: the stealthy, light touch of tiny feet walking across your blankets at night. The skunk left my head, tiptoed into a paper bag, and grabbed a loaf of bread. Then it backed out of the bag, dragging the plastic-wrapped package in its teeth. Tail up, watching us with eyes flashing an electric green, it continued to walk backward, moving with the deliberate control of a ballet dancer. Finally, it disappeared into the shrubs and shadows on the periphery of our campsite.

The next morning, a shredded plastic bag and a few crusts were left as evidence of the evening raid. We repacked our belongings and headed back into the wilderness, where the animals were less likely to think of us as a walking garbage can.

At Columbus, we had started our walk at an altitude of 4,000 feet. At the cliff dwellings, the altitude was 6,000 feet. Two days later, we climbed to the top of the 10,770-foot Mogollon Baldy—a climb that was the climatic equivalent of walking to the Arctic Circle. Standing on the summit, we had a view that extended 60 miles in any direction. The temperature hovered around the freezing point, and we put on every piece of clothing in our backpacks. On the north-facing slopes, the snow had not yet melted. In the distance, we could still see the desert.

As a rule of thumb, walking 1,000 feet uphill is the equivalent of traveling 170 miles north. The specific formula varies: Mountain chains make their own weather; ocean streams and wind currents collide; so do pressure systems and rainfall, all of which have an effect on what can grow and live in any particular place. Unlikely as it sounds, you can find arctic conditions—snow, ice, lichens, rocks—on the equator. All you have to do is find a mountain and walk 15,000 feet uphill.

Since the beginning of our trip, we had walked 230 miles. As the crow flies, we had come only about 150 miles due north, not enough for latitude to make an appreciable difference. But ascending 6,000 feet made all the difference in the world. From the creosote and cactus, we had climbed to sagebrush, then to mixed piñon-juniper forest. In the Gila, we had risen farther, to oak and ponderosa pine; then finally Douglas fir. Now, on the summit of Mogollon Baldy, we were at the very top of the so-called Hudsonian zone. To find a comparable life zone at sea level, we would have had to travel to the northern part of Hudson Bay in Canada.

Mogollon's summit is a cold and windswept place, an unlikely spot for a cabin. Regardless, a log cabin perches on top of the mountain, serving as the summer home of the firewatchers. Nearby, a fire tower pokes itself another thirty feet into the air.

"Come on up!" the fire warden called down, and we started up a ladder that led to the cab, a room perched on top of the spindly stairs and enclosed by wall-to-wall windows. Dan and Karl scampered up the stairs like a couple of five-year-olds on a jungle gym, but my stomach was visited by the familiar vertigo when I got about halfway up and looked down—straight down—over millions of acres of New Mexico.

"You get used to it," the fire warden encouraged, as I struggled to climb through the trapdoor at the top. Dan and Karl were already playing with the equipment: high-power binoculars, and the fire-finder, which is a flat table with a map, a viewfinder, and a compass that identifies precise coordinates for any place in the forest. Life in the fire tower could lead to an interesting combination of claustrophobia and agoraphobia, I thought, as I looked around and tried to banish my vertigo: On the one hand, the wardens are enclosed ten hours a day in a tiny fourteen-foot-square cab; on the other, stretched in front of them is an unobstructed view clear to forever. We could see all the way back to Mexico.

There are several lookout towers in the Gila National Forest, each staffed by a team of two Forest Service employees who are the forest's first line of defense against wildfire. We can vouch for their vigilance. On top of Mogollon's tower, we traded stories with the firewatcher, and as we described our route, she started nodding.

"Did you guys make a fire yesterday?" she asked.

"We almost always do."

"Did you camp"—she pointed to the map, to a clearing called McKenna Park—"somewhere near here?"

We had, in fact, camped exactly under her finger, in a green park where a herd of elk had joined us for breakfast. "How did you know?"

"Well, that explains it."

"That explains what?"

"The fire. I called in your campfire."

"Our campfire?"

"It's been a dry year," she explained. "Moisture content is low, and if a fire gets started it's more likely to burn. We've had a couple of suspicious blazes in the last couple of weeks. I knew your fire was man-made; there hadn't been any lightning strikes. And it had big puffs of smoke coming up from it—maybe from when you dumped water on it to put it out? It looked weird, so I called it in. They sent a helicopter from Silver City to check it out, but by the time it got to McKenna Park the fire was out."

"We were probably on our way up here by that time."

"Well, at least I know I wasn't dreaming," she said. "The helicopter guys were giving me a hard time over the radio."

Looking down into the waves of mountains, you can see why the firewatchers are so careful. On the surrounding slopes, a patchwork of vegetation tells the forest's fire history. Old burns are covered with stands of young conifers. More recent fires are easily identified by groves of aspens, with the quaking silvery green leaves of springtime. Shrubs cover the charred slopes of the newest burns, and sun-loving plants like wild roses bask in light that no longer has to fight its way through the canopies of evergreen trees. But on some slopes the scars have not had time to heal, and the wounds are still raw and fresh: ashy earth, whitened tree trunks, black stumps.

Forest fires, as we all know, are something to be prevented. Smokey the Bear—a New Mexico native, by the way—taught us well: Fires are bad. Smokey taught his lesson so well that by the time ecologists realized that some fires are good—necessary, even— the juggernaut of fire suppression was almost impossible to stop.

Natural fires are actually a part of the cycle of rejuvenation and change in a healthy forest. They encourage species diversity, ecologic stability, pest resistance, and new growth by enriching the soil, letting sunlight in, and killing old, sick trees. In some forest systems, fires are not only common; they are essential. The Gila is one of these. Without fire, deadwood builds up, the forest floor is shaded against new growth, and seeds don't germinate. Some scientists speculate that certain species of trees are so adapted to fire that they can't survive without it. The cones of the ponderosa, for instance, pop open to germinate when they are subject to extreme heat. The ponderosa is one of seven species that help to cause fire by covering the ground with highly flammable, dead pine needles, which ensures that the trees will eventually burn—and that new seeds will sprout.

Now that science has caught up with Smokey, fire management has been added to the list of controversies in the West. Fires can be unpredictable, uncontrollable, and awful, and they can leave ugly scars and acres of bleak devastation—not to mention millions of dollars in property damage. Walking through a burn, you might be tempted to say—and many people do—"If this is a healthy forest, give me a sick one."

"You bet it's controversial," said Teresa, the firewatcher at Bearwallow Mountain, the next tower north of Mogollon Baldy. "Fire is a part of the ecosystem. The ponderosas depend on it. But try telling that to a logging company that has leased a stand of timber. Or to an inholder who runs a ranch surrounded by national forest. Plus, there's another problem here. You'll see it when you try to bushwhack off of this peak." She pointed down the mountain: The trails on the Forest Service map no longer existed, and we were trying to figure out how we were going to get down.

"The Forest Service used to have a policy of total suppression. If small fires had been allowed to burn, they would have consumed the dead wood that falls on the forest floor little by little. But they weren't, so all that dry fuel has been allowed to build up. It doesn't rot quickly in this climate; it just accumulates. Parts of this forest are a tinderbox."

We had noticed the abundance of dry downed wood, and we asked Teresa about the prescribed burn policy that is supposed to let fire play its role in wilderness.

"Some fires are allowed to burn," Teresa confirmed. "But the Forest Service can only let fires burn if they meet certain prescriptions: the moisture content in the trees, the weather, the wind, the amount of fuel on the ground. In parts of the Gila, the amount of dead wood is so great that I don't know if it's even possible to have a prescribed fire anymore. And in dry years like this, the parts of the forest that are really dangerous just get worse. There's no way they can let them burn because there's too much danger of a fire getting out of control. So, the pile of deadwood on the ground gets bigger and bigger. And of course, there's public opinion to worry about as well." Teresa rolled her eyes.

"Public opinion?"

"Yeah. The Forest Service doesn't want to have to explain to an angry group of ranchers and loggers why a fire that could have been put out when it started got out of control. People around here can be pretty critical of the Forest Service. Anyway, you'll see how bad the deadwood is when you try to bushwhack off this mountain." Teresa pointed to a thin cut, a speck just barely visible through the trees. "See that?" she asked. "It's a road. That's what you want to head for."

<hr />

In books about orienteering they tell you to point your compass in your direction of travel and pick out a landmark to walk toward. When you get there, you repeat the process. It sounds simple. It is, in fact, simple—if you are walking across a flat plateau toward a distant peak, or following a drainage along a mountain valley.

But walking through forests is a different matter entirely, especially forests where the trails are so old and neglected that there is barely a trace of their ever having existed.

You determine your direction and set your compass, which points you toward a tree. But between you and that tree are a thousand obstacles: a fallen log; and another, fallen on top of that. Then there are branches to duck under, and underbrush to step over, and more fallen trees, and as you move farther and farther through the maze, you realize that all of the trees in front of you have started to look remarkably similar and you have no idea which one you were heading toward.

At a snail's pace, you continue on, climbing and ducking and doing battle with the deadfall: dry, spiky branches that clutch at your hair; disintegrating logs that crumble into a pile of dust when you step on them; and the ubiquitous fallen trees that lie in your path at just precisely a height that is, at the same time, both too high to climb over and too low to crawl under.

Teresa had been right: The forest was a mess.

It took us two hours to find the road at the bottom—two hours to travel not much more than 2 miles. Karl and I were the map and compass team, and we both took readings to find the way down. Dan followed behind; his job would begin at the bottom, when Karl and I announced that "the road ought to be about here somewhere." Dan had a good sense of where a trail might logically be constructed, and he had the strength and willingness to go and look for it. At the bottom of the hill, he went jogging off. Within minutes, he was back: He had found the road that would lead us out of the forest to the small town of Reserve, where our next food box was waiting for us at the post office.

≋≋≋≋

Reserve, New Mexico, population 600 and seat of Catron County, was originally smack in the middle of Apache hunting grounds. Hispanic settlers to the area came next, settling nearby Upper San Francisco Plaza. They were followed by the United States government, which put the land into the forest reserves—hence the name. Today, Reserve boasts a bank, a post office, two hotels, a library, two restaurants, a general store, and Uncle Bill's (UNCLE BIL 'S, reads the sign outside) Bar.

Inside, Uncle Bill's looks a little bit like part of a movie set. Rifles hang from the ceiling, a mounted elk head stares at you from the wall, and there's a pool table in the smoky back room. In the rest room, someone had left a photocopied notice suggesting that if you oppose logging, you should "Wipe your ass with a spotted owl."

At the bar, there was a line of men with cowboy hats and leathered faces, every one of which turned and stared as we walked in and claimed a table near the wall opposite the bar. In our sneakers and bright hiking shorts, we were definitely out of place, and Dan whispered to me that among the macho western costumes, he felt like he was wearing a dress.

It took about five minutes before one of the ranchers got up and walked over, squinting suspiciously at us as we downed our beers. He was a wiry man with well-worn cowboy boots, a jaunty bolo tie, and a sun-lined face that peered out from under a cream-colored Stetson.

"How you doing?" he asked, or rather demanded.

"We're doing just fine, thanks," we said, and told him our names. "How you doing?"

The rancher was trying to be polite, but his curiosity quickly got the better of his manners.

"Who are you?" he blurted. Here was a man who, clearly, knew everyone sitting at the bar at Uncle Bill's, and, most probably, everyone in Reserve, too. He knew just where everyone fit in his niche of the world. Except us. Obviously, our names hadn't settled the problem of our identity.

"We're on a backpacking trip," we explained.

He took that in for a moment. "You with the Forest Service?" he asked.

"No, we're not with anybody. We're just hiking. We've walked here from the Mexican border."

He seemed to relax when we said we weren't with anyone. As far as he was concerned, we were a "type"—a type that isn't like ranchers. On top of that, we had East Coast accents. There was no telling what mischief we could be up to, and I suppose he was relieved that whatever our intentions were, they weren't backed by an organization.

"Why'd you think we were with the Forest Service?" I asked, taking the lid off Pandora's box with the most innocent expression I could muster. Teresa had mentioned that we might get the Old West gospel at Uncle Bill's; I was interested in hearing it from the horse's mouth, so to speak.

"There's a lot of Forest Service people 'round here. Forest Service is looking at cutting our allotments. Figured maybe you was some of 'em." He still wasn't sure.

"Nope."

"Mind you, we don't object to Forest Service. Some of them's good people. What we mind is when there's a bunch of outsiders from Washington trying to tell us how to work our land. Can't tell a cow from a horse, but they think they can come to Catron County and tell us how to run things."

"Sounds like there's some conflict," I said in what I hoped was a neutral tone.

He had his response ready before the sentence was out of my mouth.

"I'll tell you what," he said. "It's because of all this environment crap. This damn spotted owl business. The environmentalists want to kick us off our allotments because of a goddamned owl." He said the word *owl* as though it were a curse. "You one of them spotted owl lovers?"

The way he looked at us, we could tell this was an important question.

Dan was up to the challenge: "Nope," he said. "I never heard of a spotted owl in my life."

It was the right answer. What a stranger thought about the Mexican spotted owl was a litmus test in Reserve—and we had passed it. The rancher pulled out a hundred-dollar bill, ordered us another round of eighty-five-cent beers—no, make that a pitcher—and proceeded to tell us about timber, ranching, and the interference of the federal government in Catron County, New Mexico.

Like most westerners, our companion started by telling us how long his family had occupied this expanse of dusty brown earth—since the 1880s. You could tell that he thought this was one of the earth's great places, and the issue, as he saw it, was simple: The spotted owl people were out to ruin his world.

On the surface, the Mexican spotted owl hardly seems to merit the legendary wrath of a western rancher. Ranchers have waged a long war against inconvenient wildlife, but their targets have generally been more worthy opponents. The wolf, for instance—exterminated in the Southwest in what can only be called an all-out war. The grizzly bear met a similar fate, decimated first by the predator-control program and then by human encroachment on its territory. Coyotes and mountain lions continue to be vilified, although they still prowl the Gila. Black bears survive, too—we had seen one back at Mogollon Baldy—and although they are neither hated nor feared, they are hunted for sport. Among such large and powerful sylvan cohabitants, the Mexican spotted owl seems barely worthy of notice.

It might never have attracted any attention at all, except for the mischief of its notorious cousin. That cousin, of course, is the Oregon spotted owl, a raptor whose home territory—the humid, green, lush, mossy monster forests of the Pacific Northwest—could not possibly be any more different from the sagebrushed fields, piñon-juniper forests, and ponderosa highlands of Catron County.

The "endangered species" status of the Oregon owl has been used to all but shut down logging in the old-growth forests of the Pacific Northwest. The Endangered Species Act requires that federal agencies establish policies to protect habitat that is necessary for the survival of any species listed as threatened or endangered. Simple enough. In the case of the Oregon spotted owl, a single nesting pair is thought to require between 2,200 and 3,800—the data is still incomplete—acres of old-growth forest in order to breed. A single old-growth tree can yield anywhere from 1,000 to 10,000 board feet of lumber; an average acre of old-growth forest might go for $48,000 "on the stump"—that is, the amount a timber company pays the Forest Service for the right to harvest the timber. In other words, if you assume that a breeding pair of owls requires 3,000 acres of old-growth forest, the cost of maintaining a habitat for a single pair is $144 million. Hence the controversy.

It's not the owl's fault that its habitat is worth so much money. The immense economic value of the forest and the owl's inflexible needs negate even the possibility of compromise. How much is a spotted owl worth? ask the loggers. It doesn't matter, counter the environmentalists. No one, for any amount of money, has the right to render a species extinct.

This is not one of those arguments where men of goodwill who disagree sit down over a beer or two to talk it over. There is too much at stake for that. There are places in the Northwest where it is not safe to wear a T-shirt with a wilderness slogan; there are places where owls have been nailed to signposts. There are environmentalists—some would say terrorists—who spike trees; and so-called eco-warriors who pour sand into lumber truck oil lines. And there is the not entirely unfounded suspicion that even if there was no such thing as a spotted owl, the environmentalists would try to invent it, because their real agenda is to shut down the logging industry.

In the Gila, the owl was being studied as a possible threatened or endangered species. We had met a team of researchers the previous evening; they were counting owl populations by making birdcalls, listening for responses, and marking the locations of returned calls with tape. Not much is known about the Mexican spotted owl— about its territorial requirements, or its population figures, or its adaptability to new habitat. Preliminary data suggest that the smaller Mexican owl requires less territory and is less dependent on old-growth forests than its northern cousin.

In Reserve, those are all irrelevant issues: There could be a single breeding pair left, or there could be a million. The mere fact that the owl is being studied as a possible threatened or endangered species is enough to put it smack in the middle of a maelstrom that is likely to last for years. Loggers, miners, and ranchers have had plenty of opportunity to watch the scene play out in the Northwest, and they have no intention of letting it happen here.

The ranchers in Reserve know all about the Endangered Species Act. They know that it is being used to appeal and cancel timber sales in the northwest part of the Gila, where there are high concentrations of spotted owls and large tracts of harvestable timber. They know that the Reserve district produces half of the Gila's commercial timber. And they also know that the lumber mill downriver from town just lost a major sale because six owls were found in timber that was supposed to have been logged.

Our companion at Uncle Bill's didn't want to talk about ecosystems—about what keeps them healthy and why that's important. He wanted to talk about land—about who owns it, and who works it, and who depends upon it, and who should manage it. He wanted to talk about the money he's put into water development and fences on his leased government land, and about the shape the range is in, about all the elk that come down to winter on it, and about how that ought to give him more of a say in managing and using that land than people in Washington.

He was quick to say that he's never expressed an opinion on how New York City should manage its affairs—all he wants back is the same courtesy. And when we pointed out that a good part of this land is federal, he had a ready reply: Then give it back to the states and let it be managed by the people who live here. The Sagebrush Rebellion lives on.

He doesn't object if a few nature lovers like owls. They're welcome to study them all they want, though God knows why anyone would waste their time on a damn fool thing like that. But he doesn't know why the spotted owl can't just go fly around in the wilderness, which is too big as it is. He doesn't want to hear about critical habitat, or minimum-size-of-ecosystems research, or wildlife niches, or, God forbid, mating habits. He doesn't believe that the spotted owl is endangered. He saw one just last week.

He may have been a stereotype, with his rhetoric and his clothing and his hat-tipping yes-ma'am western manners, which had re-emerged as soon as he got his fix on us. I could have written his speech without ever having met him. And that is unfortunate, because it's hard to really hear someone through a stereotype.

Stereotype or not, we would hear echoes of his voice throughout the rural West. His perspective is not the only one; it is rather more extreme than that of most ranchers we met. But it reflects the values of the old-time power structure, and it has caught the ears of small-town folk, who are struggling to survive a recession in a resource-dependent economy while trying to preserve a valued way of life. If the ranchers and the loggers are loud, if they sound a little desperate, there is a reason: They are not being paranoid when they say the old ways are under attack.

In addition to logging, grazing has become increasingly controversial, as environmentalists attack the system that allows ranchers to lease federal land for grazing cattle at a cost far below what a private lessor would charge. In New Mexico, the ranching industry depends on Forest Service and Bureau of Land Management grazing allotments. As we hiked through miles of barren sagebrush and piñon-juniper forests, we had plenty of opportunity to think about cattle and public land: Not a day had gone by that we hadn't shared the landscape, the trail, and sometimes our campsites, with bovine companions.

From a purely personal standpoint, our hike would have been impossible without the cattle: Most of our water in southern New Mexico had come from windmills that were built to supply stock with water. And it is certainly true that, as land use goes, grazing cattle is more environmentally sound than, say, developing shopping malls. On the other hand, badly managed grazing can have—and historically has had—a disastrous effect on highly erodible, dry western land. In areas that do have water, such as the Gila, cattle can cause even more damage: Trampled streamside vegetation increases flooding and widens streams, turning them from fast-running, healthy, cold-water habitats to murky, swampish channels; in the Gila, all of the streams were infested with *Giardia*.

And so, the environmental movement has taken on the western ranching industry, although it should be said that different environmental organizations have different positions on the issue. Earth First! predictably has the most extreme slogan: "Cattle Free by '93," and some members caused all-out ruckus when they suggested—they later claimed it was in jest—that people shoot cows during the hunting season. Other environmental groups take less extreme positions, although some ask whether cattle ought to be grazing on federal land in the first place: Aren't below-market grazing fees really a form of welfare subsidies to an industry that isn't needed by the public and doesn't do the land any good? Should marginal land even be used for cattle, considering how much land is used to produce such a small percentage of the nation's beef? And why, if ranchers are such good stewards of the land, does so much of the range have such severe damage?

In the middle of the mess is the Forest Service, which has been dragged into the environmental limelight with about as much zeal as a schoolboy forced into after-hours detention. Charged with managing forest resources for sustainable use, the Forest Service finds itself attacked from both sides: by groups focusing on the "sustainable" part of the mandate, and by groups focusing on the "use" part. Also in the equation is the Forest Service's traditional interpretation of multiple use, which is heavily prejudiced toward selling timber and grazing cattle. (The Forest Service was moved to the Department of Agriculture from the Department of the Interior in 1905. This move still strikes most easterners—who are more familiar with the Forest Service's description of itself as the "nation's playground" than they are with its cow-timber-mining operations—as somewhat odd, and most westerners as perfectly logical.)

Our companion at Uncle Bill's knows—and this may be the crux of his resentment—that the urban easterner, who is questioning his grazing allotments and spouting environmental doctrine, does not have to worry about ecosystems and spotted owls in his or her daily life. "To you," he told us, "these are luxuries. Putting the owl on the endangered list doesn't affect how much money you earn."

He has a point. Those of us who make our homes in large urban centers may support environmental causes; we may discuss them with some familiarity—passion, even—but there is no sacrifice associated with taking an environmental position. We may turn down the thermostat a couple of degrees or recycle our newspapers, but new environmental regulations have little to do with how much money we make or how we go about our daily lives.

Nor is the typical rancher sympathetic to the back-to-the-land set, the urban refugees who have moved to the country and embraced the newish eco-philosophy of bioregionalism. Bioregionalism involves a symbiotic connection with land and place, and its proponents have a parlor game that they trot out for urban guests: Can you name five edible plants that grow near your home? Six kinds of grasses? Seven native animals? The point is that to reestablish the relationship—and responsibility—that man has to the earth, you first have to know the nature of the spot of earth you happen to call home.

True enough, but this is nothing new to western ranchers, who don't need to prove their bioregional sensitivity in a parlor game. It is neither a philosophical position nor a game for a rancher to know exactly what watershed he lives in, how much rain fell last spring, how the grasses are doing. And as far as wildlife goes, there's too damn many coyotes. A rancher knows his land, every sunburned acre of it, and if you're going to come in talking about grazing fees and spotted owls and riparian habitat, you had better be able to tell the difference between grama grass and locoweed, and you had better have some dirt under your fingernails. And you had better not be wearing a T-shirt with a picture of a wolf or an owl or a grizzly bear. The old-time ranchers here have circled the wagons and are taking turns on watch. If you are an urban transplant turned eco-philosopher, you're going to have to earn the right to come inside, and it's going to take a long, long time before anyone listens to a word you have to say.

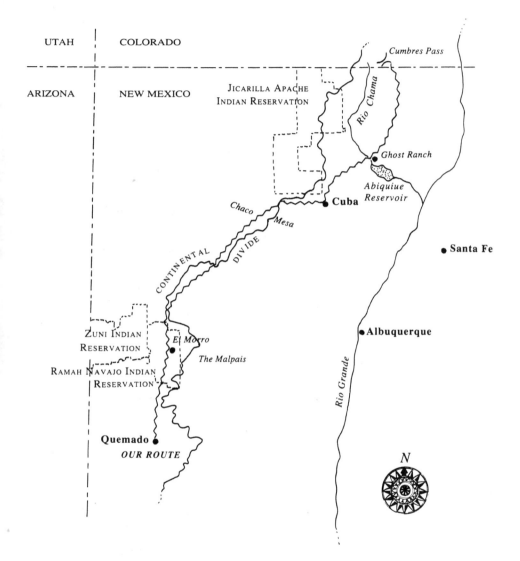

3

≈≈≈≈≈

LAND OF THE WILD ONION

≈≈≈≈≈

Long-distance hikers get used to being celebrities of a sort. A journey like ours touches a nerve; people want to be part of it. Not because they want to walk 3,000 miles—most don't—but because our journey was one of those epic dreams that most people have hidden away somewhere. It's the dream of climbing mountains, running in the Olympics, sailing around the world. It's the dream of breaking away.

There were also those who were neither dreamers nor rebels, but were simply kindhearted folks who thought that anyone who was trying to walk across the country ought to get some encouragement along the way—even though they might be crazy. It seemed that there was a fair amount of debate about our sanity that summer.

Long-distance hikers call it trail magic, this incredible generosity that finds you like a magnet in the middle of nowhere. It took some getting used to. As urbanites, we had grown up knowing a set of inviolable rules: If someone approaches you on the street, you look the other way; if someone is being unusually nice, he probably wants something. In New Mexico, we were to learn new rules. In this country of harsh environment and few people, folks do for each other.

North of the Gila, the elevation drops again and the land goes back to sagebrush. It isn't particularly well suited for anything: There's a little farming, a little mining, a little ranching, and a lot of nothing in between. For natives—primarily ranchers and Indians—seeing someone on foot is a sure sign of trouble, and the rules of the rural West are simple about that: If you see someone in trouble, you stop and help.

Not that there were many people. Our route through central New Mexico followed jeep tracks and overgrown roads, with a few pack trails and a lot of cross-country to link it all together. It was remote country, seldom traveled. But occasionally, someone would appear as we walked along a road or across a ranch, and when they did, there was trail magic: "Want a can of Coke?" "How about a beer?" "You need a ride? A meal? A place to stay?" We'd trade our story for a drink or a snack, and walk on, refreshed and uplifted, our sore feet soothed by a stranger's solicitude.

All of which explains why, on the afternoon of Memorial Day, we were walking hard, trying to get to the Quemado Lake campground. Quemado Lake is a drive-in recreation site on a gravel road, and, for New Mexico, it gets heavy use. (Any place in New Mexico with water gets heavy use.) It was the last day of the holiday weekend, and we were, I am ashamed to admit, rushing down an impossibly steep slope in the hope that we would arrive at the campsite in time to be invited to someone's holiday barbecue.

The campground was a few minutes' walk past the lake, and by the time we got there, it was empty—save for the garbage bins, which were overflowing with refuse from the weekend feasts. We had accurately predicted the activity, but we were too late to join in. Setting aside our gluttonous expectations, we faced a bigger dis-appointment: We hadn't filled our canteens at the lake, thinking that there would be a water pump at the campground. There wasn't, and the next water was at a spring about 2 miles down the road. We kept walking, obeying the unspoken creed that a couple of miles forward was always preferable to a couple of hundred yards back. It was going to take us long enough to walk to Canada without running in circles.

By the time we reached the spring, we were tired and cranky. Quemado Lake had been one big disappointment. We unrolled our sleeping bags and blew up the air mattresses, which, as usual, immediately started leaking air, victims of repeated abuse from cactus needles and flying embers. We could count on the repair patches we had applied to work for only half the night. By morning, we'd be flat against the ground again, poked awake by rocks, sticks, or pinecones, depending on how carefully we'd chosen our site.

The next morning, however, it wasn't the ground that jolted us awake at 5:30. It was snow.

Snow! It didn't seem possible. We were in central New Mexico, the elevation was only 7,000 feet, and it was the twenty-ninth of May. True, the desert nights are cold—we were accustomed to waking up in the morning to find a layer of ice in our canteens. But ice in a canteen is one thing; snow on a sleeping bag is quite another. It is not supposed to snow in late May in New Mexico. But the sagebrush and cactus surrounding us confirmed the world order gone amuck—they were covered in white.

And it was real snow, not just a few misplaced flakes. These clouds meant business. They were low, completely shrouding the surrounding hills. In the few minutes it took to devour some oatmeal and stuff our possessions into our packs, snow had actually accumulated. There was no indication that it was going to stop anytime soon.

We started walking, fast, to keep warm. Dan and I were wearing our Gore-Tex rain gear, which we had been carrying for twenty-six dry, hot desert days. There is nothing that irritates a backpacker more than an unused piece of equipment. Emergency supplies—things like rain gear and first-aid kits—of course, are never unnecessary, but in the desert, we could have made a case for leaving the rain gear behind. Caution (aided by previous experience) had won over laziness, but we had resented the extra weight every day as we packed the rain gear, knowing that the chances of needing it were about nil.

Karl, on the other hand, had taken the opposite approach. In his endless quest to not carry a single ounce more than necessary (unless it was edible), he had taken only a thin red poncho, which he now tied around his waist with a piece of clothesline. He looked like the "what not to do" example in a film about hypothermia. Or, Dan said, like a conscript in a third-world guerrilla army. The getup wasn't any warmer than it looked: Karl was so cold that when he stopped to use a Forest Service outhouse, he was barely able to resist the temptation to stay there all morning.

The snow forced a change of course on us. With no visibility, we didn't want to do the short cross-country stretch our planned route required. The low-lying clouds blocked the mountaintops, and navigating was going to be difficult. The alternative route was longer; worse, it was on a paved road—the least attractive, most monotonous kind of walking. To add insult to injury, we'd have to backtrack past the lake. On the plus side: We wouldn't get lost.

Snow accumulated for a couple of hours, then in mid-morning turned to drizzle before it stopped altogether. Within half an hour, the sun was out, burning snow into steam, making the hills look like a giant overheated pressure cooker. By mid-afternoon, all evidence of snow, or even rain, had evaporated. The ground was as parched as ever, the air as dry.

The small town of Quemado, twenty-four miles away, was our next food drop. We had planned to camp just before town, pick up our food in the morning, and go on. But now it looked like we might have to go all the way in—the road was bounded on both sides by posted private property, and there didn't look to be any likely places to camp. The only thing we knew about Quemado was that it was small. The map showed a few buildings clumped together at a junction. The junction was a good sign—it meant that there was likely to be a store. Maybe even a motel.

The walk was monotonous, with the same sagebrush, a few windmills, and scattered ranch houses set off from the road. And cows, of course. To make the miles pass more quickly, we started fantasizing about the delights that awaited us in Quemado, if we could make it there that day. Road walking is easier than trail walking; it's much faster, and compared to hiking trails, the grades are not steep. But the regular gait—the same motion stride after stride—and the continual pounding on hard pavement punish leg muscles and ligaments. Urging us on to Quemado was the possibility of a town stop: At the very least, we hoped, we could get some fresh food at a campground.

At this point in our journey, we had developed a preoccupation with food that made us behave like barn-sour horses, who enjoy the trail just fine until they catch a scent of home. We had quickly learned that when you are walking every day, all day, you can't get enough to eat. We were always hungry, always, it seemed, looking at the bottom of a bowl that had been full just moments before, always craving the fresh fruits and vegetables we couldn't carry with us on the trail. In town, we took to ordering two breakfasts apiece just to save time—and these were western-diner-sized breakfasts, which are designed for gluttons in the first place. One waitress asked if we needed more chairs and flatware, and if she should wait until the rest of our group arrived to bring out the food.

As we got closer to Quemado, we picked up bits and pieces of information, doled out by motorists who periodically stopped to offer us rides. There was a trailer lot where we could probably camp. Some road workers confirmed there was a store. Visions of a barbecue with burgers and Cokes pushed us on for a few miles. Then a couple of Indians in a pickup said they thought there might be a motel, but they didn't know if it was open. We chewed on that for a few more miles; by lunch, we'd managed to convince ourselves that if there was a motel, it would most probably be open. In addition to the burgers, now our hearts were set on showers and a sink to rinse some clothes in. It took a few more miles to add a bath and a Laundromat to the wish list. And so it went; the hamburger turned into a steak, the Coke machine into a bar, and the campground into a Hilton.

There was no Hilton. There wasn't, as far as we could see, much of anything, except a trailer lot and a plaque that told us that Quemado was first settled by Jose Antonio Padillo, a sheep farmer, in 1880. Our fantasies were evaporating as quickly as the snow had, and we were about to turn in to the trailer park when a couple of men stopped to talk. They pointed down the dusty street to some unpromising-looking buildings. "Main part of town's down there," they told us.

Quemado (derived from the Spanish word for *burned*) was the stereotype of a small, middle-of-nowhere western town—a few haphazard buildings surrounded by miles of emptiness. But it was plenty good enough for a trio of filthy hikers, exhausted by a marathon road walk. There was indeed a motel; not one, but two, restaurants; a bar; a general store; and a Laundromat. In short, there was everything a long-distance hiker could want, and, to top it off, the town was so small it wasn't more than a two-minute walk to any of them. As we walked down the main street, we were accompanied by a tumbleweed, which bounced against the pavement, hit our legs, and rolled down the highway. As we watched it make its meandering way along the empty road, it occurred to us that, at that moment, we probably had more in common with the tumbleweed than with most people we knew.

≋≋≋≋≋

Quemado sits in the middle of BLM country—big country, with vast tracts of mile-square sections. On a map, the sections are colored white if they are privately owned, yellow if they are federal, and blue if they belong to the state. The ownership patterns are clear enough on paper; the map looks like a tri-colored checkerboard. But on the ground, the distinctions are less obvious. Ranches extend for miles in any direction, and often include leased public land. Sometimes, it's impossible to tell when you are trespassing and when you aren't. We had tried to write to the larger landowners in advance for permission to cross their property, but we had met with mixed success. No one had refused to let us pass; the problem had been identifying who to write to and where to find them.

This is dry country, and in the draws that slope down from the Continental Divide you are more likely to see cactus than water. As in the southern part of the state, the only reliable water is found in windmill tanks, and then only if the windmills are working. Cattle dung was a sure sign that somewhere, nearby, windmill blades would be spinning. As we had learned in the first days of our hike, where there are cows there is bound to be water.

Fenced with barbed wire and No Trespassing signs, the ranches seem unwelcoming at first. The people, however, are another story.

The western value system places two contradictory requirements on the rancher: to defend his private property rights and to be hospitable to strangers. Every rancher we met had the knack of communicating two messages in the same breath: "You're on *my* land—and how can I help you?"

Despite the hospitality to which we had been treated thus far, we were still a little wary that we would meet a rancher whose main concern was the first part of the message. There was always that moment of uneasiness when a pickup truck cleared the horizon, slowed down, and a cowboy-hatted face scrutinized us for evidence of God knows what. The car would shift into neutral and stop; we'd lean on our walking sticks and answer the invariable questions.

"Yes, sir, we are on foot on purpose. We're just passing on through on our way to Canada."

There'd be a pause, and a double take.

"Yes, sir, we did say Canada. We've walked here all the way from the Mexican border. Four hundred miles, as we figure it."

After that, most of the time, the ranchers moved on from the "my property" business to the "how can I help you" part. It was, we were learning, the way of the West.

≈≈≈≈≈≈

There were no pickup trucks or people at the Adobe Wells Ranch. There was no sign of recent use on the roads, no sign of life near the old buildings. As we came closer, we saw that the ranch was abandoned. The well hadn't been working in years. Nor had the farm machinery, which rusted slowly in the yard. The old wooden buildings were silent, but the doors of an outhouse swung, creaking, in the breeze. There was no rancher here to question us. And no water, either.

We walked on, up to the top of a mesa, and then slid down the other side on a steep sandy gully. When we arrived at the bottom, we looked around us, quite as disoriented as Alice going down the rabbit hole. We were standing in the dry streambed of the plateau's runoff. From the evidence, we were lucky not to be there when the water roared through. The runoff had scoured a rat's maze of deep arroyos through the soft sandstone, and all we could see were their walls. Somewhere in this mess, there was supposed to be a spring, but we couldn't even figure out exactly where we were, much less which way to go to find the spring.

We split up, each exploring a different part of the arroyo's maze. The soft sand made walking difficult. After fifteen minutes, I decided that if there was a spring, I couldn't find it, and I headed back to find that Dan had come to the same conclusion. But Karl was still missing.

He was, in fact, lost. Having walked farther than either of us, he had missed a turn in the arroyo to get back. We heard him whistling, but the sound was distorted by the labyrinthine canyons. We called back, using the police whistle we carried for just such occasions. Back and forth: whistle, shout, holler, whistle. The sounds bounced against rock walls, first sounding hollow and close by, then thin and far away. When we finally regrouped, we continued walking in a direction that would have been downstream if there had been a stream, toward a windmill that the map told us was our next source of water. It greeted us with still, broken blades and a bone-dry tank. We consulted our map again: A couple of miles farther was a containment dam, this one marked in solid blue.

It, too, was dry.

Now we were worried. We were getting near the end of the day; the next windmill was five miles off. We were about out of water, and about to be out of daylight.

In the distance, off our route, we saw a white speck. It didn't fade when we blinked. A house? A trailer? We couldn't tell. The map showed a little box, a sign that a house was—or once had been—there. Where there is a house, there tends to be a water source. The white speck was a couple of miles away. We changed course.

As we got closer, we could see through our binoculars that it was indeed a house. Whether inhabited or not, we wouldn't know for a while longer. Our hearts rose at the sight of a windmill, then sank a few minutes later when we saw that the blades weren't turning. Our hopes rose again when we could make out the reflection of car metal near the house, then sank when we got close enough to see unpainted buildings and sagging fences. And then we heard the dogs.

Rural western dogs have the same sense of space as rural western people: They lay claim to areas as large as your basic East Coast suburb. Plus, they are a good deal more serious about trespassers than their owners, dispensing with the "what can I do for you" business, and getting right down to "this is mine, stay off." During the walk, I had developed a deep distrust of dogs running loose. These dogs, however, were welcome to bark as much as they wanted.

The people standing in the yard looked at us warily as we approached, but they made no move to either greet us or send us away. We had left our packs at the gate, self-consciously uncertain about coming into this impoverished-looking compound with our gaudy, high-tech equipment. As we walked past the dogs, someone called them away from us; the first acknowledgment anyone had made to us. But as we moved farther into the yard, most of the people backed away and slowly dispersed into a field behind the house. We looked at each other, not knowing what to do. Finally, an older man approached. There was no welcome in his eyes; he was polite but clearly distrustful. He spoke only a few words of English. Fortunately, *agua* is one of my few words of Spanish. In sign language, we managed to communicate that we were walking from Mexico to Canada.

Trail magic!

The old man went off to get us water, and one or two people peered out from the doorway to the house. We tried to show how friendly we were by smiling a lot and making friends with the one person who seemed to have no hesitation about approaching us: a two-year-old who greeted us with hands crossed over his chest and the most impressive scowl I've ever seen. From his expression, it seemed as though he was taking it upon himself to get rid of us, since neither the dogs nor his elders had managed to do so. But he finally warmed up enough to tell us that his name was Tito. We knew the ice was broken when he offered to show us his plaything: a dead bug.

We parted with everyone smiling—genuine, profuse thanks on our part and, from the looks of things, genuine relief on theirs. We went off into the sagebrush to find a place to camp. In the half-light of evening, we could see the people who had faded into the field cautiously starting to return to the farmhouse. We watched them, wondering who they were: Squatters? Illegal aliens? They lived a hard life there. How much more difficult to live in fear.

The next day we crossed a fence and entered the Ramah Navajo Indian Reservation. Karl was the only one with legs long enough to actually step over the fence—Dan and I had to wiggle under, which Dan did accompanied by his own rendition of the limbo song. Just as Karl had one leg on BLM land and the other on the reservation, a Navajo horseman rode up.

Being caught trespassing is one thing: You can always claim that you're lost. It is, however, hard to declare your innocence with one foot on either side of a barbed-wire fence. Fortunately, the Indian's interest in us was pretty much the same as everyone else's had been: Someone on foot attracts attention, because someone on foot, most likely, is in need of help. The fact that we were climbing the reservation fence seemed not to concern him in the least.

Actually, although it looked like we were trespassing, we weren't: With us, we carried a letter from the superintendent that gave us permission to hike through and camp on the Indian lands. The letter was friendly and matter-of-fact; the superintendent had thought it prudent to provide a list of medical facilities and hospitals in the region, along with a few other bits and pieces of information. Under a heading titled "Insect and animal life," he had listed mosquitos, gnats, and rattlesnakes. There were, he noted, no hiking trails on the reservation, but there were two functioning windmills near our route. The letter ended cordially: "It is hoped that your trip will be enjoyable and uneventful as far as unforeseen and unwanted experiences."

Unwanted experiences?

The land we were passing through sits just to the west of the Divide, and just west of the malpais—the badlands. The terrain is punctuated with the symmetrical cones of extinct volcanoes: Cerro Alto, Cerro Florio, Cerro des Mujeras. The debris they once spewed still litters the ground, lava cooled into a dark, porcelainlike mass, sharp and brittle; if you step on it, it breaks with a high-pitched snap. But this fragile rock, born from the churning violence in the guts of the earth, is not without a power of its own. It absorbs the rays of the sun, magnifies and concentrates their heat, then throws them insolently back at the sky, searing anything that dares to live there. We could feel the heat on our legs as the reflected rays burned into our skin. If the volcanoes are dead, geologically speaking, then it must be their ghosts that continue to torment this land.

This is the land of the Dineh—the name the Navajo use for themselves; like so many other Indian names, it means "the People"—and they call it T'ochini, "Place of the Wild Onion." It's an unfortunate sign of the times that the onion is now a rare species in New Mexico, a victim of overgrazing, which is no less a problem on Indian lands than it is on large Anglo ranches. There have been too many sheep, and to a lesser extent too many cattle, grazing on too little land for too many years. The result is poor forage and fewer native plants—including the onion.

The reservation is dotted with small groups of eight-sided hogans; the entrances to these traditional homes face east to the sun. There are also mobile homes, less carefully placed. On the ground, we saw irregular piles of stones, looking quite random to the Anglo eye. Still, they were put there by someone—for prayer or ritual—as were pieces of clothing strewn on tree branches. Back in the bush, the homes are simple: dirt floors; no electricity, plumbing, or sewage. Firewood is scarce; it must be brought in by pickup truck. So must the water—hauled in fifty-gallon drums over dirt roads that are close to impassible in bad weather.

Sheep are the mainstay of this subsistence agricultural society: a measure of wealth and a source of food and wool for consumption and barter. Women in long skirts and full blouses cajoled their herds across our path, aided by dogs that looked at us suspiciously, then rounded up the strays. A young man on horseback, barechested, rode bareback through the sagebrush. When he saw us, he galloped in a wide, fast circle in a dazzling display of horsemanship, clearly intended for us. It occurred to me that when I was a teenager, I would have thought his was the luckiest lot in life. Perhaps I had the right idea back then, I mused, as I watched him, the dust swirling behind, his long hair blown back by the wind.

Bringing us back to our own century were the pickup trucks that periodically careened along the bumpy road. Invariably, the drivers offered us rides. No one seemed interested in whether or not we had a permit.

This insouciance regarding our presence in the middle of the reser-

vation is noteworthy. The Navajo, at least if they use history as a
guide, have little reason to welcome outsiders. Certainly, they have
nothing to gain from helping a group of scruffy backpackers through
the heart of a land that has cost them so dearly. The story of the
Navajo, their land, and the newcomers who laid claim to it does not
encourage hospitality.

The United States government was one such newcomer when it
gained title to the Southwest through the Treaty of Guadalupe-
Hidalgo in 1848. The United States won title from the Mexicans,
who had inherited it from the Spanish, who had, in the manner of
European colonialists everywhere, claimed sovereignty over the land
as though the people who already lived here had no claim of their
own. By the time the United States signed the treaty, the Navajo
had been in these mesas and mountains at least 500 years, and the
new government found that it had inherited not only the land but its
history of hostile relations. The Navajo were a people whose life-
styles and values were both incomprehensible to Anglos and incom-
patible with Anglo settlement. The new government had a final
solution.

The Navajo were ordered to move to a government reservation,
and those who didn't were attacked by the American army. The few
Navajo who weren't killed or didn't surrender retreated to hiding
places in the canyon country of the Four Corners area. Under the
command of Kit Carson, the American military came looking for
them, and burned Navajo crops, killed Navajo livestock, and ultimately starved the Navajo people into coming out from their hiding
places in the cliffs and arroyos. The few survivors of the atrocities
were forced to abandon their sacred land and move into the western
equivalent of a concentration camp: Bosque Redondo, a name now
notorious in Navajo history. Under the patronage of the United
States, the Indians would settle in this hated place, give up their
nomadic life-style, and learn agricultural skills and European ways.
In the parlance of the day, the savages would become civilized.

In Spanish, the verb meaning "to civilize" derives from the same
root as the verb meaning "to reduce." In that case, *civilize* is the
right term for what happened to the Navajo interned at Bosque
Redondo. Separated from the land from which they drew strength,

the land where their spirits lived in a parallel, unseen universe, the Navajo were indeed reduced: in number, in strength, by disease, and by camp conditions. Finally, even the government recognized that the experiment was a failure, and the Navajo were given a choice. They could stay at Bosque Redondo or they could move to the well-watered Arkansas River valley in present-day Oklahoma. Or, they could return to what was left of their home. All the fertile land had been taken by whites; of the rest, the orchards had been burned, the livestock killed, the fields decimated. Who would want this land, so worthless and desolate? Who could even hope to survive on it? The Navajo decision was unanimous. Barboncito, a headsman, spoke for all the tribe when he said, "I want to go and see my own country. . . . If you should only tie a goat there, we would all live off of it, all of the same opinion." The decision was indeed unanimous; the day after the treaty was signed, the Navajo began their long walk home.

Seven families settled in the Ramah area, in sight of sacred Tsoodzil—we know it now as Mount Taylor. Today, 2,400 Indians (as well as 800 non-Indians, most of them Mormons) live on the 156,000-acre Ramah Navajo Reservation, which is separate and distinct from the "big" Navajo reservation to the northwest. It is ironic that the Southwest's most evocative monument to its settlement by European intruders lies in the middle of "the place of the wild onion."

The monument is called El Morro, and we entered it the way we entered most property in New Mexico: We climbed a fence. Which, as it turned out, caused a problem.

Sue and Gordon were waiting for us at the campground. They have a national parks pass valid for up to six people traveling with them, so when we went over to the monument itself, we didn't bother digging out our money from our packs. But when we told the clerk at the entrance about the pass, she disappeared into the supervisor's office.

"I don't know whether to charge them or not. They're with the people with the Missouri license plates," we heard her saying, which seemed a little odd. How did she know what kind of license plates Sue and Gordon had?

Sue had become the focus of the Park Service's attention because she had been engaged in an apparently unheard-of activity: walking around the grounds. And every time she and Mac set out for a walk, a ranger would appear and demand to know what she was doing. Her answer—that she was taking a walk—was met with an uncomprehending stare followed by a stern warning about straying onto the reservation. Sue dutifully promised not to wander across the barbed-wire fence.

Our involvement with this group of subversives was, apparently, a matter for a supervisor, who came out of his office with a frown.

"You're with the people in the white van?"

We nodded.

"You weren't here yesterday when they came."

"No, we weren't," we agreed.

"Well, then you have to pay. Each vehicle has to pay for itself."

"But we don't have a vehicle," we said, and started to explain about our hike. The supervisor wasn't interested.

"How'd you come in then?" he demanded.

"We, uh . . ."

"You walked in from the south?"

We admitted we had.

"Well, you must have come in through the reservation, then. You're not allowed there." Was it just our imaginations, or did he sound pleased to have uncovered this transgression?

Our response—that we had a letter of permission—seemed to spoil the supervisor's fun, because his expression darkened.

The situation appealed to our sense of the ridiculous. It seemed more than a little ironic that we had felt more welcome on Indian land than here at a national monument that commemorated, among other things, European encroachment on Indian territory. We were torn between borrowing a couple of dollars from Gordon and Sue and waiting to see how the impasse would end. Cussedness won over reason.

The supervisor continued questioning us. "So you didn't enter the monument grounds together in the van?"

No, we agreed, we hadn't—we had climbed a barbed-wire fence.

"Well, then you have to pay. It says right here in our rules" (we

were to learn how very much the national parks people like to say
"right here in our rules") "that the pass applies to a group traveling
together." We refrained from asking what the rules said about people
who climbed fences, and focused instead on the traveling together part.

"But we are traveling together." Which was true—at least, as
much as Sue's illness allowed. "Technically, we could all just leave
the grounds, meet on the road outside, and drive back in together.
But that's sort of ridiculous, isn't it?"

In the end, we were rather grudgingly informed that, although we
were "taking advantage of the system," we could go in without
paying the three dollars. "Long live the system," we grumbled, and
headed outside, toward the monument.

But our bad moods dissipated as we reached the white bluffs and
looked upon the spectacle in front of us. For to stand by the pool
of water at the base of El Morro is to stand by history writ in stone.

≈≈≈≈≈≈

The story begins with water, with a pool of deep green at the base
of a white bluff. To understand the significance of this small quiet
pool, you must first be thirsty. You must know what it is to walk a
long way with your mind obsessed with the amount of water in your
canteen and the mileage between water sources ground into your
thoughts. You must know how many liters you need to drink in
order to walk in the sun for a day, and how many you need to cook
your dinner at night. And you must know what to do when a water
source runs dry.

In the days before windmills, the significance of this shaded pool
would have been greater still: If you were a Spanish Conquistador,
for instance, the last reliable water would have been 30 miles back.

Around the pool, words have been carved into the rock. Graffiti,
you might call it, except that when graffiti is 300 or more years old,
it becomes something else: in this case, a monument. *Pasó Por Aqui*,
the wall reads. Passed by here: Don Juan de Oñate, and Don Juan
de Eulate, and Diego de Vargas. The names reach across the centuries; the inscriptions tell of their hope and ambition. Passed by here:
looking for gold and glory. Passed by here: governors, soldiers, and
priests.

It was gold they came for first, with dreams fueled by the fortunes stolen from the Incas and the Aztecs. By the sixteenth century, Peru had been plundered, and Mexico, too. Now, new hope, new rumors, and new lies lured the Spanish north.

The first reports had been vague. In 1528, a party of shipwreck survivors had landed somewhere on the east coast of Texas near present-day Galveston. It had taken them eight years, but they had finally made their way through uncharted territory, and they had returned to Mexico with tales of hair-raising adventure. They told other stories, too. A mere forty-day journey to the north, they said, they had heard that there were villages of gold, inhabited by workers of precious metals.

The rumors were repeated, and the more they were repeated, the more certain the conclusion. These were—they had to be—the Seven Cities of Cibola. According to legend, seven bishops who had fled from the Moorish invasion of eighth-century Spain had each gone far away to found a city of immense wealth. Was it not possible that the priests had somehow found their way to North America? Hadn't the travelers confirmed that there were seven villages to the north? Could such a thing be mere coincidence? The conclusion was obvious.

And so, northward! A Franciscan priest named Fray Marcos de Niza was sent to investigate, under the pretense of evaluating whether missions should be established on the northern frontier. Could he find these cities, these golden pueblos?

Traveling several days ahead of Fray Marcos was his servant, a Moorish slave named Estéban, who had been among the original shipwreck survivors. Estéban had taken to masquerading as a god, and, as befitted a god, he traveled in high style, with a coterie of women and all the pomp and ministrations suitable to his elevated position. His arrival at the Zuñi pueblo of Hawikuh marked the first contact between Pueblo Indian and European cultures in what was to become the United States. It was a confused and stormy beginning to a confused and stormy relationship. For one thing, the European in question was not European but African. For another, the Zuñi were evidently unimpressed with this self-proclaimed god. They might have been offended by his antics and demands; they might have wanted to test his claim of divinity. The Zuñi solved the problem by killing him.

When Fray Marcos learned of the death of Estéban, he scurried back to safety in Mexico. But he faced one small predicament: He had not only failed to visit a city of gold, he had turned back before even glimpsing one on the horizon. This, of course, was not what his patrons wanted to hear; they wanted to know where the cities were located, who lived in them, what they looked like, how rich they were. Perhaps Fray Marcos was an obliging sort; perhaps he was afraid. Perhaps he had begun to believe that the golden light of a New Mexican sunset really had been the reflection from a distant golden city. Or perhaps he was an irredeemable liar. In any event, he provided the travelogue expected of him: He had indeed seen the mythic Seven Cities of Cibola, and they were filled with more wealth than anyone had yet imagined. And so new life was breathed into an old myth, and a story that had originated in the Spanish middle ages came to roost in the barren country of the Zuñi, polished by deceit and fueled by greed.

Francisco Vásquez de Coronado received the royal appointment to claim this next Inca empire for Spain. In 1540, sixty-seven years before Jamestown and eighty years before Plymouth Rock, Coronado, along with 300 Spaniards and 800 Indians, set out to find the riches that lay just beyond the horizon.

They would have been an odd apparition to the Zuñis. For one thing, there were the animals: 1,000 horses and mules, and 5,000 sheep—animals that the Indians had never seen. For another, there was the strange idea of riding on the back of one of these creatures. And then there was the clothing: Coronado's soldiers traveled in full Spanish regalia, wearing chain mail, which weighed between twenty and thirty pounds, or complete suits of armor, which weighed sixty-five to eighty pounds. Imagine the bright light of the New Mexican sun glinting against iron helmets; imagine the heat and the long waterless stretches. Imagine the hottest, driest, sunniest, dustiest day you have ever known; and imagine traveling through it encased in a suit made of metal!

Their weapons, too, would have caused commotion: The matchlock muskets might have been inaccurate, but what a show they put on! With their flash and fire, their puffs of smoke, and their loud roar, they were so terrifying that bullets were almost incidental. And there were other weapons, too: gleaming metal stilettos and elegantly worked daggers, as well as more practical tools like the *espada*, which functioned not only as a sword but could also cut firewood.

History would make a fool of Fray Marcos: There were no golden cities, in Cibola or elsewhere, and sooner or later, Coronado would learn of the holy man's treachery. Coronado would lose his fortune, his son, and his health in the deserts of New Mexico. He would return, empty-handed, brokenhearted, and cursing the priest, to Mexico.

But the Spaniards would try again. They would establish missions and attempt to convert the Indians—in the process, decimating the population. And they would continue to bring with them the symbols of their hope: weights with which to measure precious metals, mercury for refining gold and silver, and tools with which to work them. More than a century after the magic name of Cibola was first whispered in the courtyards of the governor's palace, the myth still retained its allure, tarnished by years of disappointment, but glittering nonetheless.

So, imagine for a moment that you are a member of the first party to etch its names into the sandstone. You are a Spanish soldier in the service of Juan de Oñate, whose mission is to establish Spanish dominance over the pueblos. Now, in 1605, you are returning from an expedition to the faraway Gulf of California (you would have called it the South Sea). In your heart, you care neither for colonizing the natives nor discovering new oceans: You are here for gold.

You are at home in this country of high desert and searing volcanic debris. You have only the most rudimentary of maps, but you know the way from those who have gone before you, from landmarks like the tall, perfectly round mountains and the black earth of the malpais. You know, too, of a long mountain range with two pronounced notches, identified first by Jaramillo of the Coronado expedition, who wrote: "All the springs, rivers, and arroyos we have found as far as Cibola, and perhaps also those one or two days beyond, flow to the South Sea, and those farther on to the North Sea." Jaramillo may have lacked a complete understanding of the geography of the terrain and of where the waters went, but he understood what he was looking at: the Continental Divide.

The significance of the Divide might escape you in your thirst. The direction and drainages of dry streambeds are irrelevant abstractions, for there is not much water for the Divide to send to distant oceans. The watershed is mighty only in theory. You are far more interested in El Estanque del Peño, "the pool by the great rock," a natural cachement of clear, cold water surrounded by the telltale signs of cattails and green grasses.

You wouldn't admire the height or the sheerness of the cliffs around you. You wouldn't notice the incomparable blue of the sky, or the colors of the rock: bleached white, deep red, and bright orange. You would find the rock they call El Morro—the one that shades the pool from the thirsty heat of sunlight. You would put your face into the water, and you would drink.

Perhaps later, when you had drunk your fill, you would look around and notice the strange marks on the sandstone bluff: pictures of geometric patterns, of hands, and feet, etched in the stone. Long before the Spanish came to New Mexico, the Anasazi—from the Navajo word for "the ancient ones"—drank the waters of El Morrow. They left their mark: Even today, ancient petroglyphs carved into the bluff give directions to the pueblo ruins on the cliffs above. Atsinna, it is called by the nearby Zuñi, who may be among the descendants of the people who once lived in this mesatop complex. Like the Gila cliff dwellings, Atsinna was built in the thirteenth century; like the Mogollon people, the Anasazi disappeared soon after, leaving evidence of their passing, but no trace of where they went.

Perhaps you would climb to the top of the bluff, to the ruins, from where you have a view for miles in any direction. Searching the distant horizons, you can almost see the golden spires of the legendary Seven Cities of Cibola—or is the shimmering vision merely a trick of the heat waves? Previous expeditions have returned empty-handed, but you have high hopes that your luck will be better, and you might carve your name in the rock: a long braggadocio's inscription, announcing your intentions to claim this land for your king and its people for your God. You would probably keep silent about the wealth you intended to claim for yourself.

Centuries later, American settlers would come—California-bound miners, military men, missionaries, and dreamers of all descriptions—and they, too, would leave testament to their aspirations etched in the same rock, over the same pool of still water.

And still later, the tourists—and us, a thirsty trio of backpackers. But although we had walked across the same desert, we couldn't add our names, nor drink the water. There are fences around the pool, now; if you're thirsty, you can buy a soda for fifty cents at the visitors' center. There are campgrounds, public rest rooms, a museum exhibit, and brochures for modern-day pilgrims to this primeval place. There are parking lots for the air-conditioned Winnebagos with their cargoes of comfort: radios and generators and barbecues and ice chests that make it possible to ignore the desert entirely.

We drank our sodas and put up our tent. Like the Indians, the Spanish, and the settlers, we had walked across this land. Like them, we had felt its heat and its thirst; we knew, in a way that you can only know if you depend on it, exactly where the next water was. Like our predecessors, we had become desert creatures, transformed by the heat and the sky and the clear dry air. And like the Spanish, and the Anglo-Americans, we would stop at El Morro to rest and to drink.

Pasó por aqui, we wrote, drawing the letters with a stick in the dirt by our campsite. We passed by here, too.

≈≈≈≈≈≈

When we started our journey, Karl had planned to walk with us for about a month. The month was up: We had now been on the road for thirty-one days. We had taken three full days off, a couple of half days, and had walked precisely (as far as we could figure) 444.4 miles.

The rhythms of long-distance walking had gotten into Karl's blood. He might not have planned it that way, but the hike had taken over and he was part of it, plain and simple. As we left El Morro, setting our compasses by the Continental Divide and its two landmark notches (appropriately called Big Notch and Little Notch), he was trying to figure out how to tie up the loose ends of work and home so that he could take an impromptu five months off. Karl was Canada-bound.

Thirty-six trail miles north of El Morro is the town of Continental Divide, New Mexico. Town, however, is a relative term. Even to us, Continental Divide didn't look like much. Just off the interstate exit ramp there's a store promising wholesale prices on Indian jewelry and firecrackers. Farther down the street is a small hotel and a smaller grocery store. At Stuckey's, you can buy souvenir patches from all fifty states, or, if you prefer, key rings and plaques with flowers on them, as well as animal knickknacks that have "New Mexico" etched into their bases and look exactly the same as the ones they sell in Oklahoma or Pennsylvania that have "Oklahoma" or "Pennsylvania" written on them. I stood around for a while, waiting to see who would buy one, but no one did.

We had two reasons for hanging around in Continental Divide: our food package, which was waiting for us at the post office; and Dan's friend, Dave Plum, who would be meeting us there. Dave and Dan had met on the Pacific Crest Trail, and, the last we had heard, Dave planned to join us in Continental Divide. We'd been in sporadic contact, mostly via postcard, for the last few weeks, but true to his word, Dave showed up, on schedule and ready to walk. Our group was now four.

Dave had joined us for a stretch that only a long-distance hiker would walk. There were no trails, just a network of unmarked and sometimes unmapped jeep tracks through the sagebrush, arroyos, and mesas. Every so often, we'd pass a small community of makeshift homes clustered near a well, and we spent a fair amount of time negotiating fences. Water was still determining how far we would go each day; the windmills were unevenly spaced—but always miles apart.

On this flat terrain, we had gradually raised our average mileage until a 20-mile day was nothing unusual. The walking was easy, and the navigating tended to be straightforward since we could generally see where we were going. But we had been hardened by almost 500 miles on the trail. Feet were tough and muscles were tight; any extra pounds the group carried had been shed. Anyone joining us at this point was going to have trouble keeping up, although Dave was a good candidate—a solidly built rugby player with the endurance of a long-distance runner. But he was also new to the trail in a section where water dictated how far we would walk. On his first day, that was 20 miles—and 20 miles is a long way, no matter how fit you are. By the end of the day, Dave had developed huge blisters and was popping aspirin to dull the pain of sore muscles. But he hadn't uttered a single word of complaint.

Our destination for the day was Smith Lake—although to call this bowl-shaped indentation in the earth a lake is highly misleading. Grass grows in it, jeep tracks scar it, and the last time it held any water at all was eighteen years ago, according to the proprietor of the Smith Lake Trading Post. Still, Smith Lake it is to the people who live there and to the mapmakers at the USGS, who color it seasonal in dotted blue.

There are two kinds of trading posts in the Southwest. There are the trading posts that sit off interstate exits and well-traveled tourist routes, announcing "wholesale prices on Indian jewelry" and selling, as well, postcards and beef jerky and firecrackers and T-shirts. But in the mesa country north of Continental Divide there is another variety of trading post, used by the Indians themselves. These outposts on dusty roads often offer the only telephone for miles, as well as a limited selection of food and drink.

At the Smith Lake store, we were, as far as we could tell, the only cash-paying customers; the regulars kept a tab or traded—a woven doll for a tank of gas, a pair of earrings for a bag of groceries. The merchandise was eclectic: groceries, farm tools, and wool, as well as some jewelry and kachina dolls for the occasional tourist or wholesaler. Otherwise, the barter system was intact. Indian crafts were pawned, or traded for goods, and sheep products—wool and meat—were a medium of exchange.

The proprietor at the trading post let us sleep in his barn and shower in his mobile home, and we sat up looking at pictures of his wife and infant, who were away visiting relatives. Clearly, he missed them, and he was glad to spend the evening with company, going over our maps and pointing out where we would find other trading posts. The trading posts would be a source of small luxuries, interspersed among some of the harshest terrain we had yet seen. They would also be among the few sources of water for the next several days, and they would give us shelter, too, from the blistering midday sun.

We followed jeep trails and dirt roads through the reservation, past herds of sheep and cattle and small communities of several houses or trailers set together. Children waved enthusiastically from schoolbuses, and later we passed the school itself: a modern building, with signs in both Navajo and English. Grown-ups stopped their trucks, sometimes out of curiosity, sometimes to offer us rides, and as we chatted with the smiling, helpful Navajo, we remembered all the people who had suggested that we think about carrying guns on our trip.

The walking was easy on the jeep roads: soft dirt, even footing. But jeep roads don't go up places like the south side of Chaco Mesa, a long plateau that rises 500 feet above the valley floor. The steep southern face is treacherous sandstone that was never meant to be climbed; the soft rock crumbles as soon as you touch it.

The route we had penciled on our map was supposed to lead us up a gully to the top, but instead it led into a box canyon, clearly a dead end. We backtracked, looking for a way up, but the mesa didn't offer much hope: Wherever we looked, we were confronted by the same steep, sandy cliffs. Dan and Karl went off to scout possible routes, and Dave and I watched from across a dry streambed. From where I stood, they looked like spiders on a wall.

Neither Dan nor Karl is inclined to admit defeat, which meant that they were both likely to find a route up the mesa, whether there was one or not. I had a feeling that I was going to be either left at the bottom or coaxed into a terrifying ascent. I watched both of them, trying to ascertain which route was easier. Karl's route looked possible, until I noticed how much trouble he was having climbing a rock that was much, much taller than he. And if he was having trouble, with his long limbs, I knew what was in store for me. But I cared even less for Dan's route: Dan had disappeared behind a rock outcropping, and I couldn't see what kind of a mess he had gotten into. Karl was still halfway up when Dan came back down, without his pack, and announced that he had found a way up. Taking one last glance at Karl's impossible gymnastics, I quickly changed my mind and decided that I preferred the route I couldn't see to the route I could see. I followed Dan and tried not to look down. This vertical business was not my forte, I decided, as we scrambled on the rocks, hugged the cliff, and gambled that the sandstone wouldn't disintegrate under our weight. At the end, there was a leap over a rock crevasse, and then we were on top of the mesa.

Chaco Mesa, we call it today, a place that looks like the very end of the earth. On its crest is a network of old jeep roads—the kind they use in truck commercials. Several miles to the west, the mesa ends, sliced by a deep canyon. It is a remote place, difficult to get to. But in centuries past, it was the very center of the Anasazi civilization, a hub that dominated the surrounding 25,000 square miles. We have no idea what its name was then.

As always in New Mexico, the landscape is what dominates: the bigness of the sky stretching from one unobstructed horizon to the other, the weird and fantastic shapes and colors of the sandstone. But hidden between canyon and sky are the ruins of whole cities that may once have held several thousand people. Only in the New Mexican desert can you be staring at an entire city and not even see it. Sandstone bricks blend into sandstone cliffs, and the reds and coppers and yellows merge into the backdrop like a desert toad camouflaged to look like the desert floor. Like the Gila cliff dwellings, the pueblos of Chaco Canyon seem more like something that sprang from the earth than something that was constructed on it.

The largest of the towns is Pueblo Bonito—650 rooms big, containing large ceremonial kivas, the circular rooms that were so important to Chacoan spiritual life. Also in the canyon are other pueblos, and plenty of evidence of the Chacoan way of life: ramps and stairways, evidence of irrigation and cultivated fields, and— mysteriously, since the Chacoans did not use a wheel—remains of roads, sometimes 30 feet wide, that extended for hundreds of miles.

Today, Chaco Canyon is empty. Wind whistles through the canyons, water—occasionally—rushes down from the mesa above it. And the people who once lived here? Where did they go? It is speculated that they left during the great droughts of the twelfth century. It is speculated that they became the forebears of the Pueblo people. But what is known, for certain, is only this: They once lived here. And now they are gone.

Karl left us that evening. He needed to keep walking in order to arrive in the town of Cuba in time to catch a bus to Albuquerque in time to catch a plane to Houston. Karl was going to continue his hike on the Continental Divide, but first he was going to have to take care of all the loose ends that need to be tied up before one can disappear into the wilderness for five months. From Houston, he planned to fly back to Albuquerque, take the bus to Cuba, and resume walking north on the shortest, most direct route possible. If all went as planned, he would catch up with us somewhere near the Colorado border. He was going to have to walk fast.

We were going to have to walk fast, too. Our trek through New Mexico had turned into a race with summer, and summer was winning. The heat waves were more than visible; they were tangible, almost, undulating in slow, lazy, hypnotic waves in front of us, yet always just beyond our reach. At 18 miles per day, we had only a slim chance of reaching Colorado before the full onslaught of summer.

We were on a stretch of BLM land just south of the Jicarilla Apache Reservation. The Divide here is not much more than an unimpressive hill; at 200 feet high, it looks like any other ridge of sagebrush-covered brown dirt, and its function as the divider of watersheds is more theoretical than anything else—most of the scanty few inches of rain that does fall evaporates before it even has an opportunity to find the nearest ocean-bound stream. Still, 200 feet is high enough in a landscape more noted for its horizontal lines than its vertical contours. From the ridgetop we could see for miles. What we saw was a land so big and empty that the only thing that made the space real to us was the physical reality of having walked across it one step at a time.

We were looking for the Ojo Encino trading post. It wasn't on our map, but some tiny squares showed the existence of a small community right on the Divide. We found the hamlet, a small collection of ramshackle houses. One of them had a gas pump outside, along with a small cactus garden and a few carefully tended geraniums. An elderly Indian woman came out onto the porch and directed us to a room on the other side of the house.

She followed us inside. Our eyes adjusted slowly to the dark room. The dusty shelves were virtually bare, each containing only one or two items: a few bags of flour, some basic staples, a scanty assortment of canned vegetables and soup. An antique refrigerator held some six-packs of soda and a tiny freezer offered orange Popsicles. We bought two cans of soda each and followed the woman back outside.

She looked at us quizzically, and between slurps we explained what we were doing. Her expression turned incredulous, and in a soft voice she called into the house for her husband to come out and meet us. An elderly man with a wide, gap-toothed smile and strongly accented English joined us on the porch.

A beat-up old car pulled up, with five kids rolling around in the backseat. They spilled out of the car and ran around the gas pump, pummeling each other, pointing at us, and giggling. "Most of the time, they see only Navajo people," the proprietor explained. "Not too many white people come here." We waved at the children, and got shy smiles in return.

For most of the afternoon, we sat on the porch in the shade, getting up only to go back into the store for more soda. Aided by a pair of binoculars and frequent consultations in Navajo with his wife, the old man helped us figure out a route that would take us past another water source. We weren't in any hurry to leave; the shady porch, the company, the sodas all lulled us into staying longer. But finally it was cool enough to walk again. The couple filled our canteens with water—especially generous, since they had to haul their water by pickup truck in fifty-gallon drums. Someday, they told us, they planned to drill a well. Someday, they would have running water.

We went back into the store for one last can of soda and some snacks. Smiling, the woman added two things to our purchases: a tube of Ritz crackers, which she tucked into our bag with wishes for our success, and a postcard, which she asked us to mail to her when we reached Canada.

Trail magic, again.

North of Cuba is, I think, the greenest place in New Mexico. San Pedro Peaks Wilderness may be the greenest place I have ever seen. Certainly, it seemed that way after the unrelenting brown of the past weeks. And there were so many differnt kinds of green: the emerald green of long, lush, ungrazed grass; the rich deep greens of well-watered conifers; the light green leaves of riparian shrubbery. Where did all this green and the water it implied come from? Just a day out of Cuba, we were in a different country.

For the first time since the Gila, we were walking on marked hiking trail. Not only marked hiking trail, marked Continental Divide

Trail. Unfortunately, the trail only lasted as long as the rather small San Pedro Peaks wilderness area—a day and a half's worth of walking, at the most. At the wilderness boundary, the markers abruptly ended, leaving us to fend for ourselves through a network of unmapped logging roads.

We followed the roads down, out of the wilderness, and then found our way back up to another mesa, walking in the tracks of what must have been a humongous black bear. Here, again, the creeks held plenty of water, and the landscape was rich and green.

Two Chicano ranchers stopped to chat with us. They had been driving around to check on their cattle, and when we told them we were walking to Canada, they informed us that we were going the wrong way. Not, they quickly added, that we weren't walking in generally the right direction—that is, north—but how, they asked, did we intend to get down the other side of the mesa? We had rather been hoping that they would tell us that, we answered, but they shook their heads. No roads, and no trails, they said. And a hell of a descent, to go cross-country. Did we know how steep it was?

We had a feeling we were about to find out.

The descent to the Chama River was a frustrating scramble down impossible ravines, following narrow streambeds choked with plants that didn't want us there. At the bottom, when the route was finally flat, the plants were even nastier, particularly the wild roses and horsetail, a vicious, leafless plant with a thick woody stem covered in thorns. My skin had been scraped raw by the prickles and needles, and every nerve screamed as I pushed my way through the shrubs and bushes. Ahead of me, Dan was shouting; he sounded happy, and when I reached him I saw why: He was standing next to a CDT marker. Unbelievably, our navigation during the two-hour cross-country scramble had led us precisely to the trail that the Forest Service was just beginning to build. I didn't envy the work crews the task ahead—to finish the trail up to the mesa.

We followed clearly marked Continental Divide Trail all the way to the Chama River, a fast-running torrent that cuts through the bright reds and pinks of New Mexico's northern mesa country. The Chama is a major tributary of the Rio Grande. This part of it is also a Wild and Scenic River, which gives it the riverine equivalent of wilderness status—protection that has been granted to only .2 percent of America's river miles.

Wild and scenic status completely stops hydro development on protected segments of a river. But downstream from the Chama's wild and scenic stretch is the Abiquiu Dam, built by the Army Corps of Engineers—dam builders par excellence. Abiquiu Dam controls the heavily silt-laden river, preventing downstream flooding. It also stores water for irrigation and power generation.

As you walk along the Chama toward the Abiquiu Reservoir, you leave the protected segment for a stretch of river that shows the effects of the dam ahead. The river channel widens, and deepens, and the flow of the river becomes sluggish. The water becomes warmer, and its oxygen content decreases, sometimes so much that the new habitat is unsuitable for some native fish. By the time you reach the Abiquiu Reservoir, the water has slowed to a placid lake, strange and out of place among the dry mesas. For here, the sand-stone formations are dramatic, and huge. As the sun moves across the sky, it brings out different shades of tangerine and salmon and mauve, and the rocks take on colors usually reserved for flowers and tropical fish. The terrain looks less like an actual landscape than like an idealized image of a landscape, so true is it to our mental picture of the color and size and scale of the Southwest. It is at turns both brilliant and subtle, both hostile and seductive. And next to it, the reservoir looks like what it is: a man-made intrusion on the grandeur of nature.

A few miles away from the Abiquiu Reservoir is Ghost Ranch, a place of gentle visions and small greatnesses. Owned and operated as a conference center by the Presbyterian Church, it has, over the years, attracted artists and philosophers, archaeologists and geologists, theologians and writers, tourists and college students.

But Ghost Ranch is more than a creative conference center, or a spiritual retreat, or a summer camp for grown-ups. It is all of those things, but it is also, I think, a magic place. Even those of more prosaic temperaments would have to concede that it is stunningly, unforgettably beautiful.

The local villagers—at least the older generation—would tell you that Ghost Ranch was once an unlikely place for such tranquillity and peace. El Rancho de los Brujos, they called it originally: the Ranch of the Witches. There were tales of wailing babies, a giant snake, a murderous brother, and a flying red cow, although no one had actually seen the cow—for the sensible reason that the only people who saw it died immediately after.

It takes a long time before evil spirits abandon a place they have come to call home, and it takes even longer for people who have grown up with evil spirits to concede that they are finally gone. Most of the local villagers now agree that the witches of Ghost Ranch have moved on—although a visitor to the area might wonder if the evil spirits that once haunted this place have merely transformed themselves into the ranch's biting flies.

Georgia O'Keeffe painted here, capturing the colors of the New Mexican desert: the blues of the southwestern skies, the orange cliffs, the skulls bleached white by an unrelenting sun. But a painting is, after all, only a reflection of the real thing. The sky here is even bluer, the cliffs more saturated with color. And to see bones on your path is somehow different than to see them on canvas. Suddenly, you understand why one would paint them in the first place. They speak of life and death here; of the power of the sun.

Georgia O'Keeffe was not the only visitor to the Ghost Ranch who took an interest in the desert's macabre souvenirs. At the same time that she wandered the grounds with paintbrushes in hand, other visitors were also searching the desert for the remains of its previous residents. But these visitors were not artists; they were paleontologists. And they were interested not in cattle skulls, but in dinosaur bones.

Dinosaurs once roamed across Ghost Ranch, when the arroyos were swamps and the sagebrush plains a verdant marshland. Coelophysis, the oldest known dinosaur, was found here, one of the most spectacular fossils ever unearthed, with a perfectly articulated skeleton, complete to the bones in its stomach not yet digested from its last meal. A modest fellow, by dinosaur standards, he now lives in New York's Museum of Natural History, unremarkable among his monster-sized brethren.

There are plenty of other dinosaurs who remain at the Ghost

Ranch, many of them still hidden among the canyons and the mesas. More than a thousand, from hatchlings to adults of a variety of species, were found here in a single ancient quarry. The site is one of the most important dinosaur discoveries in the world. Back at the ranch's paleontology museum, another coelophysis takes center stage, slumbering embedded in an eight-ton block of siltstone. Visitors can watch as a staff paleontologist painstakingly chips away at the rock with dental tools and fine-haired brushes, exposing the skeleton one tiny, ancient bone fragment at a time.

Outside, the story of time is told not in small bone fragments but in bold strokes of color. The mesas are a brilliant kaleidoscope: oranges, reds, purples, yellows, and whites, stripped bare by erosion from the wind, in their nakedness revealing their history in neat rainbow stripes.

For those who can read it, the story is rich. It begins at the bottom, with the oldest layers, left from 3.5 billion years ago—the Archeozoic era, the age of old rocks. Above them lies newer matter—from the Proterozoic era, when the most advanced forms of life were simple organisms like sponges; a little higher, Paleozoic rock marks the beginning of the fossil record. The 300-million-year-long age of reptiles is next, represented by a virtual rainbow of rock layers: the deep red of the Chinle formation, which contains a treasure trove of dinosaur bones and petrified wood; the fine-grained golden cliffs of the Entrada formation, protected from erosion by the harder, younger rock above it. There is a thin white layer of limestone containing fossil fishes; and above that, the long, purple slopes of the Morrison formation, formed when New Mexico was beneath the sea. The dun sandstone of the Dakota formation marks a time of immense change, when the land rose, the continents changed, the dinosaurs vanished, and the earliest mammals took their first tentative steps. And capping it all off is a slender top layer representing, in comparison to the rest, a mere instant of time—the 60 million years of the age of mammals. To this layer, we humans are relative latecomers, occupying only the thinnest tippy-top portion of this thin, topmost slice. We have not, one sees very clearly, been on this planet a very long time at all.

Short though it may be—at least by comparison to geologic standards—human history in New Mexico is as rich and colorful as the story told by the rock cliffs, and it, too, is celebrated at the Ghost Ranch. A small museum of southwestern anthropology contains a fine collection of protohistoric and contemporary pots, as well as other artifacts and crafts from nearby pueblos. Also displayed are artifacts representing local Hispanic culture.

With all the richness of its geology, paleontology, archaeology, and cultural history, Ghost Ranch could be excused for focusing on its past and on the luminaries that come to the ranch to give workshops. But instead, it ventures into the real world of its immediate community, determined to be a good neighbor to the old Spanish Catholic communities of the Española Valley. There is a swimming pool here, open for use by local children; ranchers from nearby communities graze a limited number of cattle on Ghost Ranch rangeland for below-market prices; and a local outreach program provides services to the largely Chicano community. A high-desert research farm experiments with cereal grains native to the Third World, in the hope of learning new techniques to produce food in arid environments.

But perhaps the most distinctive of the ranch's undertakings has been its attempt to help some of the region's oldest families regain title to lands that have been lost through the tangled land ownership problems in New Mexico.

The original land grant to the Ghost Ranch dates from 1766—ten years before the Declaration of Independence. According to the Treaty of Guadalupe-Hidalgo, land titles recognized by the Mexican government—for instance, traditional land grants made by the king of Spain—were to be honored by the new American government. In the tradition of the *ejidos*, or commons, grants of title went to each family for its small living area; the *ejidos*, used primarily for grazing, were held in common. The United States government, however, respected only official titles, and over the years much of the *ejidos* ended up in the hands of large Anglo ranchers or the U.S. government itself. The ranch took it upon itself to redress some of these old injustices by initiating an unprecedented land trade with the U.S. Forest Service. After obtaining title to the disputed lands, Ghost Ranch signed them over to the descendants of the original owners.

One hundred and twelve families thereby gained title to lands long thought lost forever.

At nearby Echo Amphitheater, the land grant problems have not been so peaceably addressed. The amphitheater is a large rock echo chamber where even a whisper resounds loud and clear. Imagine, then, what it sounded like in 1966, when it was invaded by Reies Lopez Tijerina—otherwise known as "el Tigre"—and his Alianza Federal de Mercedes, land grant activists seeking legal recognition for what they claimed were traditional rights. Echo Amphitheater was once part of the San Joaquin del Rio Chama Land Grant; now, it is a Forest Service campground. The activists "arrested" Forest Service rangers, confiscated their pickup trucks, raised a new flag— and ultimately ended up in jail.

To the north of the amphitheater lies yet another testament to the history of the land wars in this area—the huge Tierra Amarilla grant, which, at 3.7 million acres, is one of the largest grants in the state. Its name means "yellow earth," and every inch of its perimeter is posted. The battles over land grants here have gone so far as to involve private armies of armed guards and signs that proclaim "TIERRA O MUERTA"—"Land or Death." In some cases, the legal battles have gone on for decades. Some of these land grants were awarded during the brief period after Mexican independence, during which most of the Southwest was still part of Mexico. Others date further back, awarded by long-dead Spanish kings who never even set foot in New Mexico. The battles over these lands—the very lifeblood of the people who live here—continue. In the Southwest, history is not only part of the landscape. It is part of life.

Our route out of Ghost Ranch took us to a mule trail that led straight up the mesa and was neatly marked with wooden signs painted with bright yellow donkeys. The climb was hot and steep, and it became hotter and steeper as the vegetation got thinner and the sun climbed higher in the sky. But we didn't complain. There was a trickle of water running in the stream we were following, and there was a trail, which we hadn't expected, leading us up the sandstone, past a box canyon, and onto the mesa top.

And then we lost the trail.

By now, we had discovered that there is a pattern to getting lost. It starts innocuously enough. First, you are checking your map periodically, identifying landmarks as you pass them. There's a road on the map heading east, and you see a road, or what might be a road, heading east. Check. Then a mesa to the west; sure enough, there's a mesa to the west. Check. Then, you notice that there is the slighest disagreement between the map and the terrain. The map says there's supposed to be a notch in the mesa, and the notch isn't visible. Everything else looks okay, though; perhaps the notch is blocked by that little rock outcropping. You continue, noting from the map that you're supposed to be walking northwest. But your shadow is over your left shoulder and it's still morning, which tells you that you are walking due north. You look for reasons the sun is in the wrong place: Maybe the trail has zigzagged a little, and it doesn't show up on the map. Maybe the map is wrong (always a good excuse, because occasionally it's true). Or your compass isn't working right (not a good excuse, do you really think you have a better sense of direction than your compass?). Or—the last delusion—you can't be wrong because where else could you have gone?

You continue on. You'll know soon enough if you're on track, because you ought to pass a dry containment dam in a quarter mile or so. In fact, that might be the dam right there, that splotch of brown over to the right. Fifteen minutes later, the sun is still in the wrong place, and there's no containment dam. And finally, you allow yourself to process the mounting and finally indubitable evidence. You are standing on a canyon floor, and the map tells you that you should be on top of a ridge.

As far as getting lost goes, stumbling into a canyon is a happy circumstance, because it is easy enough to identify a canyon on a map. So to be perfectly technical about it, we weren't actually lost; we just weren't where we wanted to be—and we saw no way of getting there. Between our dry streamed at the bottom of the canyon and the flat plateau of the mesa top was a cliff of soft sandstone, virtually impossible to climb.

An alternate course was easy to figure out; the canyon headed north toward a network of jeep trails, one of which would take us back to our route. In theory, you remember, a streambed is an easy thing to follow. So we followed it, sinking into its sandy soil, climbing over deadfall that grasped at our legs with dry, sharp twigs and plants that scratched at our arms with hidden daggers of thorns. And as we fought our way through the mess of plants that depended on the trickle of water that occasionally deigned to visit this dry gully, we missed the sharp right turn the stream took and continued straight up a side gully so insignificant that it hadn't even been marked on the map.

Armed with the certainty that we were in the right gully, we bumbled on, letting imagination and wishful thinking remake the landscape. The gully we had been following had long since disappeared, but we continued to convince ourselves that we could see a vague indentation in the soil. When we were forced to accept that we had indeed lost the gully, we looked for the jeep trail that should have been at the gully's end. And—lo and behold!—our imaginations produced a jeep trail, or what might have been at one time a jeep trail. In a few hundred yards, after we had followed its twisting and turning path to a dead end where there was nothing to indicate that anyone had ever been there, let alone in a vehicle, we had to admit that what we were following was at best a game path, and more probably just a random scattering of spaces between the trees.

There are different kinds of being lost. There is the kind of being lost when you don't know exactly where you are but you know that if you keep going in a certain direction you'll eventually hit what you're looking for: a river, or a long mountain ridge, for example. There is the kind of being lost where you know about where you are, but it's not where you're supposed to be and you're not sure how to proceed. There's the kind of being lost where you think you can retrace your steps to known or knowable territory. And there is the kind of being lost where you have wandered off your map and onto terra incognita, the kind where you can't even decide to go forward or backward because you don't know which way forward and backward might be.

We were that last kind of lost.

And, not incidentally, we were almost out of water.

Out of water. Just looking at the half liter we had left for the three of us made us thirsty. We hadn't been aware of thirst while we were climbing, absorbed in our maps. Now it assaulted us, preying about the backs of our mouths, pricking at our lips.

Dan and Dave called a lunch break and decided to look at the maps over crackers and cheese. I declined—the first meal I had declined in forty-seven days of walking—because I thought that lunch would only make me thirstier. Instead, I headed into the trees with my compass, trying to find a landmark or a view that would help us figure out our location.

Just as there is a process to getting lost, there is a process to getting unlost. You start by looking at the map to try to identify prominent features. If you're lucky, there are some: mountains, bodies of water, meadows, patches of trees, man-made things like power lines or roads. If you're unlucky, you've got pretty much what we were looking at then: even ridges, a view blocked by trees, and gentle, indistinguishable hillocks.

If you can't identify your location, you start working backward, trying to figure out where you went wrong. Once you know the mistake, you can guess what you did since then and figure out approximately where you are. Then you can start working forward, trying to figure out what features you should run into if you walk in different directions. What works depends on the terrain you're in, what there is to see, and how well it's marked on the map.

Dave was the one who figured out the side gully; once he had solved that mystery, it was easy to see how we'd gotten into this mess. From there, we worked out about where we might be by going over what we had done in the last two hours. If we were right, Yeso stock tank would be three quarters of a mile down the road. No one wanted to think what would happen if we were wrong. It would mean some sort of evacuation—either trying to find our way back to Ghost Ranch or trying to get to a road that might have traffic on it. One thing was certain: We weren't going to stumble across water. We'd have to search to find it.

No one wanted to walk the extra distance. Each false start took time and energy, and we were running short of both. As usual, Dan went, leaving Dave and me to crawl under some shade and escape the afternoon sun. The logging road was hot, reflecting the heat back

at us. Neither of us said anything about water. We were saving our
last sips, trying not to think about it. I studied the map, and periodically said something reassuring like: "If Dan doesn't find water, I
don't know where we are," and, getting no reaction to that, "This
could be a real emergency." I was starting to panic—a controlled
hysteria that had been building and was only waiting for Dan to
return to explode into a full-blown frenzy. Dave didn't say much.
He's not the panicking type, but I imagine that my hyperbole didn't
help him much.

My diatribe was interrupted by the onslaught of an army of red
ants that had first dibs on my spot in the shade. They attacked in
full force, swarms of them climbing into my socks and under my T-
shirt, vicious, bloodthirsty, painful. That was the final straw, and I
sniffled back tears as I surrendered my spot to the ants.

Time crawls in the New Mexican sun. You can see the heat,
dizzy-making waves, but you can't stare at it for long. The heat
crawls into your brain, maddening, hypnotic, painful. I tried dis-
tracting myself by studying the map, turning it upside down, to see
if it made any more sense. It didn't. Finally, there was nothing left
to do but wait.

Dan came back, declaring victory. Up ahead, the roads were identified by numbers, and the numbers—miraculously—matched our
map. The tank was where it was supposed to be, filled with water,
surrounded by cattle. We celebrated with the last of our water, which
by now tasted better than champagne.

Our spirits rose higher and higher as we approached the tank, but
we were tired and walking slowly. Fifteen minutes, we told ourselves; just fifteen more minutes and we'd be able to drink all we
wanted.

We could see the water from the road: It was fifty or so feet down
a hill, sparkling blue. But for the cattle, it would have been a perfect
swimming hole.

We climbed down to it.

"We have weather coming in," Dan said. The sky above us was
still blue, but to the west was a gathering mass of purplish brown
clouds, the kind that means rain, even in New Mexico. The irony
was not lost on us, but it was easy to laugh about the rain now that
we had water.

I started unpacking, looking for a flat spot that the cows hadn't gotten to first. Dave showed up with two canteens of water, frowning. He held up the plastic bottles with hands covered in sticky brown mud, and we could see that the water was an opaque dark brown.

"No problem," Dan and I said in unison. We had been bragging about our water filter since Dave had joined us, but this was the first real chance we had had to prove it—since Continental Divide, we had relied almost exclusively on windmills, trading posts, and gifts from passing motorists. The few times we had found surface water, it had been clear and easy to filter. Dave looked on doubtfully as we began to assemble the tubes and canister.

Dan held the tubes as I pulled on the pump, feeling, immediately, its resistance. I pushed hard and a few tablespoons squirted through. "See," I said, just as the tubes exploded off of the canister, spreading brown, fetid water over everyone.

What faith we place in contraptions and machines! It must have been a fluke, we said. We reattached the tubes, tried again. And again. We tried to prefilter the water by straining it through a bandanna. We let one bottle sit untouched, hoping the scum would settle and allow us to decant the water. We tried again, still refusing to believe that the filter could fail us. Finally, we allowed ourselves to admit the obvious. We had managed to produce less than a cup of clear water, and the filter wouldn't budge. Period, end of story, that was that.

We had to go on, and looking at the map, I knew immediately what that meant—eight miles uphill. Dan and Dave continued to look at the map, as though wanting it badly enough could make a spring appear close by. "Maybe here," Dan said, pointing to another containment tank, likely, I responded, to have water exactly like the water here, and off our route as well. "Maybe there," Dave offered. But I knew, with complete certainty, that the water we would drink that night was eight miles away. Dan and Dave refused to let my distress and impending hysteria affect their belief that we might find water before Harris Bear Camp Spring.

We did, in a way: rain. It dripped down on us, teasing us with drops on our noses and fingers and clothes. It laughed at us from above, in pregnant, dark clouds; it fell just barely hard enough to make us don rain jackets, and then lightly enough to trick us into taking them off. But there wasn't enough water to collect. We tried licking raindrops off our pack covers, but there wasn't enough for that to work, either.

Twice, Dan left the road to go rummaging about in the bush, where the map promised a dam. Twice he came back with bad news: At the first, the water was even worse than that at Yeso tank, and the second dam was dry. The news didn't surprise me; I hadn't been holding out any hope.

It was past four o'clock now, and it was obvious to all of us that we had to get to the spring. We were simply too thirsty to bivouac for the night and try again in the morning.

"Can you make it?" Dan asked.

There is only one answer to that question; how we felt about it was irrelevant. But we were a miserable trio as we continued along the infrequently used dirt road. To each other, we fantasized about drivers offering us ice-cold cups of water—or any-temperature water. But there were no vehicles; nor were there likely to be. The lack of recent tracks, the overgrown weeds, the ruts in the road—all of these were signs that this remote Forest Service road was used infrequently, at best.

We kept our thoughts to ourselves, although we all knew that we all shared them. This was, after all, the fourth consecutive year of drought, and June was the month when the springs began to run dry. What would we do if there was no water at Harris Bear Camp? No one dared voice the possibility.

There are many different kinds of miles on a long-distance hike, and while they are all a mile long, they are very, very different in length. There are miles walked in cool mornings on soft dirt footpaths; there are miles climbing steep, trailless slopes covered with scree. There are miles on hot gravel roads, exposed to the sun; and there are tedious miles of river crossings and stream fords. There are miles of easy, comfortable descents; and lightning-quick miles on paved roads or well-graded footpaths.

The miles to Harris Bear Camp Spring were the longest miles on the Continental Divide.

It was nearly dark by the time we reached the road to the spring. We were so close, but too tired to pick up our pace. My mind played the same words over and over, like a broken record: Just a little more, just a little more, keep going, keep going. But nothing, not even the promise of water, could make me walk faster.

Dan reached the spring first. There was a metal holding tank the size of a watering trough for livestock. I could see him cut over to the trough, see him looking into it—and then I heard his yell of triumph and relief.

Cold water, clear water, perfect water flowing from a piped spring. As I drank—two liters, barely taking time to breathe between gulps— I knew why it was that so many people in the Southwest had bragged to us about the quality of their water. If this was my spring, I'd brag about it too.

Suddenly, a clap filled the great space of the huge New Mexican sky. From one horizon to the other, the sound filled creation. Instantly, it seemed, water flowed in streams on the ground and formed ponds in the grass. Sheets of rain forced us to run for shelter under a grove of trees, and puddles of water formed at our feet.

We had prayed for water, and nature had answered. Who were we to complain how she had done it? We looked at each other in the weird purple light of the storm. We were soaking wet, and we'd have to settle for a cold dinner. But none of that affected our sense of the ridiculous. Or our sense of relief. We had what we needed, and that was enough.

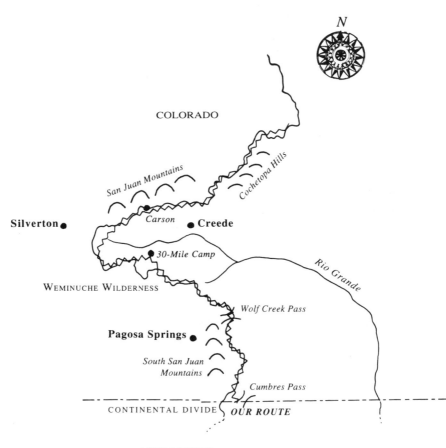

4

COLORADO!

The first thing you do at the Colorado border is look up. Colorado doesn't waste any time revealing itself; its mountains have all the subtlety of a mile-high wall. They loom in front of you, above you—towering, monolithic. The only way to go forward is to go up.

We had walked 750 miles to get here. We were strong, broken in to the trail, at ease with the packs and the miles and the rhythms of a life spent entirely outdoors. We owned the trail now. We impressed ranchers, shopkeepers, and rangers with our tales. And we impressed ourselves.

The San Juan Mountains were not impressed with us.

At Cumbres Pass, Karl joined us again, and the four of us headed north, into the mountains. A sign directed us: CONTINENTAL DIVIDE TRAIL; BLUE LAKE 22 MILES. We started up, lulled into complacency by the promise of marked trail. Hiking would be easier in this back-packer's paradise.

Two miles later we were hopelessly lost in a maze of dirt roads, all of which went the wrong way. The choice—to continue on the roads or to head cross-country—was an easy one. No matter how fine the road, it doesn't help much if it goes to the wrong place, so—reluctantly—we turned into the woods. Scrambling along a creekbed, doing battle with branches and brush; then climbing, up, out of the timber to the open high country of snow and scree, we became acquainted with Colorado's idea of a late-spring hike: one step up, one slide down, compasses out, maps flapping in the breeze, and no trail in sight.

When, some time later, we found it again, the trail was still point-ing uphill, to the 12,187-foot summit of Flattop Mountain. It's one of those names that you run across frequently throughout the West; there are countless Flattop Mountains, just as there are countless Spring Creeks and Gunsight Passes and Apache Canyons and Elk Parks. Usually, the names say something about the terrain, and, indeed, the top of this particular peak was flat. But getting there was another story: The ascent was unforgivingly straight-up steep, and it catapulted us into a new world of rock and ice and thin, thin air. To find equivalent conditions at sea level, we would have had to travel to the Arctic Circle.

In just a few miles, the rules had changed completely. Weather, water, elevation, temperature, footway; here in the alpine tundra nothing was the same. In New Mexico, our general route of travel had taken us through desert and semidesert; to see trees, we had had to climb. We wouldn't spend much time walking among the trees in the South San Juans, either, but for a different reason: They were far *below* us, and from here on we would travel largely above tree line.

The trees that did manage to cling to their tenuous hold on life were hardy fellows, the marathon runners of their species. Their feats test the outer limits of endurance as they eke out a fragile existence in cold rocky soil, hurricane-strength winds, and months of frigid blizzarding winter. And, like marathon runners, they are far too preoccupied with their struggle to worry about what they look like.

Krummholz, they are called, a name as awkward and graceless as their appearance. It means "crooked trees" in German, and crooked they are: Contorted by the wind into grotesque, deformed shapes, these stunted spruce hug the ground or crouch against the lee side of boulders. Somehow, they hang on. Trees, as we would see again and again, have an immense will to live.

From the summit, we could look back into New Mexico—mere foothills from this lofty vantage. We were standing at the gateway to Colorado's high country. In front of us, the view extended over valleys, down glacial cirques, across to more mountains, and then, again, to even more high, snow-tipped peaks. There were no towns, no power lines, no highways, no lights—only the endless mountains over which we proposed to walk. It sounded preposterous.

In fact, we had no way of knowing yet whether it was even possible. Still south of the highest ridges, we had so far only seen the warmer, south-facing slopes. The north slopes remained hidden from our view; we had no idea how much snow would be lying on the cold, shaded sides of the mountains. Enough to stop us? We knew that we'd have the answer only when we reached the first ice slopes, the first cornices.

There were other differences, too; the abundance of water stood out the most. Water was everywhere. It rushed down from the peaks, gurgled in streams, trickled out of ice fields, and seeped into meadows. No more planning our days by windmills and containment dams; no more thirsty climbs on rationed water. All we had to do was reach down and dip our canteens into the clear running streams.

There was snow, too: huge, icy patches that melted every afternoon and froze again every night. The walking took on new, uneven rhythms: slow and cautious in the morning, as we made our careful way across the hard, icy slopes; awkward and ungainly in the afternoon, when we broke through the sun-softened crust and sank down, thigh-deep, into stinging, wet slush.

And the climbs! This was a completely different kind of walking. This was weight lifting, this hauling of bodies and backpacks up 1,000 feet, then down again, then up once more. Some deep recess of memory provided the tidbit that the Empire State Building is 1,000 feet tall, give or take the radio tower. Following Colorado's

Continental Divide, we would climb anywhere from 3,000 to 6,000 feet in a day, rarely less. As we struggled uphill—and it seemed that we were always walking uphill—our bodies clamored for attention, demanding that we notice the thinner air, the strain on our muscles, the mechanics of motion.

We had walked into a new weather pattern, too. As if to punish us for the temerity of being so close to the sky, the clouds pelted us with rain, hailstones, and lightning. Walking astride the backbone of the continent, we were far higher than any trees, completely exposed. Above us, the mountain gods told us, with booming pyrotechnics that brooked no argument, exactly what they thought of our trespass into their high abode.

※※※※※

Lightning. When it strikes close—say, right next to you—you smell it, feel it, hear it, all at the same time. Just exactly as it rends the air, an instinct older and deeper than conscious thought throws you to the ground; the earsplitting crack echoes off the mountains, reverberates in your brain.

To the Maoris of New Zealand, he is Iko; to the Pygmies of tropical Africa, he is Kvum; the Dakota Indians of North America call him Wakan. He is the god who controls lightning, and he is to be feared.

Like any other god, this one has his preferences, at least according to folklore and myth. He is attracted to cats and dogs, and repelled by pregnant women and infants. He likes oak and ash, but avoids aspen and elder. Bibles, candles, bells, and salt are said to afford protection, and the safest place of all is on a feather bed.

We carried a little bit of salt, but no candles, Bibles, or bells. And alas there are no feather beds on the Continental Divide.

Lightning seeks the earth, yearns for it. It sends out forks of electricity—branches that search for the air current offering the quickest route to the ground. When it strikes, the temperature can be as high as 30,000 degrees Kelvin—hot enough to separate air molecules into their component atoms (and thus transform the usual form of oxygen, O_2, into ozone, O_3, which is the oddly acrid "burned" odor one smells after a strike). And it is hot enough to kill. It strikes the first thing available, often the highest point. Too often, the highest point was us.

And then, there is the thunder, not a boom or a rumble, but a resounding in the sky that sounds like an announcement of the end of time. Engulfed in the noise and power of the storm, completely at the mercy of a random bolt of electricity, you don't think of the statistics—that to be struck by lightning is, in fact, very rare. On the contrary, you think of metal ice axes and metal backpack parts, and it seems that your escape has been nothing short of a miracle. You are somewhat surprised to find yourself all in one piece.

The Sherpas of Nepal believe that to climb a mountain brings bad luck; it makes the mountain gods angry. Avalanches fall, storms gather, young men may die. It may be that Colorado contains some misplaced Himalayan peaks. Take Montezuma, for instance: At 13,150 feet, it's a modest mountain, by Colorado—let alone Himalayan—standards. The state has some two hundred summits that rise above it. We aimed only for its shoulder; our trail contoured around, and 500 feet below, the summit. But even that modest goal angered the gods.

Scientists, of course, have a different explanation for Montezuma's behavior: orographic effects, they call it, when mountains create their own weather. Either Montezuma Peak engaged in orographic legerdemain, or, godlike, it conspired with the skies. Whether you believe the ancient myths or modern science, the effect, for us, was the same.

≋≋≋

The storm came in while we were eating lunch, comfortably ensconced against the rocks of a high, flat boulder field. The clouds didn't so much gather in the sky as fly across it. We could see them coming, fast, purple-brown, carrying a sheet of rain, hurling hailstones at the ground. But we couldn't run fast enough to escape, and even if we could, at 12,000 feet, there wasn't anywhere to hide.

The how-to books tell you that if you're caught above tree line in a storm, you should crouch among the boulders, which sounds like a good idea when you're reading about mountain safety in the comfort of your living room. But when you're cowering among rocks barely large enough to shelter a child, your perspective is considerably different. The best we could do was cross the field and huddle near an upslope until the storm blew down the valley.

The purple clouds moved on to other peaks, and perhaps to other hikers, but Montezuma had not yet finished with us. In front of us was a small ice field, fifty yards across, perhaps, no more. But its slope was steep, covered with half-melted snow and edged by a cornice that had already started separating from the rest of the ice. Sooner or later, and by the looks of things, sooner, all that snow—and anything or anyone on it—was going to end up in a rocky gully several hundred feet below.

The urge not to backtrack kept us staring at the cornice for another half hour, as though our eyes could bore a safe path through the ice. It lured Karl out onto the ice, where we watched, scarcely breathing, as he put first one foot down, then the other, testing the snow, walking out as far as he dared—which, by the rest of our measurement, was a good deal farther than was safe—to be absolutely certain that a detour was really and truly necessary. It sent Dave scrambling around a nasty-looking rock outcropping to see whether there was a way to climb around the other side of the ridge. Eventually, we allowed ourselves to accept what would have been patently obvious to your basic urban apartment dweller: We would have to find another way.

The other way was hardly an improvement. It descended in a wide arc a few hundred feet into a drainage, then followed a creek back up the other side. This route had a few traps of its own: a near-vertical rock scramble, a glissade down an ice slope, and then, because—in the Colorado Rockies, at least—what comes down must go back up, a climb to regain the 400 feet we had lost by descending into the drainage. It was slow going as we climbed over a tedious series of boulders and scree. As the crow flies, the ice slope and the shoulder of Montezuma Peak were separated by a mere half mile. It took us more than an hour to get there. At that rate, we'd make it to Canada sometime in the next decade.

And Montezuma had not yet exhausted its arsenal! The anger of the storm and the treachery of the ice were behind us; but in front of us was a trail hidden by snow. Trickery was the mountain's weapon of choice this time, and we fell into its trap with a thud. It wasn't until the end of the day, when the map and the terrain ceased to have anything in common, that we realized that we had been lured down the wrong trail to a clearing 2 miles from our destination. When we finally got back on route and stopped for the night, we were completely exhausted and far short of our goal. We were also short of food.

In everyday life, food can be an excuse for a social event, the center-piece of a celebration—it can even be an art form. One plans a meal, considering all kinds of questions: How attractively is it served? How good does it taste? How well do the components of a meal complement each other?

On a long-distance hike, food is fuel, and human bodies are gas-guzzling automobiles. Carrying a pack at high altitude and walking at a fair pace over difficult terrain, a hiker uses up about 300 calories a mile. To walk 15 or so miles per day requires at least 4,500 calories just to keep going. There is only only question on a long-distance hike: Does the meal fill you up? The answer, usually, is no.

There are almost as many culinary strategies as there are hikers. Some people take the easy way, subsisting on freeze-dried dinners, light to carry, simple to prepare. Others carry heavier loads in order to vary their diet or satisfy personal preferences. There are the do-it-yourselfers who dehydrate foods at home, and the supermarket gourmets who rely on prepackaged foods. Our sacks contained a little of everything. Always concerned with the weight of our loads (and just why is it that the foods that taste the best weigh the most?), we nonetheless felt that variety in our diet was necessary, not only to appease our taste buds, but also to keep our bodies healthy.

The old-time mountain men, of course, didn't dine on freeze-dried Louisiana beans and rice. They lived off the land, a romantic notion, to be sure. But the land now is different from the land then. There are more people and less wildlife. There are also game laws and fishing regulations, reflecting the fact that fishing and hunting are more often a matter of sport than of survival. And, perhaps most important, living off the land requires knowledge, skill, patience, a willingness to change your route to follow your quarry—and a lot of energy. Not to mention an acceptance of the fact that the fish you plan to eat for dinner may not be in the mood to be caught when you cast your rod into a lake or a stream. Finding fresh mushrooms, picking berries, or catching a fish are wonderful treats for backpackers; many hikers do, in fact, carry light collapsible rods with them. But, given the enormous caloric demands of hiking and the general state of exhaustion at the end of each day, most backpackers prefer to rely on food they can carry, not on food they can catch.

As we examined our near-empty food bags, containing a few ounces of cheese, some crackers, a couple of candy bars, and some packages of oatmeal, we imagined all kinds of delicacies. Karl fantasized about fresh-caught trout frying on the fire, and decided to buy a fishing rod at our next town stop. Dan and Dave declared that once they got to town, they would be more interested in today's pizza than tomorrow's fish, and they began negotiating the subject of toppings ("everything," I think, was the final decision). And I daydreamed about salad. We had 16.5 miles to walk before our next road crossing, at Wolf Creek Pass, from where we would hitchhike into Pagosa Springs. In the meantime, we would have to be satisfied with fantasies, not food.

≈≈≈≈≈

Even in late June, snow lingers on the side of the road at Wolf Creek Pass. At 10,857 feet, this passage through the Continental Divide is the so-called bearcat of mountain passes. Receiving an average of 460 inches of snow a year—and sometimes almost twice that—it boasts a small downhill ski area that gets more snow than any other in the country.

Compared to the alternatives in the rugged San Juan Mountains, the pass is accessible. If you had lived in southern Colorado 6,000 years ago, you would have traveled over this pass to follow game to the San Luis Valley. If you were a French trapper, you might have crossed the Divide here in search of beavers. As a nineteenth-century miner, you would have come looking for gold. And in the

1930s, you might have made the traverse in a Model T—quicker than walking, to be sure, but even so, a trip of two days. Fortunately for us, the modern internal combustion engine is a good deal more efficient. We stuck out our thumbs and a Navajo Indian named Joe promptly pulled to the side of the road and told us that yes, he'd take us all the way to the post office in Pagosa Springs.

Joe told us that he made ritual objects for Navajo religious ceremonies, and he showed us some eagle feathers, meticulously decorated and carefully stored in a fabric-lined box. When we told him about our journey, he asked us to send him any eagle feathers we might find in Montana. "They're getting so rare around here," he said sadly. We took his address. But although we didn't forget our promise in the months ahead, we would find no feathers to send back to Colorado.

Once in Pagosa Springs, we had more to do than refill our food sacks, eat pizza, and find a fishing rod for Karl. It was time to reevaluate our schedule and our gear for the high country ahead.

Since Elwood Pass, 16 trail miles back, we had been walking more west than north, following the Divide as it begins a huge hairpin turn around the headwaters of the Rio Grande, swinging first almost due west, then north a bit, and then back almost due east. From Elwood Pass to Spring Creek Pass would be a 135-mile walk by trail; as the crow flies, it was a mere 35 miles north.

In New Mexico, Dan and I hadn't worried too much about our schedule; we had covered the miles much faster than we had anticipated. Karl, too, had been unconcerned about our pace beyond the basic issue of getting to the next road crossing before we ran out of food. But since rejoining us at Cumbres Pass, Karl's relationship to the hike had changed: He was Canada-bound now, and he had figured out that unless we increased our mileage, we were almost certain to be stopped by snow in Montana. So Karl had come up with a new schedule, as well as a shortcut that would avoid the Divide's long arc in southern Colorado. He figured that if he averaged at least 18 miles a day, he could make it to Canada by October 15. Did we think, he wanted to know, that we could pick up our pace a little so we could all continue to hike together?

There were two problems with that proposal. The first was that the shortcut would have eliminated some of the most spectacular scenery on the entire Divide. The second was a more practical problem: During our first few days in Colorado, I had discovered the exact nature of my relationship with gravity—and it wasn't a friendly one. Gravity wasn't going to let me walk 18 miles a day in these mountains.

The guys had no such problems. Karl's long legs ate up the miles with little apparent difficulty; Dan had no problem doing big mileage, big climbs, or any combination of the two. And Dave, although not seduced by the miles-per-day mind-set of many long-distance hikers, loved the straining of muscles against mountain, and attacked each challenge with gusto and confidence—and usually a smile. "I've got my boogying shoes on," he'd say, passing me on the way uphill, headed for the sky. In Colorado, the guys were in hog heaven, hollering at the tops of passes and whooping at the big views. The harder the climb, the louder the caterwauling.

"CO-LO-RA-DO!!! YOU GOTTA LOVE IT!!!"

I'd hear them celebrating the mountains every time they got to the top of a climb, their shouts echoing against the canyons. Down below, still inching upward, I was finding the climbs debilitating. One hundred steps, then rest. Fifty steps, then rest. Try not to look up and see how much more climbing is still ahead. Try not to believe that the next hillock is the end of the climb. And do not, under any circumstances, think about Canada.

Step-breathe-step, step-breathe-step.

"CO-LO-RA-DO!!!"

Step-breathe-step, step-breathe-step.

Since we had crossed into Colorado, we had averaged 16 miles a day, and by evening I was so exhausted I could barely stay awake through dinner. I simply didn't think I could go any faster. Nor was I willing to give up the occasional rest days in town.

So Dan and I made a different decision. We would go north on trail as far as we could and then, when the snow, inevitably, made it impossible for us to continue—probably somewhere in Montana—we would continue to Canada on a lowland route. The next summer, we would return to finish hiking on the Divide itself.

The decision was an important one, because it allowed us to set two goals that could otherwise have been contradictory. The first was to walk from Mexico to Canada. The second was to follow and savor the best possible trail through the high country. We wanted to enjoy ourselves; to stop and take pictures; to watch the elk and the deer; to really see the country through which we were walking. We wanted the process of walking to Canada to be more important than the act of getting there.

So at Pagosa Springs we repacked our gear so that Dave, Dan, and I were sharing communal supplies, and Karl was equipped to go out on his own. We would all hike together for two more days, until we reached the junction with the shortcut trail; then Karl would go on ahead, alone. We were going to be sad to see him leave—the four of us got along well, and he had been with us since the very beginning of the journey. Karl didn't want the group to split up either, and he made one last attempt to pull us along, encouraging me up hills, waking us up an hour earlier than usual, and proposing that we walk a few miles after dinner. I reacted like a recalcitrant donkey.

The terrain continued to torment us with steep climbs. We were staying on the crest of the Divide for miles at a stretch, obediently following it as it went up and down and up and down, a thousand feet at a time. Finding a level spot for a campsite was a problem. Up on the actual crest of the Divide, water was a problem too: We could see it below us, but getting it meant scrambling off the Divide—when that was possible—or filling our canteens with snow. And the thunderstorms continued to plague our afternoons as we raced across high, bare ridges, trying to reach shelter before a storm reached us.

We had added a few additional pieces of equipment at Pagosa Springs: heavier waterproof boots for slogging through the snow; gaiters for covering our lower legs; and extra layers of clothing for the cold evenings. Most important, instead of our walking sticks, we each carried an ice ax. Now, at least, if we slipped on an ice slope, we had a chance of stopping the fall.

And there were so many opportunities to slip; so many ice slopes on so many steep, steep hillsides. Sometimes it was hard to believe that a trail actually existed through the rock outcroppings and the unstable scree. At the Knife Edge, a near-vertical spur ridge that looks about like it sounds, we stared hard, asking each other where the trail could possibly be taking us, until we finally followed it through a sort of hole in the rocks. On the other side, the path was blocked by more ice fields, each of them much bigger than the one that had stopped us at Montezuma Peak.

This time, bullheadedness triumphed: Tired of detours and armed with our ice axes, we headed across. Dan led, and he made it to the other side of the first patch. As we followed—slipping and sliding, grasping at the slope with our axes, and trying to find stable footholds—the scree and slush seemed intent on taking itself and us down to the base of the slope. We carefully and slowly kicked steps into the soft snow that clung to the mountainsides. Below us, there was a stern reminder that a fall could be fatal: A dead horse lay a hundred feet or so down from the trail.

Any hope of further forward motion ended when Dan announced that, from his vantage point, the next patch looked even worse. Bullheaded we might have been, but the mountains hadn't driven us to suicide: We backtracked again. To Karl's delight, this detour, to Trout Lake, was a shortcut to the shortcut trail he had been looking for. Karl decided to set up camp by the lake; in the morning, he would head north alone. In the meantime, he pulled out his fishing rod in the hope that the lake would live up to its name (it didn't). For our part, we made the choice we had promised ourselves we would: to continue on the long arching route around the very farthest headwaters of the Rio Grande. As Karl continued casting into the lake's cold, still waters, we waved good-bye, and climbed back up to the north slope of the Divide.

≈≈≈≈

There are dozens of different kinds of campsites, and the Continental Divide has them all. There are sites along streams, sites near meadows, and sites overlooking lakes. There are soft, sandy cradles along riverbanks, and gravelly beds on rocky mountain ridges. And then there is the tundra, with its crisp winds, cold clear skies, inhospitable crags, and crystalline air.

The tundra does not beckon to the hiker with promises of comfort and protection, but you can find both if you look hard enough. You can squeeze in among big boulders or, if there are any, among shrubs and bushes. There are flat spots for your tent, although you might have to remove some rocks. The water is ice-cold and shockingly clear, and the sunset paints the mountains in a soft, dreamlike rose. The higher you go, the more difficult it is to find wood for a fire. Out come the backpacking stoves, sputtering about the altitude, fighting the cold with their tiny blue flames.

At first acquaintance, the high country appears a cold and barren place, but there is no lack of life here. Marmots chatter and whistle, or, if threatened, dive into their burrows among the scree. When they think it's necessary, which isn't often, these short-legged, wide-bodied critters are surprisingly quick, considering their improbable physiques. Exactly how do they get so fat? one might wonder. What do they find to eat on this bare, rocky ground?

There are elk, too: fleet, graceful, galloping effortlessly, exempt somehow from the laws of gravity, not to mention any danger of twisted ankles. Even a tiny fawn, awkward and ungainly on uncoordinated legs, can run circles around us earthbound humans. And any elk can bound, in minutes, up a hill it would take us hours to climb. To these 600-pound animals, a fall is nothing more than a short jolt in the rhythm of their gallop; a scrambling of hoofs, a spray of snow, and they are up and running again, graceful as ever. Silhouetted on the ridges, their dark forms stand out against the sky as they continue their roaming, so much fleeter and swifter than we.

But more than anything, the tundra is a place of beauty, both stark and subtle. Camped on top of the Continental Divide, with the San Juan drainage to the south and the Rio Grande drainage to the north, we had a view of miles and miles of surrounding wilderness, with not a single sign of man in sight. Below us, an alpine lake reflected a blue the exact color of ice, and the evening shadows moved across the gray rock walls of the mountainsides, creating weird and fantastic shapes. And later, at night, the clear air brought the stars so close it seemed that if only we could reach a little farther, we might touch the Milky Way itself.

The high country exacts a price for its beauty: The price is exhaustion. We had been averaging 3,000 feet of climbing per day since the Colorado border, following the Divide in its endless dips and rises. The day after we left Karl, we decided to take a two-day detour from the ice slopes and the climbing by following the lower, longer, and easier of two parallel trails down to a Forest Service campground and a small wilderness resort.

The long even slopes were a treat—a welcome break from the ups and downs of the ridge. Unencumbered by scree, or ice, or muscle-wrenching angles, we reveled in the rare pleasure of walking at an even, comfortable pace; of feeling our muscles working effortlessly and rhythmically. On the descent, we met the first backpackers we'd seen in Colorado—in fact, the first backpackers we'd seen since the Gila Wilderness, 650 miles ago. They were part of an organized group, and they were having trouble with the hill. We didn't have the heart to tell them that they had just begun their climb. The leader was in the front, doing his best to make it clear that he did not share the rest of the group's difficulties. Most of the other hikers were beginners; the sneakers and blue jeans betrayed both inexperience and bad leadership. I shuddered at the thought of trying to cross the scree and ice in sneakers, let alone getting caught in an above-tree-line thunderstorm while wearing blue jeans. You'd be better off naked than wearing wet cotton—except that then you'd have to carry it, and wet denim is very, very heavy.

"Where did you start your hike?" the leader asked. There's a sort of ritual exchange of information in the backcountry, a combination of camaraderie and muscle-flexing, depending on the people involved. "Where ya headed, where ya coming from? How many miles a day do you do? Been out long?"

Yeah, we'd been out long.

After a few more exchanges, our questioner told us, with calm assurance, that we wouldn't make it to Canada. "Maybe you'll get to Wyoming," he said, with a certainty born of I'm not sure what. "But you won't get to Canada."

That question settled, he told us that he was leading his group in the direction from which we had just come, and could we tell him about possible campsites up ahead?

We could.

There was a lake about 10 miles farther, just on the south side of the Knife Edge. To earn the Divide and then negotiate the detour around the ice slope would be quite enough for anyone's first day out, but the leader didn't want to stop there; he wanted to put the group ahead of schedule by doing a few more miles. The problem, we told him, was that the lake was the last possible campsite for a long, long way; after that, the trail stayed almost entirely on the crest of the Divide.

"What about water?" he asked.

"You'll find a few trickles down these slopes . . ." We showed him on the map. "But no places to pitch a tent."

"Oh, if there's water, we'll find something," he assured us.

"No, you won't," I muttered under my breath. We had just been over that terrain: After the lake, there was nothing but steep slopes and exposed ridges. Fortunately, the group didn't look like it would have much extra energy once it got to the lake—if it even made it that far. Sometimes it's the weaker members of a party that keep a hike safe.

As we continued to descend, we began to see more and more people: folks with fishing rods and day-packs and clean clothes. There were couples sunning themselves on the rocks lining Squaw Creek, children playing, and families picnicking. We were within a sprint of the road head at 30-Mile Camp.

30-Mile Camp is, rather predictably, so called because it is 30 miles from somewhere; in this case, that somewhere is the small town of Creede, Colorado, population 500, and seat of Mineral County (an honor, according to local legend, that was wrested from the original county seat of nearby Wason when a few of Creede's upstanding citizens stole the county records). Creede was the next town stop on our schedule; however, it would take us another four days to get there because of the Divide's indirect path. From 30-Mile Camp our route back to the Divide actually had us walking in a southwesterly direction—180 degrees away from Creede (and not exactly in the direction of Canada, either).

In the absence of a town stop, 30-Mile Camp became our temporary beacon of civilization. As usual, visions of gastronomic delights accompanied us as we walked toward this outpost, spurred on by the rumor that there was a store at the resort. But our visions of plenitude were quickly dashed when we arrived at our destination: The store consisted only of an old-fashioned wood-and-glass counter and a few shelves in the resort office, most of which contained fishing supplies. It was hard to get excited over powdered Tang and candy bars, but we took a philosophical attitude: At least we hadn't had to carry them.

≋

The Trego family has operated the resort at 30-Mile Camp for almost 50 years. Charlotte Trego, the resort manager, grew up spending her summers here on the edge of the Weminuche Wilderness, and although she has since traveled widely, she firmly believes that there is no place like home. Of course, that's easy to say when your home sits in the shadow of the Continental Divide.

On hearing of our journey, Charlotte invited us into her living room–cum–dining room–cum–kitchen for tea. While we chatted, she searched her cupboards for snacks—Fig Newtons, peanut butter, brownies, apples, crackers, and cheese—which we happily ate in random succession.

The resort at 30-Mile Camp is a simple place—the kind of retreat you don't expect to find anymore. The wood cabins are sparsely decorated in Victorian era themes; there are no hot tubs or televisions or video games. Even the power supply is Victorian. The electricity is produced by a tiny dam, a turbine, and a hand-me-down generator that began its life in an old mine; and a coal-burning boiler heats water for the showers—all of which makes the owners gleefully independent of the local utility company.

There have been changes here, Charlotte told us, not all of them good ones. The Tregos used to keep their cabins open in the winter, as a shelter for anyone who needed it. Now, the wilderness is more accessible, with snowmobiles and Ski-Doos, and vandalism is a problem. In the early days, the family kept horses here—no true westerner would actually walk in and out of the backcountry. Back then, they loaned the horses to Forest Service rangers during fire season; later, they took guests on trail rides. But the horses are gone now—during the last few years liability insurance has more than quintupled. Today, any guests who venture into the wilderness must do so on their own two feet.

Charlotte takes a dim view of hikers who take on the rugged terrain of the Continental Divide without being sufficiently prepared. There are too many uninformed, irresponsible, or inexperienced people, she said, who are "running around the backcountry, making a mess and getting into trouble."

Indeed, as backcountry recreation has become more and more popular, the wilderness has suffered from the environmental damage backpackers, like any other wilderness users, can cause. Most backpackers today have abandoned the Boy Scout methods of an earlier generation: You'd have to search a long time before you found someone who still thought that making beds from boughs, digging trenches, and burying garbage reflected a responsible backcountry ethic. But backpackers still have an impact on the land: Poor sanitation practices spread pests like *Giardia*, fire rings become backcountry dumps, and overuse turns favorite campsites into trampled, biologically dead eyesores. Even responsible hikers have an impact: carrying the seeds of exotic species in their clothing, trampling fragile vegetation, or contributing to erosion problems when overused trails become rain-filled gullies.

When we described the group we had seen heading up to the pass, Charlotte grimaced. "That's exactly what I'm talking about," she said. "There are a lot of people who are seduced into the outdoors by advertising. And some of them have no idea what they are getting into, or what to do when they get there."

She's right, of course; the outdoors has become entirely too trendy for its own good. Manufacturers of hiking gear have taken to hiring fashion designers to make their clothes chic as well as functional, and institutionalized adventure travel is big business. With a healthy enough checkbook, you can buy −30 sleeping bags, mountaineering tents, and Iditarod parkas, although your gear may never see subzero temperatures, a real mountain, or anywhere in Alaska. If you're the hardy type and plan to actually use your gear, you can hire someone to haul you up a world-class mountain or just about anywhere else your heart desires. The Amazon? Nepal? Antarctica? Hardly anyone points out that it's not adventure if you're following a trail of litter, and it's not wilderness if Coca-Cola has gotten there first.

You can also go out on your own, urged on by advertisements, catalogs, and magazine covers where the outdoors is a kaleidoscope of blue skies, bright colors, smiling faces, and healthy bodies. There are days like that, of course—lots of them, days of wildflowers and granite peaks and skies saturated in the bluest of all possible blues. There are days of clean, clear challenge; the exultation of bodies stretching their limits; the triumph of the last steps of a climb when there is nothing left between you and the sky. The photographs are telling the truth about those kinds of days.

But there are other truths to tell about the wilderness. There is the truth about nuisance: the pure cussedness of taking a tent down in the morning rain and putting it back up again in the evening rain; the smell of bodies caked in sweat, suntan lotion, and mosquito repellent; the torment of black flies that are immune to any sort of bug spray; the heartbreaking false summits at the end of endless days.

There is also the truth about danger. Jack London wrote about that truth in "To Light a Fire"; the bone-chilling truth of insidious cold and the irrevocable consequences of a single, small mistake. The wilderness is not as big as it was in Jack London's day, and it takes some doing to get yourself truly beyond help. Nonetheless, you can still get yourself killed—just ask any member of Colorado's mountain search-and-rescue teams. According to one study, measured in deaths per thousand participants, mountain hiking is one of the most dangerous kinds of recreation there is.

The common wisdom among search-and-rescue volunteers is that two kinds of people are most likely to get into trouble: those who are ignorant of the dangers and precautions, and those who believe that their strength or skill gives them a special dispensation from the rules of nature. Strong, uninformed people are at the highest risk— and they are all over the backcountry. We have seen people go out for a week without rain gear; we have met hikers who, although staggering from altitude sickness, refuse to retreat. We've seen people leave food on the ground in grizzly country, and we've watched people start climbing a 14,000-foot peak at one o'clock in the afternoon, just in time to run head-on into a lightning storm above tree line. The list goes on, and as a result, so does the work of search-

and-rescue volunteers, who too often end up risking their own lives for people who should have known better.

"In the end," Charlotte said, "the burden falls on local communities. What's infuriating is when the incident shouldn't have happened in the first place." She also pointed out that, unlike fishermen or horse packers, who use local suppliers, guest ranchers, outfitters, and guides, backpacking doesn't bring enough money into a community to compensate for the services it requires. Instead, hikers buy their gear (in a distant city), and take off (cadging a ride) for places where there is nothing to spend money on. Then they show up somewhere looking for someone to hold packages or give them access to a shower. We had to admit, as we contentedly munched our way through Charlotte's cupboards, that the scenario she described sounded awfully familiar—although we also pointed out that had there been a restaurant at the resort, we would have very quickly become contributors to the local economy.

We spent so much time visiting that we hadn't even noticed that it was starting to get dark. There were tent sites available at the Forest Service camp across the road, but Charlotte had another idea. All her cabins were full, she said, but maybe we'd like to stay in a different kind of tent for the night? She pointed to a large tepee just outside, and we eagerly accepted, feeling a little like children on a scout trip. Later that evening, Charlotte showed up with keys to the shower and fresh towels. She might not have approved of backpackers, we told her, but she sure knew what made them happy.

The next morning, we climbed back up to the Divide, not unaware, considering that we were supposedly going to Canada, that the sun was rising in the wrong part of the sky. We tried not to let ourselves think about our southwesterly heading.

We earned the ridge at Weimenuche Pass and continued west, staying high as we passed the Rio Grande Pyramid, 13,821 feet tall, a massive block of granite shaped as a nearly perfect pyramid from all sides. Close by is a cut in the Divide known simply as the Window, a square opening bordered on three sides by rock and on one side by sky. The opening is 100 feet wide and 150 feet tall, and it looks, Dave said, like a place an Old Testament prophet would choose for proclaiming his revelations. The Window has a mystical aura about it, and ephemeral wisps of fog only added to its mood. I could imagine a giant Moses, in long white robes, handing a tablet through the opening. Was heaven on the other side? The rumor that the Window acts as a magnet for lightning only made the fantasy more plausible.

The trail here was spectacular, but it was not well marked. By the end of the day, we were frustrated and tired. Unclear sections of trail had led us off course, and the first couple of lakes, where we had hoped to camp, were flooded and marshy from snowmelt. For Dan and me, finally finding a campsite—a sheltered spot that had obviously been used often as a horse packers' camp—gave us more than relief from a tough day; it gave us a place to celebrate our second wedding anniversary. As we cooked up our Ramen noodles and freeze-dried vegetarian chili, it occurred to us that most people would have had a different menu for an anniversary celebration— and they probably wouldn't have had to walk 17 miles and climb 4,000 feet for it, either.

It is sometimes said that we are loving our wildernesses to death. At Hunchback Pass, where a dirt road leads to the very edge of the wilderness, that may well be true. At least, so it seemed the next morning, when we were hit by an onslaught of holiday vacationers out to enjoy the long July 4 weekend. Horse packers, hikers, fishermen, jeepers—the improvised parking area at the trailhead was strewn with multicolored gear and looked for all the world like a movie set for filming a commercial for the Colorado tourist bureau. The commotion continued well down the road, past the old mining camp of Beartown. Never on the entire walk had our solitude been so suddenly invaded. By afternoon—as usual—it was pouring rain, but that seemed to make no difference. Hikers kept coming, and horse packers, too, in groups of twenty or more, slipping through the mud and ice at Hunchback Pass.

The horse packers were in wretched shape, shivering in their ponchos. Usually, a slight twinge of jealousy assaults me when I see horsemen taking a leisurely ride uphill, their gear lashed to the back of a mule or a packhorse. Not this time: If the riders avoided the straining muscles and sore backs of the hiker, they also avoided the body heat generated by a good climb.

In contrast, the jeep folks seemed frankly gleeful. The conditions were apparently ideal for this peculiar group, who revel in foul weather and even fouler roads. The road to Hunchback Pass qualified, judging by the mud-splattered vehicles and the exhilarated group parked at improbable angles at the base of the pass. Dan, watching the jeeps bump and buck over the rutted road, commented that he could see no difference between that form of recreation and riding in a taxicab through New York City's potholes—except that in New York, if the cab broke down, you could pay the meter and abandon it.

There were other backpackers, too. We crossed the pass with a middle-aged couple who had been out for a week, hiking from lake to lake and feasting on trout every night. What they hadn't eaten, they had brought out with them in plastic bags filled with snow. Their jeep was parked at the base of the pass, and when they reached it, they opened up a cooler of beer and soda and told us to help them make room for the fish by helping ourselves to some drinks. We gratefully obliged.

Adding to the general commotion were two large groups of Outward Bound students getting ready to finish their month in the wilderness. Most of them looked exhausted. During the last four weeks, these mostly urban and suburban dwellers had been participating in a program that evolved out of the Royal Air Force's survival training during World War II. It is safe to say they had never done, or perhaps even heard of, anything like it in their lives. They had crawled through obstacle courses made from ropes strung 30 feet off the ground; they had dangled on harnesses while climbing up and down rock cliffs in the San Juans; they had braved a couple of days and nights alone in the woods armed with a handful of matches and not much else. Now they were engaged in an activity familiar to us: They were tormenting each other with descriptions of the food they would eat once they "got out."

The students and instructors were standing in two clusters, and

although they were roughly the same age, there was no doubt whatsoever who was who. The difference wasn't visible, strictly speaking.
Everyone in the group had been out for three and a half weeks, and
they all looked a good deal like us: dirty and trailworn. But there
was a sort of settled-in comfort to the instructors; they seemed
at home splattered with mud and rain. In contrast, the students looked
as though their gear didn't quite fit right. While Dan and I chatted
with the instructors (I wasn't sure whether to puff up with
pride or check into a lunatic asylum when these tough characters
seemed genuinely impressed at our pace), Dave was talking to the
kids. "Oh, no," we heard him saying. "You don't want to start
counting down the days till you get out. You want to enjoy this
experience."

"But it's been raining every day," one of the kids protested.

"What's a little rain? Besides, when you're back home, you'll
look back on it as one of the special times in your life."

We were to remember those words the next day, when the skies
opened on us—and didn't close again for thirty-six hours.

<hr />

It comes as some surprise to most people to learn that you may be
far more at risk of hypothermia in a 32-degree rain than in a 20-degree
snow. Rain and wind are, in fact, far more dangerous than cold
alone because they rob the body of warmth. The trick is to stay dry,
to keep your gear dry, and to stay warm. Sometimes, that is easier
said than done. And it becomes particularly difficult when people
who are trying to hike together have radically different paces.

All three of us believed that we should each be free to walk at
our own speed, but that sort of individualistic laissez-faire did not
work in practice on the CDT. The difficulties of route-finding and
the lack of an incontrovertible trail forced us to stay together, or at
least wait for each other wherever the trail was unclear. In foul
weather, that meant that Dan and Dave spent a good deal of time
standing still—and shivering.

Dave must have sat at the top of a hundred passes, bundled in all
his layers, patiently waiting for me; Dan must have written hundreds
of pages of his journal while staying behind to give me a head start.

As for me: I tried not to feel pressured and miserable as I gasped my way uphill, knowing that by the time I made it to the top, Dan would have passed me, and he and Dave would be cold from waiting and ready to walk on.

We were all cold by the time we arrived at the ghost town of Carson, situated at 12,000 feet on the crest of the Continental Divide. This windswept, open, exposed place is one of Colorado's highest and most inaccessible ghost towns. It is not hard to understand why it is a ghost town; what is hard to understand is how it ever became a town in the first place—except for the fact that there is gold in these hills. Carson, reputedly named after Kit Carson's son, James, is actually two camps: the higher, a gold mine; and the lower, a silver mine. At one time, 500 people lived here, with bars and restaurants and all the necessities of a wealth-crazed mining camp. There's not much evidence of all that now. Miners have a saying that there's no such thing as an abandoned mine, just mines waiting to be reworked. But, as a layperson, I would venture to call these mines abandoned. The mountains have mounted a slow, inexorable attempt to reclaim the land, and it's amazing how effectively they do their job of erasing the evidence of man's presumptions. Now, all that is left are a few mine shafts, some listing buildings, crumbled heaps of weathered wood, and piles of tailings that make the water taste metallic.

We hadn't planned to stop in Carson, but the weather made continuing impossible. For the first time, we each wore all the clothes we were carrying: wool shirt, long johns, gloves, hat, rain gear—everything. Even so, the cold fingers of the rainy chill penetrated our layers of Gore-Tex and wool and burrowed into our bones. Worse, we weren't quite sure which way to go: The trail we had been following had ceased being marked as soon as we reached the jeep roads around the old mining camp. The visibility was so poor that we couldn't even see the mountain we were supposed to climb next—Coney Peak, which, at 13,334 feet, would be the highest point so far on our trip. As we looked at the maps, frustrated by the lack of trail markers and visibility, it became obvious that the situation wasn't likely to be any better farther up—to the contrary, the higher we climbed, the more exposed we would be.

It is said that the Inuit people who live in arctic climates have dozens of words for snow. Hikers, then, should have as many words for rain. We should have a word for warm rain, and a word for cold rain. We should have a word for the fat, swollen raindrops of a mercurial, quick thunderstorm, and a word for the needle-thin raindrops of an all-day downpour. We should have a word for rain that falls gently on a tent at night, when we are snug and dry in our sleeping bags, and we should have a word for the rain that arrives when we are in the middle of making camp with our gear strewn about on the ground. And we should have a word for the rain that fell on us at Carson: a cold, long, determined, all-day sort of rain with a few thunderstorms thrown in for good measure.

The only logical decision was to find a place to camp, but even that was no easy trick; at the end, Carson grudgingly yielded a marginally flat spot, completely unprotected in the open grasses. Our fingers were stiff and clammy as we fumbled with our tents, trying to move quickly in order to get them up reasonably dry. We failed: By the time the tents were securely staked, rain flies in place, the tent bottoms were soaking wet, and everything else seemed in imminent danger of the same fate. Quickly, we mopped out the tents with a wet handkerchief and managed to get our gear and ourselves inside. For the rest of the day, we stayed in the tents, huddled like animals.

~~~~~~~~~

The dreary misery of wet gear, wet weather, and wet bodies continued the next day. We far preferred to keep walking than to stand still in weather this bad, so we decided to go all the way to Spring Creek Pass, which would put us a day ahead of schedule. From the pass, we would drop down into the town of Creede to pick up our next food package.

About 4 miles from the pass, we started seeing tiny piles of stones on the trail, some of them holding balloons. They must have been a confusing sight to other hikers—if there were any—but they were a message for us. The balloons told us that Sue and Gordon had arrived at the pass and were waiting for us there.

Sue and Gordon had an uncanny knack of figuring out when we would actually arrive, as opposed to when we had said we would arrive, at any given road crossing. Even on a stretch like this, when we hadn't seen them in eight days, they were able to anticipate what kinds of difficulties we might encounter and what we were likely to do. Considering that we were almost never on schedule—and that, because the trail didn't even exist in many places, we often weren't even where we said we would be—Gordon was remarkably accurate in predicting when and where we would come out of the woods.

Whenever possible, Gordon and Sue tried to meet us on the trail so we could walk together for a bit and talk about what had happened since the last time we saw each other. Often, they brought in treats like fresh fruit, which our bodies craved. But by far the greatest gift they gave us was their example of courage. Sue's illness has taken so much from her; just walking up a hill that we wouldn't even notice is painful for her, and, with her limited vision, she doesn't get the reward of a view at the top. Her daily life—and, because he takes care of her, Gordon's too—is proscribed by a series of medical needs: when to eat, what to eat, insulin, dialysis, blood sugar tests. But despite all of that, Sue keeps walking, through pain that is, every day, far worse than anything we would experience on the entire trip. More than once, as I struggled up a mountain, swearing, I thought of Sue, who would have given anything to be able to be there struggling with us. Her example put our self-imposed hardships in perspective.

We picked up the balloons, on which Gordon and Sue had scrawled little notes—"Four miles to go"; "You're almost there"; "Don't take the left-hand trail, it ends in a swamp." When we arrived at the pass, Sue and Gordon weren't at all surprised to see us. Gordon had already set up his tent, but after one look at us, he took it down and drove us 30 miles into Creede. This late in the day, we had been prepared to camp out at the pass, but we didn't argue—after two days of cold rain, the chance to be warm and dry was the greatest gift we could have asked for.

Creede is a town suspended between the mining that started it and the tourism that will have to sustain it if it is to survive. In the process, it has become a stop on the summer tourist belt.

But first things first. Before Creede can become a full-fledged tourist town, it needs places for tourists to sleep. As we learned within moments of our arrival (on a Friday evening during the week of the July 4 holiday), there are only two hotels in town and one of them has only four rooms. Confronted with the news that both of them were fully booked, we stood in the lobby of the Creede Hotel, dripping water and wondering where we were going to spend the night.

Rich and Cathy Ormsby own the Creede Hotel, the only lodging establishment dating from the glory days, when Creede was one of the baddest, meanest, bawdiest, and busiest mining towns in the West. It's hard to believe that in its heyday the town had more than 100 hotels. Zang's—now the Creede Hotel—was one of the finest then, and it is a jewel of a hotel today: a restored, lovingly maintained piece of western history. And while an early guest might have written ''I couldn't sleep with all the noise . . . hollering, yelling, horses galloping, wagons chuckling, hammering, pounding, sawing, shooting,'' today's visitor has no such concerns.

Rich and Cathy offered us the use of a tiny room that might have been a maid's room once. It contained a single bed and about enough floor space for two sleeping bags. With our packs, it made for close quarters, but we gratefully accepted and, once rid of our gear and wet clothes, hurried across the street to a restaurant advertising pizza.

The Creede of yesteryear bustled with 'round-the-clock restaurants, saloons, and gambling houses. In the wake of bound-for-riches miners came the chaos and ribaldry of the inevitable tagalong coterie: card sharks, saloon keepers, pickpockets, prostitutes, and con artists. With its all-night energy, its hordes of flimflam artists, its pulsating drive for wealth, and its complete disregard for a man's history coupled with an abiding faith in his future, the Creede of yesterday had more in common with today's New York City than with anyone's stereotypical image of a small Colorado mountain town.

But not so today. To our immense dismay, the pizza place was shut. The famous refrain of an old poem has it that "It's day all day in the daytime, and there is no night in Creede." Regardless, the pizza place closes at eight o'clock sharp.

Creede's was a short, frantic boom; three years from start to finish. It was the kind of boom where a twenty-five-dollar grubstake could grow into a million-dollar fortune, the kind of boom that turned ordinary citizens into men of outrageous wealth; the kind of boom that made otherwise sensible, solid family men pack their bags and head west to dig and pick and search the earth in the kind of hysterical frenzy you see today during a wild week on Wall Street. And anyone—absolutely anyone—could be the next millionaire.

There was no time to be lost in a boom like this: The grains that run from an hourglass could just as easily be made of silver as sand. Certainly, the railroads wasted no time. David Moffat, of the Denver and Rio Grande, bought into a Creede silver mine and followed up with a narrow-gauge extension that paid for itself in a scant four months. No wonder, when up to 300 people a day were arriving in the exploding town, crammed into railway cars, sitting on each other, hanging off the platforms. Not to worry about temporary discomfort: They were all bound for riches. Not to worry, either, if you couldn't afford to pay the inflated prices of the real estate sharks: You could hang a couple of planks across Willow Creek and throw a shack up over the water. You could hang your outhouse there, too, and people did. Some of them continued to dispose of raw sewage in Willow Creek well into the 1930s.

If you preferred selling goods to the miners to hacking away at the capriciously secretive mountains, the town could accommodate you, but here, too, there was no time to waste. Creede virtually threw itself up, a hastily built shantytown of clapboard houses and canvas tents. It was said that a prefabricated bar that arrived by rail in the morning would be open and serving drinks by afternoon, and that from the time the town bosses decided to install electricity, it took exactly five days before lights all over town blinked on.

The usual suspects all came to Creede: Bob Ford, killer of Jesse James, was shot in his own bar; Soapy Smith moved in and imposed his own version of law and order, assisted by John Light, the best gunman money could buy, brought all the way from Texas. Poker Alice and Calamity Jane set up shop at the gaming tables, and houses on Creede's Second Street filled up with ladies seizing their opportunity to do a little business with the mining community. "Creede is unfortunate in getting more of the flotsam of the state than usually falls to the lot of mining camps," complained the local paper. "Some of her citizens would take grubstake prize at a hog show."

It ended about as suddenly as it began, and like so many other cataclysmic changes that have imposed themselves on the West, this one came from Washington. In 1893, Congress repealed the Sherman Silver Purchase Act, and lowered the price of silver from a dollar and twenty-nine cents an ounce to fifty cents. With a stroke of the pen, night came to Creede.

Or perhaps it was twilight. Because the town struggled on. Fire destroyed it, and the townsmen rebuilt. So, too, when floods raged down the narrow canyon. The mines continued to operate, although on a smaller scale. By 1900, the population was just over 900; and a million dollars' worth of gold, silver, and other metals was being pulled out of the earth each year.

Of course a million dollars was a pittance, compared to what the Creede mines had produced, but still, the mines limped on. They never recovered, and first one, then another, closed its doors, the miners heading for other lodes in other hills. Creede's last mine— aptly, the Bulldog—lasted until 1985, but finally it, too, fell victim to simple economics: The price of silver dropped below the price of silver production. The closing put almost one sixth of the town's population out of work. After almost a century, there were no more mining jobs in Creede.

They had been good jobs, and the town would miss them. A new high school graduate could earn some $25,000 a year, and an experienced, hardworking miner could make up to three times that— a fortune in a small western town. By contrast, the tourist jobs that sprang up to replace them pay a fraction of that, and, as the miners will tell you, it ain't the same.

Today, names like Holy Moses, Amethyst, and Golden Nugget refer to the gift shops and galleries that dot downtown Creede. The railroad depot houses the local historical society's collection of memorabilia; there isn't any need for a station. The big mine just outside of town is being turned into an underground museum. And every July 4, Creede relives its glory days in a "Days of '92" celebration, complete with contests in spike driving, hand mucking, single jacking, and machine drilling.

Only now there's no mother lode just beyond the reach of that drill. For the miners, and their families, night, finally, has come to Creede.

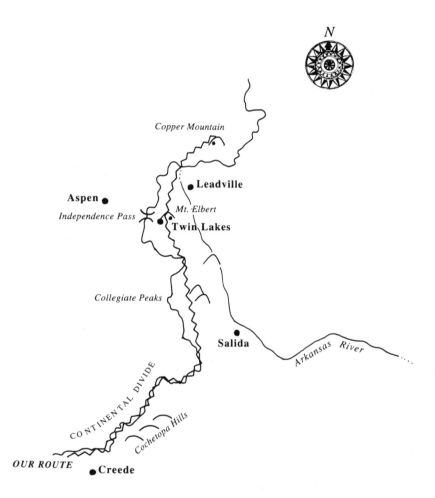

5

≋≋≋

Where the Earth
Ran Silver

≋≋≋

The Cochetopa Hills, averaging some 11,500 feet above sea level, could only be called hills in a very few places on earth. Colorado is one of them. In comparison to the massive San Juan Mountains behind us and the mighty Sawatch still ahead, they were indeed merely hills: green, gentle, unspectacular, with easy grades and wooded passes. The landscape was brown and dry and open, reminiscent of New Mexico. Out of the tundra and into the valleys, the terrain regained its horizontal component: We could, for the moment, look forward without looking up.

Cochetopa means "gate of the buffalo." There are none here now, of course, but Cochetopa Pass was once a route used by buffalo to cross the Continental Divide; it was also, therefore, a hunting route for the Ute Indians, until the Utes were shoved west by the usual series of broken treaties.

In the wake of the Utes came the miners, and in the wake of the miners came the railmen—builders of empires and creators of fortunes—looking for a way to cross the high peaks of Colorado. If buffalo could migrate over the passes of the Cochetopa Hills, perhaps the railroad could, too. As we looked down into the inviting valleys, we could understand the hope cherished by the empire builders of a century ago.

Colorado is filled with passes that once promised that holiest of western grails—a way for the railroads to cross the Continental Divide. Perhaps no other force so greatly left its mark on the landscape of the West than the railroads, and perhaps no obstacle so frustrated the ambitions of the railmen as the Continental Divide. Lured to invest in westward expansion by the promise of free land from Congress and by the nascent wealth in the mining camps, railroad companies multiplied as prolifically as rabbits, all of them competing to lay track to the communities that sprang up during Colorado's gold and silver rushes.

If Colorado was going to fully exploit its mineral wealth, it would have to move ore and equipment and men and building materials and food. To do that it would need a viable system of railway lines. And, it would need to be linked with the rest of the country. But the Union Pacific quickly turned its back on the expense and technological difficulties of building through the Colorado Rockies, and went north, instead, to the flatlands of the Wyoming Territory. By 1869, it was Cheyenne, not Denver, that was linked to the new markets of the far West; and it was Cheyenne that seemed destined to become the great metropolis of the Rocky Mountain region.

Coloradans rallied to this new challenge: If the railroad would not come to them, they would go to the railroad. They would create feeder lines to connect Colorado's communities with each other, and they would build trunk lines to the transcontinental route, as well. In that age of optimistic, unbridled capitalism, the race was to the swiftest: The town with the first branch line to the transcontinental railroad would become the major business hub of Colorado. For a while, it looked like the town of Golden would get there first. But the Denver business community threw its hat into the ring with its newly formed Denver Pacific Railroad, and formed a partnership with the Union Pacific. The new railroad obtained a 900,000-acre land grant from Congress, and the route to Cheyenne was officially opened on June 1, 1870. Two months later, when the Kansas Pacific Railroad opened a line from Kansas City to Denver, Denver had direct rail links with both Cheyenne and Kansas, and its future—as the dominant urban center of the Rocky Mountain region—was secure.

And meanwhile, the mining boom continued, and the railroads continued laying tracks into the mountains. There was no time to waste in bringing railroads to these boomtowns. The mining communities needed railroads—without them, the cost of transporting goods by wagon would be prohibitively expensive. But first, a new technology had to be developed to carry trains through the tight, winding canyons and over the steep switchbacks to mountain passes. The railmen were up to the challenge; in 1871, the Denver and Rio Grande began laying the innovative narrow-gauge railroad, a three-foot-wide track that replaced the four-foot, eight-and-a-half-inch width of the earlier railways. Traveling on the new track, a train could turn tighter corners, it could climb steeper grades; it could, in short, go where trains had never gone before.

Other railroads followed, in quick succession, announcing their intentions to the world with names that sounded like a virtual alphabet soup of destinations, passes, and cities—the Denver and Rio Grande; the Atchison, Topeka, and Santa Fe; the Denver, South Park, and Pacific; the Cumbres and Toltec; the Denver Central; the Colorado Midland. By 1878 Colorado had over 1,000 miles of rail, all constructed on the eastern slope. In the Arkansas River valley, which lies just to the northeast of the Cochetopa Hills, the fierce competition among the young railroad companies came to a head when two railroads began simultaneously laying track to the town of Leadville.

If Creede was the bawdy teenager, then Leadville was the nouveau riche adult. Born of the gold rush, Leadville came to adulthood in the silver boom, becoming a proper city—the second largest in Colorado—complete with an opera house that attracted the best performers of the day, streets lined with sumptuous Victorian mansions, and high-living first families whose excesses fueled the dreams of every miner who picked away at the earth. Huge profits awaited whoever could lay the first tracks up the Arkansas River to this booming silver city.

The two railroads were the Atchison, Topeka, and Santa Fe and the Denver and Rio Grande, and neither one of them was interested in compromise. Inevitably, the battle wound up in the courts, and finally, in 1880, it did end in compromise. In return for concessions on other routes, the Denver and Rio Grande was awarded the exclusive right to construct the Arkansas River route into Leadville, which it did—immediately.

The backdrop to all of this drama was the massive mountain chain just to the west of Leadville—the Continental Divide itself, silently mocking the railmen. For despite all of their innovation, and energy, and money; despite all of their successes on the eastern slope, the Colorado railmen had still not figured out a way to cross the mighty Continental Divide.

As for the Cochetopa Hills—they were only one more dead end in the search for a route across the Divide. For while the Cochetopa Hills themselves are gentle here, the terrain immediately to their west is protected from railroads and other incursions by severe winter blizzards, deep canyons, and rugged rocky peaks. The ambitions of mere men were not going to conquer the mountains—at least, not here.

Today, logging roads and jeep trails crisscross the timbered slopes of the Cochetopa Hills, following in the tracks of the wagon roads of an earlier time. The grades are comfortable, easy, even. For the first time in Colorado, Dave and Dan and I could actually walk together at the same pace.

Until now, our journey through Colorado had taken us primarily through wilderness areas. Even in those segments that were outside of designated wildernesses—places like Hunchback Pass and Carson— the primary land use had been recreation. But now we were in the National Forest proper, and that meant multiple use. After the high remote stretches of the San Juan Mountains, the contrast was striking.

Almost by definition, multiple use includes cattle, and this was indeed cattle country, filled with the hardy brown-and-white Herefords that dominate the western range. The land here was richer than most of the ranch country we had traversed in New Mexico; it supported

In a land of big distances and giant skies, the only thing that made the vast spaces of New Mexico's mesa country real to us was the memory of each footstep it took to cross them.

History is a constant companion along the Divide. Here at Gila Cliff Dwellings National Monument, the Mogollon people built their pueblos far above the desert floor.

Atsinna (the name of the Anasazi pueblo atop El Morro Rock). In the distance is the Continental Divide. Big Notch and Little Notch were described by a member of the Coronado expedition as a part of the ridge that divided the region's watersheds—the first time the Continental Divide was so recognized or noted by the Europeans.

Cross country walking sometimes turns to rock scrambling. Here we try to find a route up the crumbly sandstone of Chaco Mesa.

Atop Chaco Mesa.

The brilliant red-rock country of northern New Mexico where Georgia O'Keefe
once painted—and dinosaurs once roamed.

Here, in Colorado's South San Juans, Dan contemplates the route ahead. We can't tell if the lingering snowfields will stop us. The idea of walking atop these peaks strikes us as preposterous.

Afternoon thunderstorms are a daily occurrence in Weminuche Wilderness—and indeed, throughout the entire state. In Colorado, the trail's elevation averages some 11,600 feet.
Treeline is at about 11,200 feet.

This moldering building at 12,000 feet is one of the few remains of what was once the thriving mining town of Carson.

Good trail near Arapaho Pass.

North of Parkview Mountain, Colorado, fields are fed by snowmelt.

Colorado's Front Range challenged us with some of the most difficult walking of the trip, but the views were spectacular.

The clear water of snowmelt fills a tarn just below the Divide.

Home is where the tent is: here, in the high country of the Mt. Zirkel Wilderness in Colorado.

Approaching Muddy Gap, Wyoming: Our only companions in this dry open landscape were desert dwellers like antelope and jackrabbits.

ABOVE LEFT AND RIGHT Burnished gold grasses in the Wind River Range and crisp cold air told us that fall was on its way. In the distance is the famous Cirque of the Towers.

Dan displays his professorial bent and gives an impromptu lecture at Two Ocean Creek, the place where the waters divide.

Spectacular scenery in the Wind River Range makes these mountains among the most beautiful—and popular—on the trail. But in early autumn, the crowds were gone, and we had this landscape and water all to ourselves.

In Yellowstone National Park, "hell runs close to the surface." We'd been so worried about grizzlies and permits that when we stumbled on the first backcountry geyser basin, we thought the smoke must be from someone cooking breakfast.

OPPOSITE The Green River (which flows into the Colorado) comes by its name honestly, draining glacial silt from Wyoming's highest peak.

TOP Ranching, timber, and big mountains: That's Montana.

MIDDLE Forest fires can have unexpectedly beautiful results. Fed by ash enriched soil and sunlight, acres of flowers carpet the Scapegoat Wilderness.

BOTTOM Good trail in Glacier National Park near Triple Divide Pass.

OPPOSITE The 1988 fires left their mark, but the grasses and flowers are growing back.

Bighorn sheep: Our companions in the high country.

A view of the Chinese Wall, a 1000-foot escarpment that is the Divide for 20 miles.

OPPOSITE Our version of
"Windows on the World": A picnic supper and
a world-class view in the Scapegoat Wilderness.

We arrive at the Canadian border, having walked 3,200 miles, taken 6 million steps, and climbed 300,000 feet in 233 days.

more vegetation, and hence, more cattle, who made obtrusive, messy hiking companions. Unlike deer, or elk, or even horses, who retreated from us with a minimum of fuss, the cattle seemed comically stupid. The calves, skittish and wild-eyed, took refuge with their mothers, who never seemed too sure of what to do until we came close enough to violate some sense of bovine personal space; then, they would turn on their heels and run clumsily away. Considering that the cattle obviously thought we were dangerous predators, we had to wonder about natural selection. The cows generally stayed directly in front of us, on the trail, in plain sight. They neither ran far enough away to put themselves out of danger nor sought shelter off the trail, and they always seemed somewhat surprised to turn around and see that we were still behind them. Range cattle are easily frightened; they are not, as far as we could tell, overburdened with intelligence.

They are, however, smart enough to know a good resting spot when they see it. As we well knew by now, cattle prefer the very places that make good campsites for backpackers: the shaded spots near water sources. As the afternoons wore on, and we began our search for a place to call home for the night, we resigned ourselves to the inevitable. In ranchland, preparing a campsite means taking on barn duty to clear out the cattle dung.

This was dry country, dotted with sagebrush. There were few streams and springs, and most of them were polluted by the cows. We resumed our New Mexico habit of planning our day according to water sources. No more the luxury of cold running streams crossing our path at quarter-mile intervals. No more glacial tarns decorating our day like shining jewels. No more snowfields and icy traverses forcing long detours across scree and talus.

But, if the streams and the tarns and the snowfields and the ice couldn't follow us downhill, the thunderstorms could and did. Thus, it came as some surprise to learn that while we had been dodging lightning bolts and hailstones up in the San Juans, most of Colorado had been worrying about forest fires. A ranger informed us that several major wildfires were burning in some of Colorado's national forests. A sign announced a ban on all open campfires. But it seemed that wherever we walked, the drought was just ahead—either that, or we brought the cure for it with us. It rained, and it rained, and it rained. Perhaps, we told each other, we should hire ourselves out as water consultants. If our ability to attract rain in the arid West continued, we could make ourselves rich.

≈≈≈≈

A few days north of Creede, in the middle of a rainstorm at the end of a rainy day, we found ourselves in the typical ranch country predicament: We had reached our water source for the night, but the cows had gotten there first. This was water reminiscent of Yeso tank—stagnant, muddy, and brown. Fortunately, we had another choice: a beaver pond. Here, too, we'd have to treat the water, but our filters could easily handle the chore. As we explored the pond, looking for the cleanest, fastest-flowing water, we saw a cabin, perhaps a hundred feet away through the trees.

In the rain, a cabin is a rare and welcome treasure, promising warmth and shelter and comfort. Sometimes, old cabins in remote areas are left open for hikers to use. And even if a cabin is locked, it might have a porch, which offers the opportunity to cook and unpack without the hassle of trying to keep everything dry.

We started walking toward it, but we had gone only a few steps before we realized that, whatever the charms of the cabin, they were irrelevant. Through the trees, we could make out the form of a man—the odds were he was a ranger—untacking his horses and hobbling them for the night. The cabin was occupied. We continued along the trail, disappointed, and set up our camp on a flat spot a quarter of a mile or so later. After dinner, we walked over to the cabin to check it out and chat with the ranger.

To reach the cabin required crossing the beaver pond—literally. We could either wade through the murky brown water or tiptoe across the dam itself. I tested the dam with one foot to see if it would hold my weight; my boot sank an inch or so into a combination of aspen shoots and mud, and a puddle an inch deep formed around it. Good enough, maybe. I teetered across, hoping that the dam would hold me, and Dan, and Dave, until we were all safely back on terra firma.

The ranger, as it turned out, wasn't a ranger at all; he was a horse packer, out for his annual sojourn on the Colorado Trail. He had finished eating, his horses were hobbled and contentedly munching on the grass, and a small fire was crackling in the wood stove. An open bottle of tequila explained his heightened color and enthusiastic greeting. He had been done with his chores for quite some time, it appeared.

Ron ("Wrangler Ron," he told us) was the old hand here; he'd stayed in this cabin a few times before, and he gave us the grand tour with the pride of a proprietor. The cabin, he said, was maintained by the Heart of the Rockies Snowmobile Club. A note tacked onto the door welcomed visitors and gave the ground rules, which boiled down to "Please don't wreck the place."

"You guys want to stay here tonight?" Ron asked, but we shook our heads no. We already had the tents up. It hardly made sense to repack everything in the rain and move a quarter mile back.

"You sure? There's plenty of room."

Inside, the cabin was stocked with several cords of neatly stacked, split firewood; there were, in addition, a table and chairs, a wood-burning stove, and a dubious-looking mattress or two. On the shelves was an assortment of food that had been left by previous visitors: a few cans, some flour, hot chocolate mix, dried milk, a random collection of spices, all stored in reasonably animal-proof containers. True to form, we were most interested in the food that had been left out for the taking. Most of the provisions were basic staples like Bisquick or rice, but there were some Saltines and jelly, and—lo and behold!—we suddenly developed an inexplicable craving for Saltines and jelly. Ron contributed his bottle of tequila to the party, and we passed it around taking "pulls" and swapping stories while the rain pattered outside, slower now.

The little cabin was a haven of warmth. The wood stove banished any thoughts of the rain or cold outside. We sat down at the table, luxuriating in the heat of the fire, in being able to sit on something that wasn't wet, in the immediate camaraderie that springs up among strangers in the woods on a rainy night. Ron lit some candles, and we paged through the cabin's register, the backwoods equivalent of a guestbook, where people coming through can make a note of their journey. There weren't any other Continental Divide hikers, as far as we could tell.

The stories we told each other, in retrospect, probably gained some for the telling. The days were longer, the mileages more impressive, the slopes steeper, the travails tougher, and our relaxed imaginations allowed us the suspension of disbelief. After all, anything is possible—a 30-mile day for us, a 100-mile day for Wrangler Ron. It was late, and dark, when we picked our way back across the dam and up the hill to our tents. Behind us, the yellow light of the cabin was warm and inviting. But the night surrounded us in calm and quiet. The rain had stopped and the moon was out, lighting a path for us through the quiet forest. Somewhere in the night, a great horned owl called to its mate.

We resupplied in Garfield, the smallest town we had yet seen. To our north, now, was the skyscraping Sawatch Range, with more than twenty peaks towering 14,000 feet or more. Here, we had a decision to make.

For the last week or so, we had been following the Colorado Trail, which closely parallels the Continental Divide for some 270 miles. The Colorado Trail has achieved epic status in Colorado as a long-distance trail built by grass-roots volunteers. Linking together jeep trails, snowmobile paths, and hiking trails, it stretches 470 miles, from Denver to Durango. Its reputation stretches even farther—clear to the White House. In 1991, President Bush named the trail's founder and director one of his so-called Daily Points of Light.

We weren't quite as impressed with the Colorado Trail as the president had been. Of course, he hasn't hiked it, so he wouldn't know about its inconsistent markings and route-finding problems, which had stymied us in the rain and fog near Carson and had left us aimlessly wandering around the edges of meadows into which the trail had suddenly vanished. But what was of interest to us was the fact that the Colorado Trail and the CDT route, which had been contiguous for the last 130 miles, now diverged, and we needed to decide which way to go.

The two routes were closely parallel, and intersected again near the ski resort of Copper Mountain. The Colorado Trail was 10 or so miles longer, but it offered marked footway, which would present fewer logistical problems. In comparison, the older Continental Divide Trail Society route involved some cross-country travel, and we hadn't been able to obtain any reliable information about current trail conditions. We had maps and descriptions for both routes; what we lacked was information that would let us compare the trails: Was one more scenic than the other? More remote? More pleasant hiking? Forest Service officials told us that they were strongly considering using the Colorado Trail route for the CDT but that the decision had not been finalized, in part because of loud protest from the Colorado Trail volunteers, who didn't want their achievement subsumed by a national scenic trail. In the end, we decided to stick with the Colorado Trail because we had more up-to-date, complete information about its route.

In the Cochetopa Hills, the Colorado Trail had largely followed old roads and gentle trails that wound through the easy country. But that, we thought, was because of the gentle nature of the terrain itself. Now that we were headed to the Sawatch Range, we were prepared to go high again.

Unfortunately, it became apparent to us in the days ahead that the Colorado Trail had been designed according to a different hiking aesthetic than ours. As it headed toward the Sawatch, the trail stayed low, whenever possible, cowering below the timberline. There was plenty of climbing, sometimes as much as 2,500 feet at a time. But the climbs didn't lead to the expected rewards of the high country. After ascending 2,500 feet, we wanted views, tarns, rocky passes, and the feel of an alpine wind. Instead, the trail stayed above timberline only for as long as necessary to clear a pass; then it headed straight back into the trees.

We learned later that this avoidance of the high country in the Sawatch was deliberate—an attempt to minimize the risks of above-tree-line travel. The Colorado Trail is a populist endeavor, designed to be accessible to the greatest number of people. Much of the route can be done on mountain bikes, and the Colorado Trail Foundation has even worked out alternative trails for cyclists, who are not permitted in wilderness areas. The trail can also be completed in a series of day-hikes—another way of saying that it is never far from a road passable by car. In the opinion of Colorado Trail officials, the dangers posed by the high country are inconsistent with the trail's populist mission.

Nobody needed to explain to us about the dangers of hiking at or above 13,000 feet: After Montezuma Peak, the San Juans, and the rain at Carson, we knew all about Colorado's mercurial and violent temper. But we also knew that two of the three times we came close to making personal acquaintance with a lightning bolt, we were below timberline on the Colorado Trail. And we knew that, given the choice between the rigors and risks of the high country and the only theoretical safety of below-tree-line travel, we would unanimously and always opt for the former. If we had wanted to walk in a green tunnel, we complained, we would have stayed at home in the East.

By the time we realized that we had made the wrong decision, it was too late to change it. We were stuck with frustration as the trail led us safely around the circumference of the Sawatch mountains, dishearteningly below tree line, and within sight of Highway 24 and the towns of Buena Vista and Salida. We could hear logging saws squealing and dirt bikes roaring and cattle bellowing. But the peaks of the Sawatch remained tantalizingly beyond the trail, and our diaries reflected our disappointment with protests about ''easy but boring terrain,'' ''another dull day,'' and ''pointless, viewless, bland hiking.''

Regardless of what we thought of the aesthetic and design of the Colorado Trail—perhaps even because of these factors—there were lots of other people using it. In fact, since we had been hiking on the Colorado Trail, there hadn't been a single day that we hadn't encountered other people. As we walked on, we never knew what manner of recreationist would come around the next bend. There were horse packers leading mule trains, hauling in the comforts of civilization for a party of dude ranch guests. There were mountain bikers, in tight-fitting neon clothes, and camp groups of eight-year-olds with impossibly mispacked equipment. There were backpackers, some of whom had seen Karl a couple of days up the trail and carried back messages from him to us. There were runners training for the Leadville 100, a 100-mile footrace at elevations of 10,000 feet or more. There was a group of senior citizens day-hiking the length of the Colorado Trail, equipped with a van to carry their food, gear, and water to campsites up ahead. And there were dirt bikers, spewing mud and noise as they pursued their customized roller coaster rides: roaring up and down hills and around corners, making sudden stops and starts, plowing through mud puddles and streams, and digging deep ruts in the footway. We looked upon them with a combination of resentment, disapproval, and smug superiority; we, after all, occupied the moral high ground. We were the ones who appreciated the subtleties of wilderness, who left scant trace of our passing. But we might as well have turned up our noses at the queen of England—I don't even think they noticed us as they flew by on their noisy machines.

The Colorado Trail stayed low, winding around parcels of private property, passing clearcuts and grazing land. It passed through the town of Mount Princeton, a summer home community that announced its presence to us with No Trespassing signs and notices instructing hikers to stay on the paved road and to refrain from bothering local residents with requests for telephones or water. There was no need to bother residents for either water or a telephone: Both were readily available just a few miles down the road. But the signs didn't mention that.

This was the first time since we had begun the hike at the Mexican border that we had felt unwelcome, and we were struck by an obvious irony. We were hiking on an official, completed hiking trail. The people here were urban types: They looked like professionals using their free time to relax and rejuvenate in the mountains. They drove nice cars, some of them sporting environmental stickers ("DON'T DAMN THE ARK!" read one, in reference to an ongoing battle over the nearby Arkansas River). If we had been clean, we would have looked just like them—whereas no one, in this life at least, was ever going to mistake Dan or Dave or me for a rancher. So why was it that it was the ranchers' beat-up old pickup trucks that invariably slowed down to offer us a ride? Why was it that a rural Indian trading post had opened its doors to us? Why was it that so many of the people who opened their coolers, or their homes, or their hearts to us were the ones with dilapidated cars and modest houses? We had been offered rides in dozens of pickup trucks, but not a single Audi or Mercedes or even a good, new sedan ever slowed to see if we needed help. Why was it that this community of people that looked just like us needed special signs to keep us in our place?

Fortunately, the tiny town of Twin Lakes was our next stop, and it offered everything we needed to raise our flagging spirits. Traditional western hospitality, good food, beautiful scenery, and genuine European feather beds were the fare of the town's only hotel, the Nordic Inn.

Twin Lakes is off the beaten path, but it has been enchanting those who find it for more than a hundred years. The Nineteenth-century writer Samuel Bowles described the lakes as "two as fine sheets of water as mountains ever shadowed or wind rippled, or sun illuminated. They took their place at one in the goodly company of the Cumberland Lake of England, of Lucerne in Switzerland, of Como and Maggiore in north Italy, of Tahoe and Donner in California, and no second rank among them all."

Apparently, there has been a remarkable lack of change since the nineteenth century, for these sheets of water are just as Bowles described. Fortunately, designation on the National Historic Register ensures that the hamlet will continue to be protected from change.

The town consists of a grocery store, where the post office occupies a desk in the back; a rafting outfitter, a few antiques stores, some cabins, and the Nordic Inn. The inn began life as the Twin Peaks Hotel, named after the mountains that dominate the view to the southwest. Back then, Twin Lakes was a stagecoach stop on the road to Aspen. It must have been quite a journey; even today, the road across the Continental Divide over 12,095-foot Independence Pass is one of the roughest rides in the state, open only in the summer months. In early autumn, the flat top of the pass blows shut with snow almost immediately, and for 9 miles the road is threatened by avalanches and rock slides. In the winter, the Continental Divide reasserts the power it has always claimed in Colorado: to split the state and make travel impossible.

In the summer, though, the Independence Pass road is merely long and slow, especially if you're stuck behind a Winnebago. Tourists drive between Leadville and Aspen, two old silver towns turned tourist villages—the one slightly tarnished, its heart still in the mines of its past; the other glittering and glistening with a newfound influx of wealth. In between them, the Nordic Inn entertains hikers, mountain bikers, and fishermen.

In earlier years, the clientele here was of a different sort. Back when the main business was mining; back when nearby Leadville was one of the most important of Colorado's mining boomtowns; back when the earth ran silver, the clientele who frequented the hotel came not to fish, or relax, or hike in the mountains, but to visit the assembly of ladies who resided on the second floor. Around the turn of the century, the Nordic Inn was a whorehouse.

The ladies are long gone, of course, but they are remembered with rooms named after them, and their biographies hang on the walls. There is more to remind the visitor of the Old West here in Twin Lakes: A ghost, we learned, frequented the hotel, although we didn't personally make his acquaintance. John, the hotel's proprietor, and his mother, however, have, and they told us about it over drinks in the inn's cozy barroom.

Noises in the night. Banging and slamming. All the windows left swinging open in the middle of winter.

It sounded, we suggested, like pranksters.

But who would have done it? The year-round population of Twin Lakes is about twenty—there are more elk than people in the winter-time. Besides, John said, he had nailed all the windows shut himself. And then, there was the small matter of the ghost appearing on the landing one night just as John's mother was walking down the stairs. Dressed in black, she told us, in cowboy garb, from head to toe. And when she turned to get a closer look, he vanished.

What the ghost is doing there is anyone's guess: Perhaps he is looking for a favorite lady. Perhaps he was cheated in a card game or swindled in a property deal. Perhaps he is still waiting to find the mother lode that escaped him during his lifetime. Or perhaps he, like Samuel Bowles, simply likes these fine sheets of water with their high mountain backdrop of some of the most impressive peaks in the country.

〰〰〰〰

Mount Elbert is one of those impressive peaks—at 14,433 feet, it is the highest mountain in Colorado. It was Dave's idea to climb it. Elbert isn't technically on the Divide, but it's close enough, and the trail-head is a scant 3 miles from the Nordic Inn. We could hardly walk past the base of the highest mountain in Colorado without going up it.

To reach 14,000 feet before the afternoon storms get there, you have to start early. At five in the morning, the air was brittle and shiny—the crisp, bracing air of a mountain morning. It was cold, too, as we started uphill, bundled in gloves and hats and extra layers of clothing.

The extra layers came off soon enough, as we climbed higher on the mountain and the sun climbed higher in the sky. Five thousand feet of elevation separated us from the summit, but we fairly flew along the trail. We carried only our rain gear, some snacks, an extra layer of clothing, and our water bottles, and without our packs we felt liberated and free. This was a whole other kind of walking; it was floating, almost—although as we approached 14,000 feet, the illusion of floating became more and more difficult to sustain.

Elbert is one of those mountains that fools the eye, a master of illusions and false promises. The trail winds around ridge after ridge, and as you obediently follow it up and up, you begin to hear the mountain's promises: "Almost there," it seems to say, luring you onward, heaven-bound. "Just over the next rise." The higher you go, the more you believe that this time, at last, the mountain is telling the truth. After all, all mountains have summits somewhere. But there is always just one more rise, just one more curve, just one more ridge, and by the time you finally figure out where the top is, you're just about standing on it.

The summit of Elbert is cold and windy, and we shared it with half a dozen or so other hikers—not surprising, since Elbert attracts several thousand visitors every year. The register at the top is so full of names there was hardly room to squeeze ours on the list. There's even a redoubt, an ambitious rock wall behind which hikers can shelter themselves from the bitter wind while swapping snacks with others.

But it was the view that kept us there—a heaven's-eye panorama of ridges and ridges of rocky peaks, most still holding bits and pieces of snow, more mountains than you can imagine for as far as you can see. The sky is the deep, saturated blue of high altitude; the air is as clear and sparkly as a fine diamond. La Plata is a solid wall to the south; Mount Massive lies to the north, and some 30 airplane miles to the west is Snowmass, easily identified as the mass of snow in the distance.

Before us was Colorado—the mountain state. Perhaps nowhere else in the United States has human history been so inextricably linked with a state's physiography. From the earliest Native Americans, whose seasonal travel was dictated by the patterns of game migrations and climatic variations, to this year's migrations of skiers and tourists; from the trappers of beavers to the miners of metals; from the builders of railroads to the users of water, Colorado's mountains have shaped human lives. Standing on Elbert, looking down on the rest of Colorado, we could see, firsthand, just how huge a force and an obstacle they have always been.

But what shaped the mountains? What colossal forces thrust and carved and moved and broke these miles and miles of endless rock?

If we had climbed Elbert some 20,000 years ago, our view from the summit would have been about the same. Colorado as we know it is only some 20,000 years old, in geologic time, a mere infant. Sitting on a weak zone on the North American continental plate, between a more stable mass to the east and a less stable mass to the west, Colorado is vulnerable to the spreading of distant sea floors and the moving of massive continents.

It was just such a disruption that formed the first Rocky Mountains some 300 million years ago. The North American Plate shifted somewhere over the Atlantic Ocean and, here, 2,000 miles away, a mountain range was born. Over the next 200 million years, this range— our ancestral Rocky Mountains—eroded down to nothing. Then, some 60 million years ago, when the first mammals were making their appearance on earth's evolutionary stage, the plate shifted again. Today's Rockies arose, and, as mountains will, almost immediately began to erode. Finally, during a period spanning from 35 to 5 million years ago, the whole state was uplifted another 5,000 feet. The result of all of these great geological upheavals was a range of mountains that we might recognize today.

But it was left to the glaciers to carve this country into its final form—to create the lakes and the rivers and the cirques and the passes and the morraines that awe those of us who come to see them. The glaciers were the agents of change, and from Elbert's summit you can admire their work. If they were people, we would call them sculptors, and the mountains they have carved—we would call them art.

Glaciers are merely big patches of compacted snow and ice. There are two things, though, that differentiate a glacier from a snowfield. First, a glacier lasts through the year, because the snow that falls in the winter replaces the snow that is lost to summer heat. And second, a glacier moves.

A glacier moves because of gravity. As new snow falls, it eventually melts and refreezes and crystallizes into ice. As more and more snow falls, the pressure on the layers of ice below the new snow becomes greater and greater, and finally the ice begins to slide downward. You can't see a glacier move, although if you stand at the base of a truly large glacier on one of the world's great mountains, you can hear it crackle and rumble as it slowly—glacially—shifts. But if you could film a glacier over time, and then speed up the motion picture, you would see the ice moving, unexpectedly fluid, like some huge plastic blob.

A glacier is pulled downward by gravity, but on its way—like any other river or stream—it must carve a path through whatever obstacles it encounters. Some parts of the rock are softer than others. Some of the slopes are steeper. Some of the rock succumbs readily to the glacier; some of it resists. Like a river, the glacier finds the path of least resistance; like a river, it carves a path. As it does, it picks up bits and pieces of rock and clay and silt, ranging from the smallest of sand particles to the biggest of boulders. The sand and boulders join the falling ice, and they, too, become sculptors, polishing the rock beneath them like a piece of giant sandpaper. When they reach the bottom, the snow and ice melt into streams and tarns, leaving the rocks in piles, called morraines.

And above, high on the glacier, more snow falls, melts, freezes, crystallizes, sinks, and begins its downward slide. What we saw in front of us now was the fruit of glacial labor. The scoured valleys and sheer rock walls and giant cirques and icy tarns. The rivers we drank from, the passes that we climbed to, the scree we tripped over, and the views we yearned to see. These were the glaciers' artistry— the result of snowstorms that began a million or so years ago, and ended, by geological time, only yesterday.

Hikers were still coming up as we began our descent from Elbert's summit. We virtually flew down the rocky trail, floating again, running almost, our breathing effortless in comparison to the hikers who were still huffing their way to the top in the step-breathe-step pattern, so familiar to us.

As we got farther down the mountain, we noticed a change in the people climbing toward us. In the early morning our companions had looked a lot like us: hard bodies, sun-toughened skin, good used gear. They knew, like we did, that to climb to 14,000 feet safely, you must start at first light and be on your way down by noon.

We were about at the bottom by eleven o'clock, but people were still climbing up: family groups, mostly, and a few teenagers dressed in everything from blue jeans to military camouflage costume. "What's it like up there?" someone asked, as if it would be the same for them when they arrived, hours later, just in time for the daily midafternoon storm.

We saw a man marching purposefully, head of the family, determinedly holding the hand of an overweight little boy, maybe ten years old, who was lagging behind. The boy was stumbling uphill in the way kids have of doing something they don't want to do, and his thoughts were clearly concentrated on his misery. He looked at us with the most wretched expression on his face. They wouldn't make it to the top, but that was little consolation. The poor kid would probably develop a lifelong hatred of the outdoors.

The last group we saw was a party of Texan teenagers, thirty of them, just starting up from the trailhead. They were already breathing heavily, stopping and panting every few steps. The top of Elbert was 5,000 vertical feet away—almost a mile straight up—so this early heavy breathing did not bode well for their summit attempt. They informed us that they were going to camp near the top and "take the summit" the next morning.

Elbert is a sleepy, accessible sort of giant, but he has a touch of Himalayan mountain god temperament. He was good-tempered enough with most of us, but I think he objected to this "take the summit" business. That, at least, was our explanation the next day when we looked up and saw that a blanket of snow had covered the upper elevations during the night.

In Colorado, they say it can snow any day of the year. Snow once blocked the railroads, now it closes mountain passes to automobiles. It fills the reservoirs and it blankets the mountains. Snow is a natural resource, and like any other natural resource in the West, it is a source of wealth. Coloradans have become rich from beaver pelts, from gold, from silver, from range grasses, from lumber. It should come as no surprise that they also have become rich from snow.

The ski resort of Copper Mountain was our next town stop, and it greeted us like a vision from another planet. A sign on the road warned us of an impending "GOLFCART CROSSING," bulldozers were busy churning up ground, and chic stores offered fabulous discounts on five-hundred-dollar ski jackets. Like other ski resorts in the United States, Copper Mountain is trying to make a go of the business of being a four-season vacation spot, but it has a lot of competition: Summit county is one of the most heavily developed recreation areas in the country. A mere hour or so from Denver, the ski resorts of Summit County include Breckenridge, Keystone, Arapahoe Basin, and Copper Mountain; in summer, all of them are open for business.

It's big business, and the resorts go about it in grand style, luring visitors with golf courses, tennis courts, and cut rates on condominiums. Nor is the business limited to the ski resorts: Chambers of commerce put out newsletters announcing the offerings. The entire county is a backcountry amusement park: You can take your pick of windsurfing, sailing, kayaking, canoeing, rafting, mountain biking, horse packing, hot tubs, hot springs, triathlons, road races, jeep tours, or a high-altitude burro race, all advertised in glossy four-color brochures.

Copper Mountain, though, looked like a scantily clothed skeleton, despite the golf course, the tennis courts, and the livery stables. Without their blanket of snow, the ski slopes looked like a series of clearcuts through the trees. A few children puttered around the pond in paddleboats; others stayed on the banks with fishing poles. In all, the place was quiet, peopled by a few vacationing families. The staff looked like tennis and ski instructors the world over: tanned, healthy, young, fit, and squeaky clean. A young man wandered over to us. He was a ski instructor in the winter; I don't know what he did during the summer. Just at the moment, he was wearing purple-and-green roller blades. He spoke to us in what we could only assume was English: He wanted, he said, to "fly a kite" off some slope on the mountain. We looked at him blankly until we finally figured out he meant hang gliding. He asked us what we were doing at Copper Mountain, and we told him about our trip. "Hey man, that's really rad," he told us. "I mean, like, you guys are really positive." It seemed a compliment, but I felt old.

He skated away, and I thought again of the outdoor magazines: the pictures of beautiful young women sitting on top of a mountain wearing bright matching colors, unscuffed hiking boots, and perfectly applied makeup; or young men with blow-dried hair and the same immaculate appearance. They would fit right in at Copper Mountain, where you could take yourself and your mountain bike up to the top via a ski lift, and ride back down without ever spoiling your outfit.

Need we say that our outfits, if you could ever have called them that, were spoiled? No matter what we did to keep clean, after two days in the woods we looked like ragamuffins. Our clothes were stained with sweat, mosquito repellent, and suntan lotion. No wonder resort owners didn't care for backpackers, we thought, as we caught a glimpse of ourselves in the window of the post office, where we went to pick up our packages.

We sat at a picnic table outside to read our mail. Karl had sent a note asking us to call him at a number in Denver; he had, he wrote, decided to wait for us so that we could all hike together again. He missed the fun he had been having with our group, and he decided that he'd rather have a good time walking to Canada—and risk not making it—than arrive there all alone. But by the time we called him from Copper Mountain, Karl was in the process of packing for home. He had had an accident playing volleyball, and his knee was so badly injured that he couldn't even walk. Karl was no longer Canada-bound: He was headed home for surgery and a long convalescence.

We packed up our new box of food and shouldered our packs. The Colorado Trail had turned east, toward Denver. We continued north, climbing back to the high country, into the mountains of the Front Range.

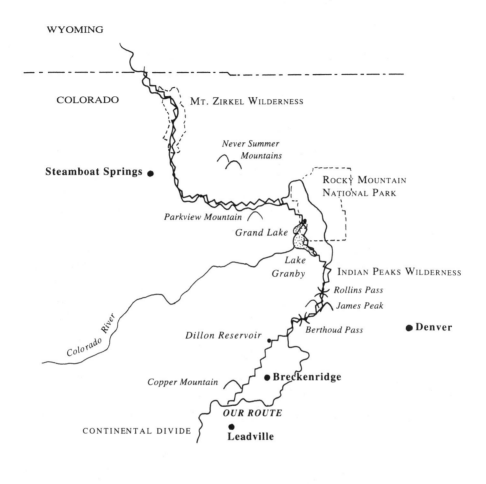

WYOMING

COLORADO

MT. ZIRKEL WILDERNESS

Never Summer
Mountains

Steamboat Springs ●

ROCKY MOUNTAIN
NATIONAL PARK

Parkview Mountain

Grand Lake

Lake
Granby

INDIAN PEAKS WILDERNESS

Rollins Pass

James Peak

Dillon Reservoir

Berthoud Pass

● **Denver**

Colorado River

Copper Mountain

● **Breckenridge**

OUR ROUTE

CONTINENTAL DIVIDE

● **Leadville**

N

6

HIGH COUNTRY

Colorado's Front Range takes its Continental Divide responsibilities seriously. There is no question where the Divide goes. The ridge is as clear and sharp as a razor's edge, and when it rains, which it does every afternoon, you can see exactly which ocean the water is headed to.

Water is a serious subject here. Initially, it is the Divide's decision which water goes east and which water goes west. But the Divide has only the initial say in how the water is apportioned; its decisions, at least here in Colorado, are immediately challenged by humans. Water is not something that can be entrusted to the whims of mere geography. Just ask any member of Denver's powerful Water Board, and he'll tell you about the inequitable job the Divide has done. The complaints stem from a simple imbalance: While 80 percent of Colorado's population lives on the eastern slope, 70 percent of the water falls to the west. Only two river systems, the South Platte and the Arkansas, drain water into the urban communities of the eastern slope and the flat plains farmland beyond, and both of them put together have far less water than the mighty Colorado River.

As if to add insult to injury, the Divide boasts of its power, rearing up in back of Denver in a massive 13,000-foot barrier between the urban metropolis and the rest of the state—between thirsty communities and western water. The Front Range issues a challenge to all who approach from the east. Cross that, if you can!

Paradoxically, the Front Range is one of the few places where a great deal of water actually does cross the Divide—not naturally, of course, but through man-made tunnels. In 1872, the Colorado Supreme Court ruled that "in a dry and thirsty land, it is necessary to divert the waters of the streams from the natural channels, in order to obtain the fruits of the soil, and this necessity is so universal that it claims recognition of the law."

The court's decision was only one in a long line of decisions that emphasized that water goes to those who would use it. As western water law evolved, it solidified into three related doctrines: "first in time, first in right," "use it or lose it," and "beneficial use." Being first in time, however, didn't offer protection to those who committed the sin of wasting their rights; those who didn't use their water rights forfeited them. And the use itself had to be beneficial: Making hay, feeding cattle, and watering lawns were all beneficial, but it wasn't until 1972 that water's role as a component of a natural environment was recognized as a legitimate beneficial use. Legitimate—but one of many. Even Colorado's wilderness areas must compete for the right to water.

Eastern slope communities were quick to respond to the Colorado Supreme Court's ruling because it meant that there were no longer any legal barriers to diverting western slope water. But although the supreme court could remove legal barriers to Colorado River water, it had no power whatsoever against the natural barrier of the Continental Divide. For a community to obtain western slope water for its faucets, toilets, bathtubs, and lawn sprinklers, it needed to divert, store, and transport the water across the Front Range. Denver communities rallied to the challenge. In the hundred years since the landmark decision, Colorado's waters have virtually been turned into one large plumbing system of tunnels, dams, siphons, conduits, pipelines, reservoirs, pumps, and hydroelectric power plants. Tunnels have been drilled through the mountains to divert water, devastating streams and riparian ecosystems; the entire town of Dillon was moved—lock, stock, and barrel—to make room for the Dillon Reservoir; and still eastern slope communities cast covetous eyes on any water they might have a chance of appropriating for their own use. Meanwhile, water from the Colorado and its tributaries must be shared among not only Coloradans but also among the residents, farms, and businesses of California, Arizona, New Mexico, Utah, and Wyoming—and Mexico. The river provides half of the water for Los Angeles, San Diego, and Phoenix; it irrigates farms in Arizona's deserts and in California's Imperial Valley. It provides electricity for Las Vegas and artificial snow for Colorado resorts. The Colorado River, born in the snowmelt of the Front Range, tumbling 13,000 vertical feet—2.5 miles—to the sea is itself arguably the most litigated and embattled river in the world.

Up on the crest of the Divide, of course, there isn't any water. In summer, the rainfall goes downhill immediately; in winter, most of the snow blows off the crest into lower, more protected valleys and cirques. What is left on top is a harsh, windswept environment not unlike a desert, and it seems strange that this high, dry ridge owes its importance to a substance that is so notoriously absent.

Our plan—to walk right on top of the Front Range—meant that we would have to be as concerned as any Colorado farmer with the question of where we could get some water. We filled our water bottles at the old gold-mining site at Bobtail Creek, and carried them 2,000 feet up the switchbacked road to Jones Pass. Several hundred feet underground, more western slope water—much more—was being carried east, underground, through a tunnel.

Jones Pass is a dip in the Divide, elevation 12,450 feet. A dirt road winds its way steeply up to the pass, and then goes back down the other side. At the top, the pass was completely blocked with snow. This road over this pass is a symbol of the dogged persistence with which Coloradans have always approached the challenge of traveling through these mountains. Even so, given its condition in the middle of July, one has to wonder, exactly when during the year did the builders of this road think that it would be used?

From the pass, we left the road and turned north onto the snow. The Divide stretched for miles before us, undulating gently, or so it seemed. From the crest of the Divide, we could see more mountains than you would have thought existed, waves and waves of them, like rough-ocean whitecaps, shining tips pointing at the sky. To either side of us, the slopes dropped down steeply, and we stayed slightly to the west of the crest itself, to compensate for the wind, which seemed determined to blow us clear to Denver. Even our backpacks betrayed us, turned by the gusting wind into sails that flung us about like badly handled marionettes.

We could see our route ahead of us as it followed the crest. But the apparent ease of our path was another trick of the mountain gods, who duped us, this time with scale and distance. Our easy, gentle undulations became backbreaking ordeals as soon as we started walking. We fought to maintain our balance, fought against the steep angles of the slopes, fought against the rocky, ankle-twisting terrain and the persistent, noisy wind. We fought, simply, to keep walking.

Not much had managed to survive the wind's unceasing assault up here. There were no trees—not even the stunted krummholtz—no shrubs, not even much grass. There was no tread through the piles of rubble and rock, but our route was, surprisingly, marked. On slopes so precipitous that we had trouble simply standing on them, someone had done a backbreaking job of building waist-high stone pyramids to mark the route. These cairns seemed almost extravagant now: On this open ridge, the route was obvious enough. But the cairns were only a luxury so long as the sky was blue and clear; if a low fog came in, obscuring the route, they could very quickly turn from luxury to lifesaver.

By lunchtime, we had covered 8 miles, and we were already tired. We took shelter on the lee side of some huge boulders, eating quickly, in deference to the weather. The clouds were building, almost imperceptibly, but steadily nonetheless. In an hour or two, we knew, the sky would be ugly and dark. We looked at the map, counting the bumps and dips, trying to determine how far we had yet to go and how much more climbing still lay ahead. It seemed that we had one more big climb—we could see it in front of us—

then, the map promised some easy upland walking followed by a final, steep descent to Berthoud Pass.

We climbed the next 400 feet, encouraging ourselves with the promise that it was the last major ascent of the day. But we had read the map too quickly, as we learned when we reached the top. The ridge was what they call a knife-edge, with steeply sloping sides. But worse, in front of us the trail dropped so precipitously that it appeared to simply end in space. It looked like a medieval vision of the far end of the world—a drop into nothing. Only when we walked nearer the edge and peered over could we see the next cairn, down, down; the trail descended 1,000 feet, so straight-down steep that we'd have to climb backward, using our hands, to get to the bottom. And after the climb down, the ridge continued—where else?—back up, rising another 750 feet. As far as I was concerned, that 750 feet could as well have been Mount Everest.

This was not the level walking promised by the map—but then, we immediately realized that the culprit was not the trail, nor the map; it was our careless navigating at lunchtime. As so often happens, and it always happens on the hard days, we weren't as far along as we had thought. For me, the feeling was as if I had reached the 26-mile marker in a marathon and been told to tack on an extra 6 miles.

It wasn't, of course, a marathon, and it wasn't Mount Everest, either: It was just one more bump in the Divide. And we climbed it, of course—we had, after all, nowhere else to go.

By the time we finally descended the rocky, hummocky ski slope that ended at Berthoud Pass, we were exhausted. Sue and Gordon were waiting for us, and we rode with them to their Forest Service campsite, just down from the pass. The road was paved, but, like the Jones Pass road, it was a tortuous, twisting affair, steep even by the standards of Colorado. Unbelievably, even this ridiculous pass was once—briefly—considered as a possible route for a railroad. Fortunately for all concerned, the notion was quickly abandoned. What staggers the imagination is that it was ever considered at all.

The next day, we followed the Divide as it rose again from Berthoud Pass, climbing 1,100 feet up a well-graded road to Colorado Mines

Peak, elevation 12,493 feet. Only when the road ended did the climbing begin for real, one ascent after another: Mount Flora, 13,142,
then down; Mount Eva, 13,130, then down; and so on, up and back
down, to Parry Peak, 13,391; Mount Bancroft, 13,250; and finally,
James Peak, 13,294.

The trail was pathological, alternating between steep climbs and
difficult descents on rocky, treacherous terrain. And always, there
was the crazy-making wind, a wind that invaded the very center of
my skull. The wind made it impossible to talk, impossible to hear,
impossible, even, to think. After a day in this wind, I could understand exactly why the French will accept "le Mistral" as a defense
for murder. A wind like this could drive one mad.

As usual, Dan had stayed back with me, and by the time we
reached Mount Bancroft, the fourth of the five 13,000-foot peaks,
neither of us could see Dave, who had gone on ahead. We couldn't
see any trail markers, either; nor could we, we suddenly realized,
identify the Divide, which, on a map, shows up as an incontrovertible, dotted line. There was no line here on the tundra, and as we
stood on the cold northern flank of Mount Bancroft, our route seemed
to have completely disappeared.

We stopped. To our left was a steep slope of boulders and scree
descending 500 or so feet to a natural rock bridge. On the right side
of the bridge was a lake where bright blue icebergs were slowly
melting into deep blue-green water—Ice Lake, it is appropriately
named. To the left of the rock bridge, there was 1,000 feet of nothing. Clearly, that couldn't be the way: Even if we could get down
to it, the bridge ended in a vertical wall that looked climbable only
if you happened to be a mountain goat. We walked on, following
the more obvious ridgeline, but it turned into a dead end, and we
found ourselves standing at the edge of a cliff.

Dan looked back and down, to the rock bridge. "Dave's there," he
said, and I followed his gaze. Sure enough, the bright blue speck huddled
among the boulders was Dave, bundled up in all the clothes he owned.

"What the hell is he doing?" I demanded, and tried to answer
my own question: "Maybe he got cold waiting for us and went down
for shelter?" But even as I said it, I realized how ridiculous it would
be for anyone to climb that far down that slope to find shelter. Still,

my mind refused to entertain the notion that the reason Dave was down there was because that's where the trail went. And it also refused to remember that Dave has an unfailingly accurate instinct for where the trail goes.

"Dave! Are you on the trail?" Dan shouted. All we could hear in response was a muffled, ". . . think . . . trail . . . cairns."

"What happens on the other side of the rock bridge?" Dan yelled. Dave pointed up—straight up—and I tried to hold back tears.

"Wait here. I'll check this out," Dan said as he started down to the bridge. He's more surefooted than I am, and it didn't take long for him to get down and wave for me to join him. Meanwhile, I had pulled out the map and had determined that, beyond doubt, the Forest Service did indeed intend for us to go down *there* and up *that*. Moreover, we needed to get moving because the sky was turning its daily, angry, afternoon brown. I groaned at the 700-foot climb still ahead: Our total elevation gain would be more than 5,000 feet for the day. Five times up—and down—the Empire State Building. The difference was that we were climbing scree, not steps, carrying more than forty pounds on our backs, and looked more like kites than climbers in the 40-mile-per-hour wind. On top of all this, so to speak, there was the altitude.

There is a platitude about the high country, that to stand on a mountain peak and experience the vastness of nature somehow diminishes a person, makes him feel smaller. But for us, the high country didn't so much make us feel small as it made us feel vulnerable.

The human body is a fragile machine, and nowhere is that more evident than at high altitudes. At 13,000 feet, there is about 40 percent less oxygen than there is at sea level, and the body responds by protesting.

This lack of oxygen is what causes mountain sickness, which can affect people at elevations of as little as 8,000 feet. An unacclimated tourist driving a car over a mountain pass, for instance, might find himself out of breath if he tries to go for a short walk. At higher elevations, the effects of altitude become more serious. Headaches and nausea are the warning signs, and if they are ignored, they can lead to pulmonary or cerebral edemas, which cause the leakage of blood plasma into the lungs or brain. Edemas are usually fatal unless the victim is given oxygen or moved to a lower elevation. Almost always, acute mountain sickness is the result of ascending a mountain too rapidly, before the body is acclimated. In the United States, edemas occur at an average elevation of 12,000 feet, and they are usually preventable: Given time enough, most people can ascend to elevations of 18,000 feet without more than a slight headache. Climbers in the Himalayas, to take an extreme example, go well into the twenties of thousands of feet without supplementary oxygen— but only after spending enough time acclimating.

After several weeks of walking at elevations of well over 11,000 feet, our bodies were used to the high country. Still, spending a whole day climbing up and down at 13,000 feet is enough to make anybody feel the effects of altitude. By the end of the day, we were—again—exhausted.

We had been walking for ten hours, and we had covered only 9 miles. It was the all-time low for our entire trip for a full day of walking, and, if there had been any water any earlier, our mileage would have been lower still. We finally stopped on the north shoulder of James Peak, where some previous camper had left a small redoubt downhill from a spring. Minimum-impact advocates would no doubt frown on this obvious man-made construction, but for us, it was welcome shelter, although it was big enough for only one tent. As Dan went for water, Dave and I started digging out another spot, quickly, in order to be able to have the tents up before the inevitable rain.

But again surprise. There was no rain: Instead, we were blanketed by a fast-moving bank of thick clouds. A couple of hundred feet away from the campsite, Dan lost sight of us in the thickening fog, and found himself wandering around in a mist that made him feel, he said, like he was trapped inside a milk bottle. Fortunately, our voices and whistles carried across the windy distance, and Dan was soon safely back in our rocky perch.

In the night, snug in our tents, we heard other noises, carried by the wind. A low rumble in the earth's belly, a long low-pitched moan that sounded like a giant blowing air over the top of a soda bottle. Too tired to puzzle out the sounds, we fell asleep. It was not until we arrived at Rollins Pass the next morning that we learned the source of the noises.

The trains again—a train, tunneling through the dark guts of James Peak. It might have seemed impossible to build a railroad through the Front Range, but the railmen did not give up on mere impossibilities.

≋

The Moffat Tunnel is named after the man with the impossible dream. David Moffat was a railroad man, and like other railroad men before him, he was frustrated by the Continental Divide. The Front Range forced all of Colorado's western railroad traffic to detour either north to join Union Pacific or south to meet the Rio Grande. Moffat was haunted by the knowledge that a more direct route to Salt Lake City and the growing urban centers of the West Coast would increase profits and decrease freight and passenger costs. But how to do it?

Moffat's obsession with crossing the Divide took on the character of a personal vendetta. He began his crusade, in 1902, with what was popularly referred to as the "Moffat Road," a temporary route over the Divide at Rollins Pass, elevation 11,700 feet.

This temporary road was itself a major undertaking. It took five years and $20 million to build, and once it was finally open, the real work began: keeping it open. Thirty-three tunnels had to be dug and maintained, four engines were required to pull a train of twenty-two freight cars over the 4 percent grade, and more than 40 percent of the annual costs of maintaining the entire line from Denver to Salt Lake City were associated with snow removal at Rollins Pass. Today, all that is left are wooden beams, remnants of the trestles that once carried trains over this lunarlike landscape.

Despite the cost and the work and the time it took to build it, Moffat always envisioned his railroad over the pass as a temporary route. His ultimate goal was even more unlikely: to tunnel through the Front Range itself—an ambition that, for its day, was as unlikely and daring as going to the moon would be sixty years later. A tunnel would reduce the highest elevation along the line by 2,400 feet, would eliminate 23 miles of track, and would eliminate, too, the risk of blizzards. All that was standing between Moffat and his tunnel was 6 miles of granite.

The 6.21-mile-long tunnel—the second longest in the United

States—would take twenty-five years to complete, at a final cost of $18 million. It would reduce the distance from Denver to Craig from 255 to 232 miles, and it would reduce the time required to cross the Divide from 150 minutes to 12. Nineteen workers would lose their lives during its construction.

Construction on the tunnel began in 1905, but two years later the major stockholders in the Denver and Rio Grande withdrew their approval of the project. True to form, Moffat, who had already spent $209,000 in company funds to explore a route in the James Peak vicinity, continued on his own. But he never lived to see the tunnel completed. The project withered from lack of financial support, and after spending his personal fortune of $9 million on it, Moffat died bankrupt in New York in 1911 at the age of seventy-three.

The tunnel then entered a period of commercial and legal limbo. The Denver business community supported it, saying that Denver's future growth was inseparable from the completion of a direct east-west railway. The crusade to build the tunnel became a public issue, and in 1911 Denver business interests persuaded the legislature to approve a $4 million bond to continue the construction. But the governor refused to sign the measure, and when the issue was raised as a referendum on the state ballot the next year, it was again rejected.

Finally, in 1919 a bill was passed by the Colorado legislature to create a State Railroad Commission charged with building three tunnels under the Divide: the Moffat Tunnel would run under James Peak, and two other tunnels would cross the Divide at Monarch Pass and Cumbres Pass. The $18.5 million bond was signed by the governor, but the Pueblo business community—in competition with Denver for business and train traffic—blocked the plan when it was referred to the voters in 1920.

In 1921, a flood decimated Pueblo and its railroad, thus irrefutably demonstrating the need for a safe and direct route through the mountains. The state approved an initial bond of $6.72 million the next year via the passage of the Moffat Tunnel Act. Incredibly, one more obstacle remained. A citizens' group challenged the state law, claiming it violated recent federal legislation aimed at consolidating smaller railway lines. On June 11, 1924, the U.S. Supreme Court upheld the Moffat Tunnel Act, and two months later construction in the James Peak area resumed, with crews boring the tunnel from both sides of the mountain. On February 12, 1927—twenty-five years after Moffat declared war on the Divide—the two sides met. It took three more years to clear and level the tunnel. The impossible, finally, had been accomplished.

Today, the Moffat Tunnel continues to carry passengers and freight under the Front Range of the Continental Divide. And, if the mineral boom is over, the railroads are nonetheless part of Colorado's newest industry: They carry skiers to western slope resorts in cars specially outfitted with ski racks. One can only suppose that if Moffat were alive today, he would approve.

Shortly north of Rollins Pass, the Divide becomes impenetrable in the Indian Peaks' Wilderness. Lone Eagle Peak, North and South Arapaho peaks, Arikaree Peak, and Navajo Peak are only some of the dense masses of brown contour lines on the maps; in front of us, the brown lines came to life as great gray precipices. We could walk to the east or the west of the Divide, but these mountains were not going to permit us to walk over them.

At Rollins Pass, a giant map of the Continental Divide Trail showed the route approved by the Forest Service—a different route, as it turned out, than the one recommended by the CDTS. Once again, we had to make the decision whether to abide by our plans or follow the Forest Service into the unknown.

We approached this new decision warily. One thing we had learned was that the Forest Service has a bad habit of self-promotion, a habit that often leads its staff to place trail signs where no trail yet exists. There had been countless times when we had followed a sign only to find that the trail ended after a couple of miles in a heap of equipment. Therefore, we had agreed not to follow the route described by the huge, attractive placard unless we could determine that we had adequate maps.

A quick look at our topographic maps confirmed that the route we had planned to take and the route suggested by the Forest Service were quite close together, running roughly parallel. The trail that had been designated for the CDT was the so-called High Lonesome Trail, and it did indeed show up on our map. The guidebook route was longer and involved more elevation and some possible cross-country. After the last two days of the Front Range, I was beat up and exhausted. The maps indicated not only that the Forest Service route existed, but that it was easier.

But Dave was adamant: The last time we had decided to leave our planned route, we had ended up on the Colorado Trail's green tunnel for a week. Dave was going to stay with the CDTS route, and that was that—whether or not we were going to stay on it with him.

If I were going to climb more and walk more miles, I needed a good reason. High country scenery would have been a good reason, but the map indicated that the two trails were virtually identical in the amount of time they spent above and below tree line. As far as I could tell, the only difference was going to be that one route was more difficult than the other.

On the other hand, I had strong feelings about the group not splitting up. I gave in, but in a bad humor that lasted for most of the day. For the first couple of miles past Rollins Pass, the trails followed the same route, and it became clear that the Arapaho National Forest had done a good job of marking trail; its placard was no public relations ploy. Dave walked ahead to avoid the steam coming out of my ears, as I fumed about his delivering what I considered an ultimatum.

Fortunately, it is impossible to stay angry for long when you're hiking. If the scenery doesn't kill your irritation, exhaustion will. By the time we set up our camp by jewellike Diamond Lake and cooked dinner in the rain, we were all friends again.

≈≈≈≈≈

Colorado's high country gets a lot of recreation use, and to monitor that use, the Forest Service puts register boxes at trailheads. People sign in, voluntarily, noting where they are going, their schedule, and so on. Several of the register boxes contained lengthy legal disclaimers from the Forest Service, warning hikers about all of the dangers they might encounter. According to the Forest Service, where we had been hiking was a dangerous place indeed: "Hazards are not limited to, but include: changing weather conditions; snow; avalanches; landslides; caves; overlooks; falling trees or limbs; high or rushing water; contaminated water; wild animals; becoming lost or overexerted; hypothermia; remnants of mining and other activities involving excavation, tunnels, and shafts; decaying structures and a variety of equipment; and changing road and trail conditions.'' And as if that wasn't enough, the notice warned that we might also be ''exposed to unreasonable acts of others.'' Not that we could count on finding Forest Service personnel in the backcountry: Hikers should, we were told, make use of other information sources such as maps, outfitters, and Forest Service information centers.

Near Lake Granby, we rejoined the official route of the Continental Divide Trail right in front of one of these information centers. A rare piece of luck, to have an information center right where we needed information: What, we wanted to know, was the status of the Continental Divide Trail ahead? If it differed from the guidebook route, where did it go? What maps would we need? Had it been completed?

''The Continental Divide Trail?'' the man said, looking as though I had asked him about hiking on the moon. ''You must mean the Continental Divide. That's not in our district.''

No, we told him, we indeed meant the Continental Divide Trail. We pointed outside, toward the plate-sized blue CDT emblems right next to the information center, and to the huge, multicolored Continental Divide Trail placard ten yards away from the building's front door.

The man looked at us blankly. ''I don't know. . . . I just moved here from Kansas. But you could go down to Granby and ask them there.''

No, we couldn't, we said; we were on foot. We explained about our trip.

''Where's your car?'' he asked, indicating that he rather missed the point.

After several more exchanges, the clerk offered to issue us a wilderness camping permit, although he didn't seem to be too sure where we could use it. We wandered out carrying the permit, which had information about ''Woodsy Owl'' and what ''Woodsy Owl'' recommended as appropriate camping behavior. It seemed clear to us that if the Forest

Service thought that its efforts at information dissemination were going to stop its legal liability, it would have to do a better job than Woodsy Owl and the man from Kansas.

≈≈≈≈≈

The clerk notwithstanding, the Forest Service had actually done a good job of clearing and marking trail through northern Colorado. It hadn't yet finished, though, with the predictable result that we were never sure that the trails we were following actually went anywhere. Sometimes they didn't, and we spent a good deal of time hunched over our maps and compasses trying to find our way out of yet another dead end.

The terrain was changing here in northern Colorado, ever so subtly. The mountains were more rounded, the valleys—parks, they call them here—were much wider, a sweep of big, open space between mountain ridges. The weather was changing, too, perhaps influenced by the dry basin to the north of us. The sky was a dry blue, and the puffy white clouds held no threat of rain.

Although it was still 100 miles from the Wyoming border, Parkview Mountain was the last of the mountain state's lung-busting, soul-breaking climbs. At 12,300 feet, it's not as high as some of the others, but it makes up for that with a trailless ascent over loose rocks and crumbling talus, on a heartbreakingly steep 2,700-foot ascent.

It is a monster of a mountain, and although there are no false summits, it seemed, after we had been climbing for an hour, that we were no closer to the summit ridge than when we had begun. I found myself screaming curses into the impassive wind as I stumbled and lifted and stumbled and lifted toward the summit ridge, which looked down over a dizzying bowl of gray rock. I wondered, not for the first time, what insanity had led me to attempt this walk in the first place. And I wondered—not for the first time—if I was going to have the strength to keep going. At the summit, though, the questions evaporated, as they usually did when confronted with a glorious view. The answers were right in front of me in the vast sweep of land and the magnificence of the mountains.

There was a hut on Parkview, improbably perched on the very summit. A notebook in the hut listed the names of the people who had reached the top, as well as the names of companions who had given up and gone back down. Most of the entries raged about the ascent and raved about the view. The last person up the hill—someone identified as BD—had gotten here two days earlier. What piqued our interest was that BD had written that he, or she, was hiking from Mexico to Canada on the Continental Divide.

We had heard a few rumors of other hikers during our walk. Some of the trading post proprietors in New Mexico had mentioned seeing backpackers, and a couple from Boulder, Colorado, with whom we camped back at El Morro, had told us they'd read an article in their local paper about a pair of Boulder hikers who were attempting the walk. Entries in a trail register on James Peak gave us two other names—some guys, apparently from California, who were trying to walk the trail to raise money for the Arctic National Wildlife Refuge. But who was BD? If this person was only two days ahead of us, why hadn't we heard of him, or her, before?

Our next resupply was at Steamboat Springs, a logical place to come off the trail for food and a rest, and we thought we might have a chance of meeting the mysterious BD. The prospect of swapping stories with another hiker was intriguing: How had BD solved the problems of route selection and route finding and resupplies and weather? What was he or she planning to do later in the hike when the inevitable winter storms came to Montana? We looked forward to trading anecdotes and impressions with someone who had shared some of the same experiences.

We had identified Steamboat Springs as the approximate halfway point of our journey—approximate, because without a firm route it was impossible to accurately predict the mileage. But with 1,400 miles behind us, it seemed safe to call this the halfway point. We had walked through all of New Mexico and almost all of Colorado, and the biggest mountains of the trip were behind us now. All we had to do was walk 1,400 miles all over again. Both the distance we had come and the distance we had yet to go were so huge as to be barely fathomable.

Dan had been spending an inordinate time at night hunched over the guidebooks and scrawling numbers on his writing pad, and he announced that although our route had been somewhat different than the route we had initially planned, and although our schedule had varied over the length of Colorado, we had, in the end, taken exactly as many days as we had predicted to cross from one end of the state to the other.

This was not necessarily good news. In New Mexico, we had gained about ten days on our schedule. Colorado's mountains had forbidden that kind of acceleration, and now, looking at our projected schedule for the rest of our trip, it seemed more and more likely that we would be forced off the Divide before we reached Canada in the fall.

Hiking is the quintessential sport for anarchists. Other sports have rules, and everyone knows them. They aren't negotiable: three strikes to an out, ten yards for a first down, a free throw for a foul. But in hiking, each individual gets to make up his own rules—particularly when hiking something as indeterminate as the CDT. What rules did we have to follow? So far, we had tried to choose a route that was consistent with our original goals: to hike the most scenic trails, to take time to see the country, to stay near the Divide itself. Sometimes we had failed, because of route-finding problems, or the terrain, or, as in the case of the Colorado Trail, a bad decision. More often, we felt, we had succeeded.

But now Dan raised a new issue. What if we flip-flopped our direction of travel? We could take a bus up to Glacier National Park, start walking south at the Canadian border, and end our trek at Steamboat Springs. The strategy didn't guarantee that we'd be able to finish the trip in one season—a southbound route would put us in the Wind River Range of Wyoming during the fall, and there was no guarantee that we would be able to pass through those high mountains in the event of an early blizzard. But all things considered, there was a better chance that we would succeed if we dealt with the Glacier high country in August rather than October or November.

It was a perfectly rational plan. Logically, if we wanted to make our journey a one-season walk, the best way to do it was indeed to flip-flop now. But logic doesn't, in the end, have much to do with walking across the country. Even though the mileage would be the same, and the route; even though the walk would take us through the same mountains over the same trails, there was something about the nature of our hike—the rules, if you will, that we had set for ourselves—that told us that we had to keep walking north. We had been saying that we were walking to Canada. We wanted to be able to keep saying it.

We would have liked to learn what another hiker was thinking as he or she passed the halfway point, headed toward a north country winter. But we didn't find BD at Steamboat Springs, or anywhere else, for that matter, and we never heard of him, or her, again. We stayed in Steamboat for a day's rest, and then continued on for our last few days in Colorado, through the Mount Zirkel Wilderness, and then down, into the low, dry desert of Wyoming's Great Divide Basin, where, for the next few weeks at least, winter would be the last thing on our minds.

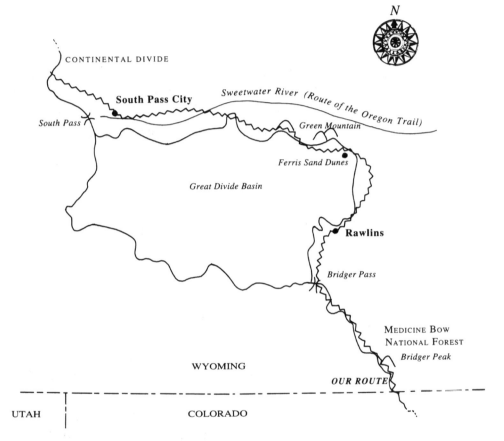

N

CONTINENTAL DIVIDE

South Pass City

Sweetwater River (Route of the Oregon Trail)

South Pass

Green Mountain

Ferris Sand Dunes

Great Divide Basin

Rawlins

Bridger Pass

MEDICINE BOW
NATIONAL FOREST
Bridger Peak

WYOMING

OUR ROUTE

UTAH

COLORADO

7

≋

THE GREAT DIVIDE BASIN

≋

Colorado ended as abruptly as it had begun, depositing us at 9,000 feet on a gravel Forest Service road, 2 miles from a reservoir that had obliterated the trail we had planned to walk on. We were back in the lands where multiple use is king.

The forest was humming with multiple use: the roar of logging trucks careening down high-quality roads, the bellowing of cows that wallowed contentedly in the streams, the squeal of chain saws slashing their way through the forests. The forests were not made up of trees; they were made up of timber—the even-aged stands looked like telephone pole factories. Those who make their living and profits from resources buried in, growing on, living in, or grazing on the national forests had left their mark here.

Of course, we had seen plenty of scars in Colorado from unwise, irresponsible, or just plain ugly resource development: the complex of condominiums around Copper Mountain; the Climax Mine, which had actually managed to take the top off Bartlett Mountain (no wonder the gods were so angry with the humans!); the obscene engine gunning of the dirt bikes; the mess of highway sprawl around the Dillon Reservoir—not to mention the reservoir itself—all stuck in our minds, etched there most deeply because of nature's incomparable background for the man-made uglinesses.

But it was also true that our route through Colorado had largely stayed in the high country. On balance, we had walked through terrain earmarked for recreation and recreation dollars. Colorado's Continental Divide is not unspoiled wilderness—there had been far too many people for that—but neither is it a victim of unrestrained development. The high country—barren, inhospitable, beautiful— had been spared a good deal of the exploitation that is typical of lower elevations.

We were back in lower elevations now. We had left the 13,000-foot peaks behind us when we left the Front Range. Parkview was the last mountain we would climb that was more than 12,000 feet high. In Wyoming, we would bid farewell to 11,000 feet, too. In fact, in a grand sense, you could say that we were heading downhill to Canada—if you ignored the 150,000 feet of ups and downs in between.

The ups and downs, of course, continued, but they were much more gentle now. The highest point in southern Wyoming was 11,004-foot Bridger Peak, just over the state line; the terrain then descended until, two days later, we crossed 7,532-foot Bridger Pass. Here, the Continental Divide does something that it does nowhere else on its route: it splits into two forks. One of the ridges heads east and the other heads west; they don't meet again until South Pass, some 200 trail miles later, where they merge to resume their job of parting the waters. But between Bridger and South passes, these two arms of the Continental Divide enclose a roughly oval basin of some 2.25 million acres, creating a kind of no-man's-land. Here is one place on the Divide that doesn't send water to distant oceans. The rain that falls within these boundaries stays right in the basin, draining into the ground or evaporating. The streambeds on maps of the basin start, meander for a while, then go dry. One might imagine that this closed sink, from which water does not escape, would be well irrigated, lush, even green. Nothing could be further from the truth. This is dry, desert country, with an annual rainfall of about seven inches. The Great Divide Basin, otherwise known as the Red Desert, has some of the harshest, driest, nastiest land in the United States—and also some of the most starkly beautiful.

There are three ways to traverse the basin. Leaving Bridger Pass, you can follow either of the Divide's two rims, or you can cut directly across the middle. For a long-distance hiker the temptation is to take the middle route, straight through on the roads. After struggling for 700 miles of Colorado's unceasing dips and rises, the straight, flat path is a chance to eat up the miles and make up time. Too, a lot of hikers don't much care for the bleak terrain. The heat bakes the sand; it shimmers in visible waves; it turns mud into a cracked jigsaw puzzle of slabs of shriveled, parched earth. It is no more kind to hikers than it is to the earth: Dry throats and burned skin are the costs of walking here.

But we had grown to love the desert: its wide skies, its open landscapes, the freedom of the wind. We were at home here now; you could tell by the way our eyes looked out toward the horizon, focused far away, comfortable with the distance and the scale. We could pick brown antelope out of brown hills by the puff of dust they kicked up as they began their headlong races across the sagebrush. We could measure the distance to peaks on the horizons; we could see the seemingly invisible contours in a landscape that appeared at first glance to be absolutely flat.

The western route had the worst water problems; the walk up the middle was the least scenic. On the other hand, while the Atlantic Rim is the longest of the three possible routes, it has some water and better scenery, and it is the route currently recommended by both the BLM and the CDTS. So, east we went, if not into Eden, then back into the familiar territory of sagebrush, jeep tracks, and cattle, back into the BLM checkerboard pattern of public and private lands. Back into the desert.

On a topographical map, green means vegetation, blue means water, brown lines mean a change in elevation, and white means that the land is barren. The snow-covered wilds of Colorado's high country tundra are shown in white. So are the deserts of southern Wyoming.

We had been walking for only five days since we crossed the Colorado-Wyoming border. Yet topographical colorations notwithstanding, the difference between the glacier-carved tundra of the Mount Zirkel Wilderness and Wyoming's Red Desert could not have been more dramatic. The only thing they had in common was that there was nothing casual about the walking. In Colorado, we had studied the map to learn about the climbs we'd have to make, or to figure out which campsites would be protected from the weather. Now, these concerns were replaced by the fanatical obsession with water that we had learned in New Mexico. Everything was determined by water: where to take a break, where to eat lunch, where to camp. We studied the maps, looking for the blue squiggles that indicated a spring, or the rare solid blue lines that promised running water, learning as we went that most of the water sources, including those that were marked permanent, were dry. Unlike New Mexico, Wyoming held no windmills on our route. Instead of searching the landscape for the glitter of a silver blade, we would be looking for surface water, for the telltale dots of vegetation—cottonwoods, willows, sometimes aspens—that crowded around even the smallest springs, and for the buckled roofs of disintegrating cabins, knowing that no settler would have built his home without a reliable source of water. We were sharing water with the cattle, and we appreciated again what we had learned in New Mexico: If nothing else, their presence was a good sign that we wouldn't go thirsty.

In this monochromatic country of brown and beige and gold, Eight-mile Lake stood out like a desert oasis. Large, almost exactly circular, it was a big splotch of blue on a map largely rendered white. The blue circle shouted its promises: a bath, a campsite, and an easy—8 miles—walk into the town of Rawlins the next day.

We could see the lake from far away. It was everything the map promised: big, gleaming blue, and completely out of place in its brown surroundings. Surprisingly, there were no cattle. Nor were there any antelope. No cattle dung, no tracks, not even birds. Something was amiss. Water is an oasis in this parched landscape; it dominates life for miles around. There was no life here.

As we got closer to the lake, the ground became soft and loamy, and our feet sank with each step, making walking difficult. The soil was wet underneath, but covered by a thin and brittle white crust. Over to the right, a lawn of red algae covered the ground, a poisonous-looking evil blanket.

We didn't have to taste the water to know what was wrong. Our oasis was an alkaline lake: salty, bitter, and thoroughly undrinkable.

If we had stopped to think, we probably wouldn't have tried to wash ourselves in the briny water. But our hearts had been set on a swim, so we ignored the fact that bathing in this briny lake, and then walking exposed to the afternoon sun, would be counterproductive and maybe even downright unpleasant.

The lake was a foot deep at the most, and the bottom no firmer than quicksand. With every step, we sank in to our knees, and then even deeper, sucked down, if we didn't move immediately, into the surprisingly warm mud. When we emerged, our legs were covered by globs of dark black muck, and the rest of our bodies were caked with ivory-colored salt.

We regarded ourselves with dismay: In addition to the aesthetics of our situation—our bath had turned us into bog creatures—there was going to be the more practical difficulty of removing enough of the mud from our feet so that it didn't cause blisters when we resumed walking. We went back to the lake to try again, but it was an exercise in futility. Each time we got near the water, we sank back into the loamy bottom. Finally, we managed to wipe most of the mess away with our bandannas, and walked on, hoping to find the only other spring on our route between the lake and Rawlins.

Or, possibly, Rawlins itself—it was only 8 miles farther. But if we were going to try to walk those miles, we'd need to stop and cook first. Our bodies had informed us, in no uncertain terms, that they didn't intend to walk another 8 miles without a fill-up, and we were out of snacks.

After 3 miles, we reached the junction with the paved road that led into town. This was the decision point: Five-mile spring was supposed to be close by (although a quick glance at the terrain looked unpromising). We could either look for the water or keep walking.

A pickup passed us as we conferred over the maps. The people inside waved, and a minute or so later, they turned around and came back.

"You folks need a ride somewhere?"

We were glad to take off our packs and chat for a spell. Maybe it's the inhospitality of the land that brings out such hospitality in its people: The folks in Wyoming had the same generosity as the folks in New Mexico, the same willingness to offer help, the same tendency to look out for each other—and for strangers, too. They were friendly and down-to-earth, even though backpackers were about as commonplace as UFOs—not to mention backpackers who had walked here from the Mexican border.

Trail magic!

There was a camper nestled into the bed of the pickup truck, and while we were talking, the woman opened the back of it and started rummaging around for whatever they had left over from their excursion. Two baloney sandwiches. Some packages of applesauce. A few candy bars. Two bottles of nonalcoholic beer, some seltzer water. It must have been like feeding bears in a zoo; she had only to hold something up and it was gone.

In between bites, we answered their questions. No, we didn't need a ride. Yes, we were walking on purpose. And no, we didn't exactly know where we were going tonight, but we thought we might make it to Rawlins, now that we had some food in us. . . . Did they know if there was any pizza in Rawlins? (That question renewed the search for food, and a few more treats were excavated from the camper.)

After assuring us that there was indeed pizza in Rawlins, the couple said good-bye and drove off. We stood around, still debating what to do. Five minutes later the pickup truck was back.

"We would of taken you out to dinner," the man said. "But we got to get on home tonight, and it's a long ways."

He paused, and there was an awkward moment as we tried to figure out why he had driven back to tell us that. We started to say our thanks when he interrupted us by sticking out his hand.

"We want to buy you dinner, anyway, even though we can't eat it with you. Here."

He pressed a crumpled wad of money—a five-dollar bill and a handful of singles—at us.

We were embarrassed beyond speech: Accepting gifts of food from people was one thing, but taking money was quite another. We tried to hand the bills back, but he wouldn't hear of it.

"Look, we'd of taken you out for pizza if we'd of met you in town," he said. "So we want to do it this way. And if you keep arguing with me in the middle of the road, you'll cause an accident."

Considering the traffic—more accurately, the lack of traffic—that was unlikely, but before we could argue again, he turned the car around one more time and drove away. The decision had been made for us. We were Rawlins-bound. As for the couple in the truck: We had never even learned their names.

Rawlins is a railroad stop turned interstate town, a dusty dry spot in the windswept middle of nowhere. It was our first food drop since Steamboat Springs, a week or so back. It was also to be the only town where we would resupply in the entire state of Wyoming. Our other food boxes went to lodges, gas stations, general stores, and the post office at Yellowstone National Park—in Wyoming, the distances were too big, the towns too far from the trail and too hard to get to. Put another way, there was the distinct possibility that Rawlins was going to give us our only real shower for the next 500 miles.

Rawlins owes its existence to a small spring, and its name to the man who found it. With annual precipitation of ten inches, it's no wonder that a good spring was enough reason to set up a town. Then the Union Pacific came through—tired, at last, of doing battle with the Colorado Rockies—and Rawlins became a stop on the transcontinental railroad. As we entered town, we saw a brightly painted caboose sitting in a picnic park, commemorating this bit of history. Rawlins grew with the railroad, becoming one of Wyoming's five county seats, each of which was on the transcontinental line, and each of which presided over a vertical slice of the state. Today, with close to 10,000 people, Rawlins is one of Wyoming's largest cities. The center of town is a national historic district; its frontier prison— which once housed horse thieves, cattle rustlers, and train robbers— is the main highlight. On either end of town, clustered around the interstate exits, is the inevitable sprawl of motels, shopping malls, and fast-food places. Freight trains still whistle through, and if you wave hello to the conductor, he'll wave back.

Rawlins was a resupply stop for us, but more important, it was where Dave's 1,000-mile journey would come to an end. After stretching his summer vacation as long as possible, Dave had run out of time. Although our route had been more or less straight, he had come, in a sense, full circle—walking from Interstate 40 to Interstate 80, from dry dusty desert to dry dusty desert. In between highways and deserts, we had walked over the high country of the entire state of Colorado.

Dave would have a rare chance to see his part of the trip in summary: His route back to Pittsburgh included a detour to Albuquerque to pick up his car, which he had left with friends. At midnight, the Greyhound rolled through town, and Dave got on. It seemed hard to believe that by tomorrow he would have whizzed through the distance it had taken us two months to cross on foot. New Mexico— it seemed a lifetime since we had been there.

≈≈≈≈≈

North of Rawlins, our route was flat and easy, following, at first, a paved road. For the first time since New Mexico, Sue and Gordon were able to walk with us for two entire days. The road led us through a deep canyon of the North Platte River called the dugway. A few fields were irrigated to a deep, rich green. The rest of the terrain wore the now familiar browns and golds. But at the Seminoe Reservoir, the color suddenly changed to bright blue as a huge, preposterous sea of fresh water appeared in front of us like a mirage. If anything is more out of place than this unlikely-looking reservoir, it is the fact that it is home to an honest-to-God private boat club.

Of course, this was the Wyoming version of a boat club, which meant that when folks weren't out fishing they were living in their recreational vehicles. It meant that instead of looking at us funny, the managers of the restaurant, which was also the store and the office, welcomed us inside. And it meant that in addition to filling up our water bottles, we were refreshed with hot showers, a couple of hamburgers, and assurances that if we thought it was windy now (we did) we should stick around till winter.

Beyond the reservoir was ranchland, heavily posted. The owners had not responded to our requests for permission to cross it. We weren't overly concerned; after walking for some 1,600 miles, a good 1,000 of which was cow country, we had finally gotten used to the idea of western hospitality. Now, we welcomed seeing the occasional pickup clear the horizon, because we were almost certain to be treated to a friendly conversation, or a cold drink—or both. But the signs around this particular ranch made us reconsider. They were especially adamant and especially abundant. We attempted to detour around the ranch, but that proved impossible: The property was simply too big. This is, after all, a region where 5,000 acres is about the minimum that can support a cattle operation.

A BLM ranger had told us that it wasn't uncommon for landowners to post property that wasn't theirs, and that a good number of the No Trespassing signs were actually on public land. The signs, according to the ranger, had more to do with hunting than anything else: This was good game country, especially for antelope, but also for deer and elk. After spending money on range improvements and water projects that attract game, ranchers justifiably want to control who gets to hunt on their land—and sometimes, they want to control who gets to hunt on land they've leased from the government, too. Some landowners charge for the privilege of hunting on their property; even those who don't are supposed to be financially remunerated by the state by means of a token system for every animal killed on their land. And, of course, it's always considered good manners to offer the landowner a part of the kill.

But by far the most compelling reason to post one's property is the issue of liability. The ranger told us that some landowners would rather have people trespassing than grant them permission to hunt, because they are afraid of being held responsible if the hunter has an accident. Remote as this part of Wyoming is, it is not so remote that it is safe from the kind of irresponsible gold-digging lawsuits that plague our court system.

No self-respecting westerner would agree with us, but as we walked through the endless sagebrush under the relentless sun, it seemed to us that land ownership is almost irrelevant here. Certainly, the land behaves as though it belongs to no one. You could see its opinion of ownership in what it had done to the scattered detritus left behind by those who had called themselves owners—people who had recorded deeds, and posted fences, and fought to scratch a living from a land that is too contrary and too hostile and too big to be owned by anyone. The slowly rusting machinery, the abandoned homesteads with bleached and buckled wooden roofs, the tangled remains of barbed-wire fences all lie forgotten and defeated. What was it like to fight this land, to wrest a living from it, to build a home, perhaps have a family, to endure the howling winters . . . and then leave? Did some confident young man, some hardworking strong woman, really think that by placing a stake in the ground they could own the vistas and the wind and the dry blue skies? Living here would not have been easy—but, after building a life in this unlikely place, the leaving would have been more difficult still. And afterward, what then? After living in the big expanse of Wyoming, wouldn't any other place seem claustrophobic by comparison? Could a person ever really adjust to the smaller spaces of anywhere else?

It seems that it would be possible to feel neutral toward this land only if you were cruising through it in an air-conditioned automobile, immune to its violent temper and unpredictable extremes. If you are walking, feeling the heat through your boots and the sun through your hat, neutrality is an option denied.

The winds, for one thing, are downright mean. They howl across the desert, picking up speed, and they make it a point to gust just exactly at the moment when you're putting up your tent. You can see where the winds have eroded some hills, and where they have built others. There is a saying about the winters here, that the snow doesn't melt; it gets blown around till it's worn out.

In the summer, it's the sands that get blown around, but instead of wearing out, they form huge piles, dunes that roll over each other like massive waves, leaving ripple lines like watermarks on an ocean shore. The dunes consume everything in their path: vegetation, roads, each other. The maps show roads that once led through here, but they now lie buried under shiny white hills of sand so fine-grained that a handful would flow between your fingers like water. Perhaps someday the dunes will roll over themselves again and the road will reappear. In the meantime, the dunes look for all the world as though they belong in the Arabian Desert. Our eyes, squinting against the violent light, picked out a herd of sheep trotting across; sand-colored, they didn't so much appear on the dunes as emerge from them, like ghosts coming to life.

Farther on, at the edge of the dunes, two cowboys were rounding up a herd of cattle. We saw them at the same moment that they saw us, and at the same moment that we turned to each other and said, "Look! Cowboys!" we heard them say to each other, "Look! Hikers!" We approached each other like alien species, and they pointed the way to where we were going—the Marvin place, they called it, as though Marvin himself would be there to meet us. The log cabin had been empty for a generation or more.

━━━━━━━

The cabin at the Marvin place is unremarkable. Notched wood logs. A spring, sometimes still flowing. A dirt road. But where did the wood come from, and how did it get here? There are no trees, and the dirt road is a rough affair. Old Marvin went to a lot of trouble to set up house; he must have had goals, reasons, hopes.

I don't know anything about Marvin. At least, I don't know the stuff of biographies: where or when he was born, and who his parents and children were, where he spent his youth, and where he lived in his old age.

But I can tell you some things about him. He came from somewhere else, probably somewhere east of here. He was tired when he got here, looking to stop. He was willing to work hard, but he didn't much care for taking orders. He had a hunger for land to call his own, and something about this land spoke to him. Maybe he got it cheap under the Homestead Act. Maybe he liked the look of the spring, or the view from the ridge to the north. He stopped here, and for a while he called it home. It wasn't an easy life. The winters were rough, with their maniacal winds and bitter temperatures. The summers were hot, and there was never enough rain.

I don't know why he left. Maybe the land wore him down, maybe it was the lonely boredom. Maybe he decided he wanted to live someplace with electricity and a telephone, or maybe, in his old age, his grandkids convinced him to move to town. Wherever he went, I bet that he never quite got used to fitting himself into a smaller

space. I bet that his eyes still had that faraway, big country focus.
I bet there were plenty of times when he walked outside, longing
for the feel of the dry wind and the hot sun. Like I said, I don't
know.

What I do know is this: Marvin's story is part and parcel of the
story of the West, and if it's history you want to learn, you come
to a place like this to learn it.

In other places, one travels to the cities to find history, to learn about
what came before, to see the places where history was made. Not here.
Because what, after all, is the history of the West? The West's story
is found in the small towns and the big ranches and the empty spaces
in between. It is found in the abandoned cabins and the rusting machinery and the forgotten projects of dreamers. The gold rushes, the ranches,
the open range, the railroads, the mines, the emigrant trails, the logging
camps, the old-time barrooms: There are stories in the weathered
beams, in the rutted roads, in the broken fences. There are stories in
the attempts to subdue a harsh land, to travel through it, to make it
yield its wealth. History is found in the places Marvin and people
like Marvin built, and the places they left behind.

In other countries, the history is old. Cities are old, art is old,
documents are old, churches are old. The history of the American
West is young. It's not book-learning history so much as it is story-
telling history—and maybe that's the romance of it. While people in
big cities lock their history in museums and textbooks, people in the
rural West still live with their version of history. They believe in it,
are inspired by it; sometimes, even, they are defined by it.

In Wyoming, history is a family affair. Nowhere is that more true
than along the Sweetwater River, which drains what little water flows
from the northern rim of the Great Divide Basin. There is, as the
local folks will tell you, a lot of history here. It's almost as though
the land is littered with its past, in scattered, random places. Something happened here, in this creek, at this rock, on this pass. Something happened—and someone remembers.

The Diamond Hook Ranch is headquartered in a cluster of buildings nestled between Green Mountain and the Sweetwater River. It
has been in continuous operation since 1879. Today, the Diamond
Hook is one of several ranches owned by the Sun family, whose

name goes back to the late nineteenth century when one Thomas de Beau Soleil, after serving in the Civil War, trapping beaver in western streams, and cutting ties for the Union Pacific, changed his name to Tom Sun and became, in 1872, the earliest permanent white settler in the valley.

In time, he also became one of its most prominent ranchers, involved, some would claim, in one of Wyoming's most infamous cases of vigilante justice: the hanging of Cattle Kate, not far from Independence Rock. Six ranchers, including Tom Sun, were accused of, but not charged with, the murder. It is still a matter of some debate whether Cattle Kate was indeed a cattle rustler—or whether she was only guilty of letting her homesteading get in the way of someone else's open range.

Although Cattle Kate's outlaw status might have been debatable, Butch Cassidy's was not. He and his Wild Bunch were wanted for train holdups all over the territory, and they had reason to fear the hangman's noose: This was a territory where justice was administered on an enthusiastic, if ad hoc, basis. The *Wind River Mountaineer* reported, in 1885, that the hanging of a certain George Cook "for the murder of James Blount . . . was the fourth legal hanging in the territory." The reporter didn't note how many illegal hangings had occurred.

Butch Cassidy was luckier than Cattle Kate; he had friends along the Sweetwater, and one of them was Jesse Johnson, the original owner of the Diamond Hook. According to local lore, Cassidy hid out in a cabin on East Willow Creek, in a place overlooking the beaver dams that terrace down from Green Mountain. The beaver dams are still there; you can see them as you climb the steep jeep road to Wild Horse Overlook. But the cabin is long gone.

Ken and Donna McMurry manage the Diamond Hook today; it's a life they wouldn't trade for any other on earth. Ken's a Wyoming native in the old western mold, a man who can ride and shoot and rope a cow, and who knows every creek and corner of this huge, beautiful country. And Donna—like so many other westerners—is an amateur historian, steeped in the legends and stories of the western landscape.

We visited with Ken and Donna, and over lunch we learned about their lives on the Diamond Hook. But most of all, what we learned was how much things change when you see them up close.

We had come to the West with some pretty cut-and-dried ideas about ranching and rangeland. For one thing, we didn't like cattle—back at home, we didn't even eat meat. Four months of dealing with cows and their calves had done nothing to make us change our minds. We still didn't think that grazing livestock was an especially good or noble use of land. We knew about the damage cattle could do, particularly to land like this, where the absence of water means that the cattle tend to gather in the few creeks that do exist, doing damage to vegetation, water quality, the water table, and soil quality.

But up close, as always, there were more shades of gray. Ranching looked different when we sat at the kitchen counter at a place like the Diamond Hook Ranch, or spent an evening watching videos of last year's roundup, or paged through a book of cowboy poetry written by a rancher's granddaddy, or read a typed and photocopied history, painstakingly prepared by an individual who cared about the past of a place. Our opinions became weathered and softened as we walked through the West; they developed nooks and crannies of exceptions and contradictions.

Bah! Humbug! The romance of the West! Critics like Edward Abbey charge that it is precisely this kind of addlepated romanticism that turns environmentalists' brains to mush and allows ranchers to keep on using—and abusing—the public land. Get the ranchers off the public lands! Get them off, now!

Unwittingly, our walk had taken us right through the middle of ranch country right in the middle of one of the biggest debates to affect the western range in recent years: whether or not the grazing fees ranchers pay to the government should be raised. Raising the grazing fees is only the latest in a series of attempts to hit the ranchers in the pocketbook and force them off the range. The government gets just under two dollars a month for each cow and calf—or "unit"—that grazes on BLM land. In contrast, grazing fees per "unit" can be as high as eight dollars on private land. Those trying to force ranchers off the public domain use the eight-dollar figure as proof that the government is subsidizing the ranching industry; ranchers respond that of course it costs more to lease private land, because private land leases provide more benefits: fencing, water, salt and minerals, stock management, less pressure from other users, and reimbursement for animals that die.

At the Diamond Hook, Ken and Donna told us that if the fees were raised, most of the ranchers would indeed be forced out of business. And that, they say, isn't right. The ranches have been here from the very beginning. And the Sun ranches, at least, are responsible stewards of the land they own and the land they lease. Ken and Donna described the ranch's stewardship program, which operates with the input of an advisory board comprising BLM people, Department of Agriculture people, environmentalists, fish and wildlife managers, range specialists, and anyone else who has an interest in how they use the land they've leased from the government. And the list is long: sportsmen's groups interested in habitat for hunters, environmentalists concerned about endangered species, animal lovers wanting to save the wild horses, biologists concerned about water quality, dirt bikers lobbying for access, nature lovers longing for solitude.

Nonetheless, in the midst of all the commotion, the stewardship program works. It establishes grazing quotas. It enforces rotation schedules. It manages riparian areas and it monitors the condition of the range. And the range is in good shape, with richer, thicker grasses than you would think land like this could support.

We left the McMurrys' home with a vaguely unsettled feeling— for me, it was the feeling that the philosophical earth beneath my feet had shifted a little.

It is true that no amount of cowboy poetry was going to make us think that recreation and cattle are compatible uses. Nor, I suspect, will we ever come around to thinking that cattle should be permitted in wilderness areas, in fragile high country, or in land managed primarily for recreation. But at the same time, ranching as we saw it here has its own validity, and history, and place in the West. There was something very right about this life, something that spoke to us seductively about open spaces and the pleasure of hard and honest physical work. There is rhythm with the seasons; with life cycles, not business cycles.

"I've spent my whole life in Wyoming and I don't want to be

anywhere but right here where I'm at,'' Ken told us. Looking around at the brilliant colors of late Wyoming summer, at the wide spaces, and that endless blue sky, we couldn't blame him one bit.

~~~~~~~

From the McMurrys' house, we climbed to the top of Green Mountain, past the beaver dams and the place where Butch Cassidy once hid. The cattle were congregated in the stream, and, as if on cue, at Wild Horse Overlook, wild horses snorted indignantly at us and wheeled around to flee into the trees.

Free-flowing uncombed manes and flying hooves; flaring nostrils quivering at our unfamiliar scent; wild whinnies that sound nothing like the calls of their domestic cousins. The wild horses are a bit of the living frontier, yet another reminder of the romance of the Old West. It seemed that everywhere we turned, the West was showing us its history and its lore.

Technically, the horses are not wild but feral, and they're not, as is widely believed, descendants of Spanish stock. Nonetheless, they have captured the public's imagination, and because of that they enjoy federal protection. Without a significant population of predators to keep their numbers under control, they have become a headache for local ranchers because they are aggressive, can be vicious, and don't limit their romantic lives to encounters with other feral stock. ''I had a mare that got pregnant by a wild horse,'' Ken had told us. ''He busted through the fence. What I wanted to know is: Can you file a paternity suit against the federal government?''

We left the wild horses up on Green Mountain, and the next day we descended the west side of the mountain to a valley road that led us through the Western Nuclear uranium mine. Here's the modern version of the buckle-roofed homesteads, the remains of one more attempt to wrest wealth from a land that is often rich, but always stingy. The mine was shut down, a silent, soulless complex of equipment shining in the desert sun. It looked like a place that was always intended to be temporary: The roads that crisscrossed the buildings and led out to the main highway weren't even paved, and neither, for that matter, was the highway itself.

The complex looks as though everyone simply disappeared one

day. The space-age machinery is still there, as is a huge toxic-green cooling pond dug into the earth. The site is ghostly quiet, the roads empty of traffic. As we walked past the buildings, we could see some of the doors were open, as though waiting for someone to blow a whistle and call everyone back to work. We looked inside one of the buildings, a prefabricated structure that looked like it had once been a locker room of some kind. The promise of shade lured us inside, and in the dark, cool room, we had to stand still until our eyes adjusted to the grayish gloom. Old work schedules and safety regulations were posted about, and some of the lockers still had slogans and posters on them. We sank down onto the gloriously cool cement floor, the most perfect, comfortable place in the world for a lunch break.

We didn't see anyone for the rest of the afternoon, not until we had left the mine and were crossing the main dirt road that runs between the uranium mines on the west side of Green Mountain and the oil fields on the east side of Crooks Mountain. Jeffrey City is 7 miles north, but with the closing of the mine, it's becoming a ghost town, just another set of buildings abandoned to the desert.

A jeep passed us, and after going up the road a bit, it turned around and came back.

"I just had to come over and find out what you're doing," the driver said by way of introduction. "My son thinks you're crazy." We could see the son in the passenger seat; he nodded. Despite the proclamation, they both looked friendly enough.

"Anyone walking through here has gotta be nuts," the son confirmed.

"I told him, there's all kinds of folks out there who do things that you might not do, and that don't make them crazy," the man continued. "So . . . well, what are you doing?"

Thus pressed to prove our sanity, we told them that we had walked here from the Mexican border. The boy shot an expression at his father that clearly said "I told you so," and even the open-minded father seemed a little taken aback.

He had been a manager for the uranium plant, he told us, which went bust partly in response to decreased demand for uranium after Three Mile Island. The mine is mostly shut down now. For a while, he worked on some of the reclamation. We refrained from saying that we hadn't seen much evidence of it.

As they waved good-bye, the son offered that he still thought we were crazy. "Where are you headed?" he asked, and we pointed to the dusty road that follows the base of Crooks Mountain. "Crazy," he repeated.

At Crooks Mountain, it was oil, not uranium, that was being pulled from the ground. Every so often, we would pass an oil well, operating on automatic cycles; inevitably, one of the wells kicked on just as we walked past, as though our presence activated some remote control device. Unnerving.

We camped in a thicket of stunted cottonwoods that night, but the vegetation was too skimpy to hide us from the road. Only one person came by, but he stopped his truck and climbed down the gully, curious about what we were doing. He was a caretaker, he told us, and his job was to check on the oil rigs every day. He had a jerrican in his truck filled with water, and he gave us a few liters, adding that we could stop at his house the next day: If he wasn't home, the spigot was just outside.

The next day, we continued walking along the flat base of Crooks Mountain on an overwhelmingly isolated stretch of dirt road. The road passed by more oil fields and herds of cattle, and the man who had visited us the night before waved as he drove by on his way to check the wells. His neat little house was right on our route, and we helped ourselves to some water. Farther on, a shepherd's rig sat by itself, looking a little like an old Conestoga wagon with its rounded roof and big wheels and wooden frame. This was home for whoever tended sheep here in the middle of lonesome nowhere, and later we saw the shepherd on horseback. But these intrusions of man were mere dots on the vast space. It was the space you saw when you looked out, and the space consumed whatever lay on the land: houses and oil wells and machinery. If you put Manhattan on this desert, I imagined, it would be overwhelmed by the sky and the space and the silence around it.

Today, a person walking through this country is cause for speculation. What is he doing here? Has he lost his mind? A hundred years ago, there would have been no speculation. A pedestrian here would have been unremarkable—commonplace, even. The emptiness in front of us now would then have been filled with wagons, livestock, and families. It would have been filled, too, with dreams. For this was the route of the Oregon Trail.

It was the most important of all the western trails used by the missionaries, emigrants, gold miners, adventurers, fur traders, and military men who filled up the West: the gentlest path across the Continental Divide, the only known route by which a wagon could travel to the ocean on the other side of the continent.

Oregon was the promised land. You could farm there, and raise a family, perhaps get rich. But first you had to get there, and to get there you had to travel through 2,000 miles of dust and heat, with bad water or no water or—only when it was time to cross a river— too much water. There was the miserable heat and the bitter nights, and the dreary tedium of the journey, endured at the plodding pace of 15 to 20 miles a day.

There wasn't much in the way of comfort. A stage station here and there offered a place to eat and to rest, although some of the early travelers were unimpressed. Saint Mary's Station, which sits in a beautiful canyon of the Sweetwater River, was one of them, described by a customer as a place that "rather added to than took from our discomfort—it was a terrible unclean hole . . . we were not sorry when the night came, but the floor was knobby, the mosquitoes seemed rather to enjoy the cold, and the bunks swarmed by 'chinches.' " Today, all that is left is a marker.

You could have seen a thousand wagons pass by here in a day during the height of the migration west, each of them filled with the necessities for a new life: clothing and spices and dishes and pots and fabric and mementos and a long list of other things that would be hard to come by ahead. The cargo rode in the wagons while people took turns walking. The wagon ruts are visible today, history worn into the ground one wheel at a time.

They were 900 miles into a 2,000-mile journey, from the last settled outposts in Missouri to points west. About 300,000 people made the trip over South Pass between 1840 and 1869. Some were going to Oregon, seeking a new life in the rich Willamette Valley. But the Oregon Trail was also the California Trail and the Utah

Trail. Brigham Young led the first company of Mormons over the pass to their new haven beside the Great Salt Lake. The Donner party passed by here, too, destined for tragedy in the early winter storms of California's Sierra Nevada. The forty-niners came by, headed for gold in Californian hills, and, if that didn't work out, for places yet unknown. So did the fast-riding horsemen of the Pony Express, traveling at the unbelievable pace of 200 miles a day. And then there were all the others, the stream of countless, faceless pioneers—seeking nothing more or less than a chance at a new life.

There was tragedy here, and we didn't have to go far to find it. A Mormon cemetery on our route tells the story of a party of 404 people, led by Captain James Willie, that was attacked by an early winter snowstorm in mid-October. Seventy-seven people died before help finally arrived. The tragedies were spread all along the trail: Indian troubles and arguments and accidents and dysentery and cholera. The route was lined with graves, approximately one every tenth of a mile, and sometimes many more than that. One in every seventeen people didn't survive the journey.

More than a hundred years later, the land is no more hospitable. Emigrants would recognize Devil's Gate and Split Rock and Oregon Buttes. The days are as hot as they ever were, the nights as cold, and the promise of a river called Sweetwater as meaningful to anyone who travels this country on foot. Today, we were walking through this country as a personal challenge, a quest to know the West. Our trip was not the beginning of a dream but the dream itself. How similar our path was to that of those early emigrants—and how different our journey.

Our route took us north of the river, and we returned to estimating how many miles we could walk on a liter of water. By evening, we were stretching the number—stretching it because the last three water sources had been dry. We needed water to camp, and we found it, finally, at a spring.

The spring was more accurately a mud puddle with a few tufts of grass poking out of the ground. Worse, the carcass of an antelope was slowly decomposing in it. We found the source of the spring upstream—if *stream* is the word—from the antelope. It was about two inches deep, and just far enough from the carcass to let us tell ourselves that we'd be okay if we boiled the water for a very long time.

We put up our tent, and were at work on dinner when we heard a motor. Seemingly out of nowhere, here in the middle of nowhere, a vehicle that looked like a cross between a golf cart and a dune buggy approached.

The driver didn't waste any time getting down to business.

"Seen any sage chickens?" he asked.

We shook our heads, a little lost for words.

"Sage chicken huntin' starts tomorrow, and I'm taking a look around," he announced. "Sure you ain't seen any?"

We assured him that we weren't holding out on him, and he puttered away, still searching the sagebrush for the evidently elusive chickens.

The next morning, we had barely started walking when it became clear that our desert solitude had ended. It was the Saturday of Labor Day weekend and the desert was aprowl with pickup trucks crisscrossing the dirt roads at 5 miles an hour, like sharks circling at feeding time. The first one on our path stopped.

"Seen any sage chickens?"

This time, we admitted that we didn't even know what a sage chicken looked like.

"They look like this!" one of the women exclaimed, and reached into the truck bed. She held up a very dead, somewhat scrawny, desert grouse.

We apologized that we had no sage chickens to report. But then, we hadn't been looking for them.

The truck drove off, continuing its hunt, and another one stopped. It was only ten o'clock in the morning, but the occupants were already deep into a case of beer.

They were, they told us, celebrating sage chicken hunting season. But since neither of them liked sage chickens, and they hadn't got a license, they were shooting at beer cans instead. Here was the catch: The beer cans first had to be empty.

It was a little early to start drinking beer, but we were getting into the spirit of sage chicken season. I took a light beer—beer and desert sun are a frankly toxic combination—and drank it slowly, while our new friend Smitty expounded a homespun philosophy that sounded suspiciously like "live and let live." With the hot sun and the beer, it seemed more profound at the time.

When we told the guys that we thought we'd end up somewhere around South Pass City that night, they told us to forget about South Pass City and come over to Atlantic City. South Pass City, they assured us, "ain't got nothing."

South Pass City is a ghost town clinging to just the slightest bit of life. A couple of people—literally—live there year-round. Reportedly, the town even supports a United States Post Office, although when we wrote to the postmaster, in care of the post office, to inquire whether we could send a food drop there, our letter was returned "Addressee Unknown."

Mostly, South Pass City is a state historic site, but we weren't sure what that meant. Would it have tourist facilities? South Pass City burgers? A place to throw up our tent? Smitty assured us there wasn't much there, and why didn't we just go down the road to Atlantic City, where he and his friends would buy us a beer.

"Just down the road" is a dangerous piece of information, especially if you are on foot and the person who is giving you directions is in a pickup truck. Add to that the scale of the West and you can have a real problem: "Just down the road" can be 60 miles. But when we pulled out our maps we discovered that Atlantic City was indeed just down the road: 4 miles away.

"You can hitch there easy," Smitty assured us. "We'll drive you back to South Pass City later if you want."

We had no doubt whatsoever that Smitty would make good on his word, if he was still conscious by the time we got to Atlantic City. Given the amount of alcohol he had already managed to consume, that was a doubtful proposition. Still, it seemed typical of the West that a complete stranger, after spending fifteen minutes with us, was already trying to do us a favor. We wouldn't be counting on a ride from Smitty, but Atlantic City registered as a possibility. We wished Smitty luck with his beer can shooting and walked on. By late afternoon, it was clear that we would make it all the way in to South Pass City; it was equally clear that we would be soaking wet by the time we got there. The skies had opened in a serious desert storm.

As we approached the town, we heard an engine turn over, and a car pulled out of an almost empty parking lot. Smitty's assurances notwithstanding, the prospects for hitchhiking didn't look good.

"Stick your thumb out," Dan said.

"Where are we going?"

"Wherever that car's going."

I stuck my thumb out and the car stopped.

"Where are you going?" the driver asked.

"Uh . . . Atlantic City," I said—it was the only place I knew. We squinted into the car to try to see who was picking us up.

"I can get you there," said the driver. We squeezed our packs into the trunk and crawled in, dripping water everywhere. As usual, the minute we got into an enclosed space, we became conscious of the dirt on us.

The driver looked like he could have stepped out of a Marlboro commercial. He was wearing cowboy boots and a work-worn leather jacket, and a cowboy hat sat on the passenger seat next to him. Steve Green is the real thing: His business card says "HAVE FORGE, WILL TRAVEL," and he had spent the day forging iron in an old-time western blacksmith's shop. A teacher during the school year, Steve is a western history buff, and during the summer he combines teaching and history by working as a volunteer in South Pass City, where he runs the restored blacksmith's shop, demonstrating how things used to be done.

His home is in Lander, some 30 miles away, and that's where he was headed, eventually. On the way was a stop at the Atlantic City Mercantile "historic saloon and steakhouse," a building on the National Historic Register that serves the best burgers in the West.

The high-ceilinged room is decorated with western memorabilia. The wall is covered with deer and elk trophies, and a moose head with a cigarette stuck in its mouth sits over the bar. The chandelier is housed in an old wagon wheel, farming implements are hung on the walls, and a pair of handcuffs dangles from the bar near the old wooden cash register.

There are usually a few cabins in the back for rent, but not this time of year. Labor Day weekend is sage chicken hunting season, the owner told us, and she could have sold fifty rooms if she'd had them.

We sat at the bar with Steve, listening to the banter of old-time friends roaming around. The topic of conversation was sage chicken hunting: how many who had got, whether they were good eating or not (Steve said not, and even Lewis and Clark, who ate just about anything, commented that the taste of what they called "the cock of the plains" was "only tolerable in point of flavour"). Nonetheless, at Atlantic City Mercantile, proud hunters were swapping recipes.

South Pass City and Atlantic City both owe their existence, what there is left of it, to the gold rush. Atlantic City almost died in the 1950s, when, with just two permanent residents, it was officially declared a ghost town. Now, thanks to renewed mining interest in the area—iron, this time—about fifty people live here, but most of them don't stay year-round.

The dream of lifting a tin plate and unearthing a golden nugget lives on in the West, and every once in a while someone tries his luck in Willow Creek. Steve introduced us to a man who had panned streams from one end of the West to the other looking for gold. "You go where the old-timers went," he told us. "And then you look some more. They didn't find it all." The old-timers found gold in South Pass City, and so had he. He pulled out a small glass vial, about the size of a test tube. It was half filled with fine-grained black sand. "There's gold in there," he told us, "gold from this creek right here." We could feel the excitement as we took the vial and looked closely: Gold! From the stream right here; a tiny speck, no larger than a grain of sand. But unmistakably, inarguably, gold. And there's more where that came from.

Outside, the rain was still coming down, and Steve said, "You'd never know it was a desert, would you?" No, you wouldn't. Sooner or later, we needed to figure out where we were going to spend the night, but there was no rush: We were comfortable and content in the restaurant, lulled into a feeling of well-being. I wouldn't have much minded just throwing up the tent off the road somewhere, but Steve had a different idea.

"Normally, I'd invite you to stay at my place," he said, "but my kids are all visiting, they're in town for a wedding this weekend. I was thinking, though, that I could drive you in to Lander: We've got some motels, and then tomorrow morning, when I come back out here, I can pick you up.''

Which is how we arrived in Lander an hour or so later. Steve drove us down the main street of town, pointing out hotels on the way.

"Look," he said, passing the third motel without stopping. "You probably want to think about where you want to stay, so why don't you come back to the house, have a beer, make a few calls, and decide what you want to do? You can just take the car and go where you want. Be back in time for breakfast— say, around nine o'clock."

As we left Steve's house and headed for town, Dan and I both looked at each other and said, "Wait a minute," at the same time.

"What's this guy's last name?" said Dan.

"Green, I think."

"Are we sure we know which house is his and how to get back to it?" We turned around and took a good look at the house and the street name. "Okay, now let's just make sure we know how to get back here."

Dan started pretending he was talking to a policeman. "Yes, sir, I'm trying to return this car and I need some help. My name is Smith. I'm from New York. We just walked here from Mexico, and we borrowed this car from a guy named Steve. Don't know his last name, but he lives over behind the school somewhere."

The next morning—after successfully returning the car and filling up on a western breakfast of biscuits and gravy—we headed back to South Pass City.

To look at what's left of it now, you'd never know that this had once been a busy, thriving community, the second oldest town in the territory, the first seat of Sweetwater County, and a candidate to become capital of Wyoming—until the Union Pacific chose a more southerly route, through Cheyenne and Rawlins.

South Pass owed its boom years to gold, discovered by Pacific-bound emigrants. In 1867, the first mines were opened. A year later, buildings stretched for half a mile on either side of Main Street. Today, most of the buildings are long gone, but about twenty-five of the original structures, made of log, frame, or stone, have been painstakingly reconstructed.

You would need the trained eye of an archaeologist to see where the more than 250 buildings once stood. Fortunately for us, there was an archaeologist on hand: Dan Walker, who works at the site. When we met him, he was crouched over a few beams in the earth, dabbing at them with fine-bristled brushes. Beside him was a detailed chart, some string, and a camera, and we chatted with him while he waited for the sun to go behind a cloud so he could photograph the floor of the old City Hotel.

The foundations of South Pass City's buildings are mostly made of rock piles that did little more than keep the buildings off the grass. They extend, Dan told us, to the top of the hill, although most of them have been covered by the earth. South Pass City is a state park now, and the state is responsible for identifying all the historic features in the area and then going about the process of restoring and stabilizing them. It's a big job, Dan told us: Remains from every cultural period in Wyoming's history have been found here, beginning with the late Paleo-Indians of 8,000 years ago. In addition to the physical remains of the buildings and artifacts that have been found, Dan relies on old photographs, records, and documents.

South Pass City is a reassuringly serious historic site, developed for tourists only in that there are brochures available and volunteers who work in the living history program to give demonstrations and answer questions. Steve Green was back in his blacksmith shop making fireplace tools; outside, a cowboy was wandering about on horseback, answering questions and reciting cowboy poetry. But aside from, perhaps, the poetry, South Pass has no gimmicks: no fake Indian jewelry to buy, no genuine souvenir gold rush T-shirts, no "pan-your-own-stream" concessions.

Dan Walker pointed us to the building that houses a collection of old photographs of the town and its notable citizens. One of them was Esther Morris, the first female justice of the peace in the entire United States. Local historians will tell you that the idea of women's suffrage originated right here in South Pass City, and indeed, Wyoming was both the first territory and the first state to pass women's suffrage legislation.

As for Esther Morris: She served a term as justice of the peace for eight months, and tried twenty-six cases. Frank Leslie's *Illustrated Newspaper* was on hand to record the historic event of her swearing in: "Mrs. Esther Morris, one of the new justices of the peace in Wyoming, is 57 years old," the paper noted. "On the first court day, she wore a calico gown, worsted breakfast shawl, green ribbons in her hair, and a green necktie."

N

MONTANA

WYOMING

YELLOWSTONE
NATIONAL PARK

OLD FAITHFUL

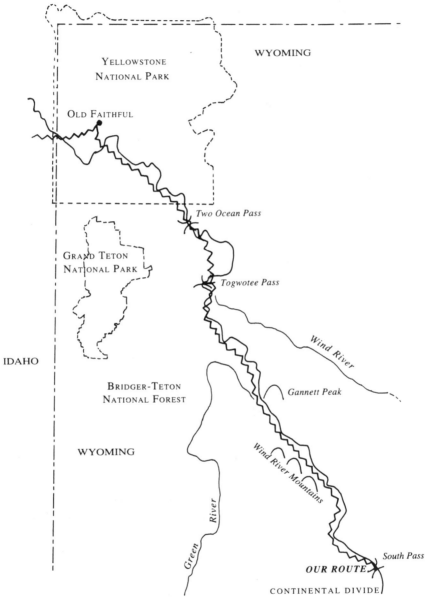

Two Ocean Pass

GRAND TETON
NATIONAL PARK

Togwotee Pass

Wind River

IDAHO

Gannett Peak

BRIDGER-TETON
NATIONAL FOREST

Wind River Mountains

WYOMING

Green River

South Pass

OUR ROUTE

CONTINENTAL DIVIDE

8

≋

GLACIERS, GEYSERS, AND GRIZZLIES

≋

While we had been meandering around the arc of the Great Basin's Atlantic Rim, autumn had come to the high country. It caught us as we left South Pass City to begin our climb from the Sweetwater River up to the Wind River Mountains.

The mountains had been growing larger on the horizon for several days. First, they were hazy purple outlines, then they grew into distinct bumps; finally, they became a severe perpendicular wall. Obvious, now, was why the settlers had chosen their dry hot route through South Pass. For them, the mountains were no haven of beauty; they were, instead, frightening obstacles to be avoided as quickly and completely as possible. The gentle, wagon-accessible climb up to the Divide at South Pass gave them a way to do just that.

For us, the mountains were the next destination.

But if our route veered from the path of our emigrant predecessors, our thoughts and concerns remained in tandem with theirs. Of primary concern to them, and to us, was the possibility of an early winter. The clear, hot afternoons mocked this newest thought with all the power of a sun still convinced of its divine right to rule. Only when the temperatures took their nightly plummet toward the freezing point did the possibility of winter become more and suddenly plausible.

From South Pass City, we climbed to the northwest, and only a slight gain in elevation made the difference between sunburned sagebrush flats and cool stands of lodgepole pine. There were aspen, too: with white trunks stark against the black earth of a recent burn and quivering pale green leaves that sounded like rustling taffeta petticoats. A couple of hundred feet above us, on the ridges, we could see more aspen; it was a degree or two colder there, and the leaves were already shimmering gold. The climb had made the difference between summer and fall.

The change of seasons caused a shift in our thinking, a shift both fundamental and permanent. A small matter of hours had put the basin behind us: No longer would we concern ourselves with heat and water and where to find a spot of shade. From here on, when we looked at the sky, we would be searching for the stern iron-colored clouds of a north country winter. For although autumn had not even officially been declared, we knew that it is the nature of the high country that once August yields to September, winter can begin whenever it wants to.

Our world changed quickly as we climbed. By evening of the second day we were camped at Little Sandy Lake, surrounded by trees, cliffs, and the sparkling diamond air of a montane evening. Despite its name, Little Sandy is a rather large body of clear water, tinged with the deep dark green that betrays glacial origins. Nor is there any sand: To the contrary, vertiginous cliffs end abruptly in the lake's still waters. It is an apt introduction to the rugged drama of the Wind River Mountains.

The far side of the lake is encircled by 1,000-foot-high granite walls. Younger, softer rock once covered the region, but it's gone now, eroded by forces much stronger than mere rock. In its place is the older, sterner stuff that once lay below. It is a rough rock, hard and dependable, the kind that won't crumble under a piton or collapse under shifting weight; a grippable rock that provides the rough-edged security of toeholds and fingerholds in its nooks and crannies. And all of this marvelously tactile granite is sculpted on a grand, acrophobic scale, which is exactly why the Winds are such an obvious and favorite haunt of rock climbers.

From the base of these mountains, looking up, the granite appears permanent and invincible. In the brief wink of human time, perhaps it is—even in the ponderous scale of geologic time, the rock is old: two billion years, give or take a few millennia. Still, there is process here, and change. The mountains have been shaped, and are still being shaped, by wind, water, snow, and ice. This is one of the few places in the contiguous United States where significant glaciers still linger, probably left over from the last ice age, still carving and sculpting. The rock and the ice are engaged in a titan's classic slow-motion war. On one side: immovable mountains. On the other: irresistible glaciers. Curving cirques, sparkling tarns, and scoured-out valleys are their battlefields, terminal moraines and scarification the wounds. And if you doubt that the mountains are being torn down in front of you, right now as you sit watching, just look down into any milky, sediment-filled glacial stream. You will see bits and pieces of the mountaintops being carried away right before your eyes.

Ultimately, if the earth lasts that long, these mountains will succumb to erosion, getting smaller at some unimaginably small rate of a fraction of an inch per year. At that rate, the glaciers will have to rely on wind and rain to finish the job, for the mighty ice fields are themselves mortal, and at current reckoning it seems certain that the mountains will outlast them—certainly if the rate of glacial recession continues as it has in this century. The glaciers of the Winds are the largest group in the contiguous United States, but, like most of the world's large glacier systems, they are shrinking.

〰〰〰

From Little Sandy Lake, a Forest Service trail sign points to Big Sandy Lake, some 11 miles away. The sign was a promising fiction. Not far beyond, the trail disappeared, a casualty of rock slides and mud slides. That the sign was still there, pointing the way to a trail that went nowhere, seemed more a matter of Forest Service indifference than anything else—certainly, it wouldn't have cost anything for the Forest Service to remove it.

The route up to Temple Pass was a tedious, ankle-twisting clutter of rocks and debris. But as always, the mountains offered compensation in the form of views that made irritation impossible to sustain. And to be fair, even without a trail, we couldn't get lost: We would have had a better chance of losing our way through a tunnel. To the west, a slope rose steeply enough to confine us to the valley floor, and to the east was the Continental Divide itself, a dramatic, crooked range that had been uplifted to look as though it was leaning into the wind. Dominating the skyline was Wind River Peak; in front of us were the Temple Peaks, with our destination, the pass between them, smack in front of us. The only obvious way to go was the right one: straight up. It took all morning to walk the 6 miles to the top.

At the head of the valley, the trail considerately reappeared, just in time to whisk us up over the 11,500-foot pass, notable because it was the highest point on our route from here to the Canadian border. That bit of information, however, was mitigated by the fact that we still had 1,000 miles of walking ahead. This was not the homestretch yet—not by a long way.

Downhill from the pass was a small glacier, full of dirt and grit, clinging to its side of the mountain as though determined to scour out the last erodible bits of rock before surrendering to gravity. We paused to take in the austere beauty in front of us: a monochromatic palette of grayish white glacier and grayish brown scree, with silver-gray pinnacles poking upward to a gray-blue sky. Ahead of us, we could see the famous Cirque of the Towers, a rock climber's paradise—and a photographer's, too—where a wall of sheer peaks encircles a rounded valley, making a sort of gothic amphitheater for giants.

The trail set off optimistically downhill, but it vanished as suddenly as it had appeared. We returned to our maps and compasses to figure out how to get to Big Sandy Lake. The navigating was again easy—guided by a major drainage and a string of lakes—but the forces of nature had been hard at work to turn the trail into an obstacle course. They had succeeded.

Of course, there is always a way to get through nature's debris, or else how do you explain the early mountain men who followed animal paths and Indian trails through the unexplored western wilderness? And for that matter, how do you explain the Indian trails? How, exactly, did Fitzpatrick and Fremont and Bridger find their way with no maps, or with rudimentary scribblings that made the maps sold by the Forest Service look like models of accuracy? And the Indians who were their guides: How did *they* know where to go? The branches that clawed at our arms and legs must have clawed at theirs; the logs that were too low for us to crawl under and too high to climb over would have stymied not only the men but their horses, too. Not to mention the mud that was as slippery as ice, and the steep cliffs that forced us to retreat and find another way down or around them.

When we finally emerged from the mess and stepped out onto the trail at Big Sandy Lake, a Forest Service sign cheerfully pointed the way back toward Little Sandy Lake.

≈≈≈≈≈

Big Sandy Lake is a beautiful lake, clear deep blue and framed by mountains. But there are plenty of other such lakes in the Winds. Big Sandy owes its popularity to the real estate maxim of "location, location, location": It is situated an easy 5-mile walk from the trailhead parking lot, where there is a Forest Service campground and a wilderness lodge. The trail to the Cirque of the Towers goes right along the lake's shoreline. When we arrived, we joined the fray: horsemen leading strings of pack animals loaded with provisions, neon-attired rock climbers grunting under pounds of hardware and coiled rope, and backpackers readjusting the straps of squeaky-clean new gear.

Accessibility plus beauty equals overuse, and overuse equals damage. Such are the simple equations of our twentieth-century wilderness, and you can see them at work at Big Sandy. Take fire rings, for example: pockmarks scattered here and there, sometimes three or four to a campsite, many of them containing burned-out remnants of cans and tinfoil. Then there is the trail itself: worn and rutted through marshy spots and wide as a highway where the ground is hard and smooth. Not all of the damage is visible. A forest ranger, who assured us that she was speaking from firsthand experience, told us that the clear waters of the lake are contaminated with *Giardia*, and the local wildlife has become habituated to human food.

It's one thing when the wildlife that loses its fear of humans is something like a curious jay or an endearing chipmunk. But at Big Sandy, the animal in question was a black bear who had spent the summer learning about the relationship between people and food. Apparently, he had been a good student, because by September the rumors were rife: The bear had stuck its head in a ranger's tent; it had run off with a backpack; it had eaten a week's worth of freeze-dried food. Whether or not the bear had done all of those things was not certain; one thing, however, was: A bear that has lost its fear of humans generally becomes a dead bear. There was already talk among the local outfitters of getting a special permit to shoot it during the hunting season.

We, however, didn't see the bear, or any sign of it, as we passed the lake on our way to Big Sandy Lodge, a wilderness retreat at the end of a gravel road that is one of only five major access routes to the Winds. The people at the lodge had agreed to hold a food package for us, so we took a quick detour to pick up our supplies and spend a day in one of the rustic cabins.

Big Sandy Lodge is a remote place; the road that leads to it is dirt, not paved, and the lodge is open, at the latest, only until November. Sometimes the weather forces it to close much earlier. "The forecasters are always talking about how cold it gets at Yellowstone," Connie Kelly told us. "But that's only because nobody tries to measure the temperatures here." In the winter, the snow here is so deep it completely covers the lodge, and the previous autumn the Kellys had ended their season by racing out on short notice to escape a blizzard that would close the mountains off for the winter.

Our packages were in a big pile near the kitchen. All of our friends, it seemed, had decided to send us parcels at Big Sandy. In addition to the three boxes of food we had shipped to ourselves, there were packages of cookies, dried fruit, and candy—even with our trail appetites, we couldn't consume all of the food. There was also a ten-pound box of maps that Karl had sent for Gordon and Sue. If this had been a normal food drop, we would have been able to share some of the goodies with Gordon and Sue, store extra food in the van, or send unnecessary gear home. But Gordon and Sue weren't here, because they couldn't take the van on the dirt road. A couple from New Jersey were coming to the end of their stay at the lodge; they offered to take our box of extra food, gear, and maps and mail it home for us.

We took a day off at Big Sandy—the only guests. Because our arrival was unannounced, and the owners had already made plans to spend the day in town, we were left in the care of the camp wrangler, who was charged with fixing dinner for us. His job was to defreeze and reheat a casserole that Connie had prepared in advance, and he was clearly nervous about the outcome. "I've never cooked a meal before," he admitted as he pulled the dinner from the oven, somewhat surprised that Connie's directions—to set the thermostat at 350 and let the casserole bake for an hour—had worked.

Without the distractions of town—telephones, televisions, stores, restaurants—our time at Big Sandy passed deliciously slowly. We washed our clothes in the lodge's big utility sink and hung them to dry near the wood-burning stove in our cabin. We also washed our tent to remove any food odors, since in a few days we would be walking through grizzly bear country. And, of course, we washed ourselves. But mostly we just rested, enjoying the fact that rain was falling on our cabin, not on our tent, and that we could read late into the night under the soft yellow light of an old oil lamp.

<hr>

From Big Sandy, the Highline Trail continues north, and the only obstacle to following it is its name. As far as we could tell, there used to be a Highline Trail and a Lowline Trail, but the old Highline Trail is now the Fremont Trail, and the Lowline Trail is now the new Highline Trail. The maps are as confused as anyone else, and it doesn't help that the nomenclature put in place by the most recent forest plan has by no means been adopted by either the local citizens or, in some cases, the Forest Service signposts, both of which sometimes use the old and new names interchangeably. No matter, the two trails go roughly to the same place, and both of them demonstrate firsthand why the Winds are so popular. Although the altitude is a heady 10,000 feet or so, the hiking is actually quite gentle (at least by comparison to Colorado) and the views are spectacular. We followed the trail downvalley, past a string of cold, quiet lakes.

Cross Lake is one of these lakes, sitting amid open uplands with a backdrop of the Divide. On the south side, there is a Forest Service cabin, which we had learned about from the wrangler at Big Sandy Lodge. The cabin was unlocked, and we went inside to explore. A handwritten note tacked to the door warned whoever used the cabin to repackage food and secure door latches to keep the animals out of the instant rice, dried soups, hot cocoa, Tang, flour, and other supplies that various groups of hikers and Forest Service staff had left behind. Another note told Forest Service rangers to leave the door unlocked so the cabin would be available to the public. It was an invitation to spend the night in primitive splendor.

For a night, we could imagine ourselves early settlers, protected from the mountains by sturdy wooden walls, our provisions stored in neatly carpentered cabinets or hung from the ceiling in cleverly designed mouseproof contraptions. The fantasy was pleasant, if historically inaccurate: At 10,000 feet in the Wind River Mountains, Cross Lake is snowbound ten months out of the year, and even the land-hungry western settlers had no use for the area beyond summer range for livestock. We cooked our dinner on a wood-burning stove, which heated the entire cabin, and then sat outside to watch purple mountains fading into a darkening sky and starlight reflecting in the still lake below us.

The next morning, we cleaned away any trace of our visit and walked on to Raid Lake. We could hear a bleating, moaning chorus that carried on the wind blowing up the valley. At the lake, we finally identified the source of the commotion: a herd of hundreds, maybe more than a thousand, sheep that were wallowing through an outlet stream.

In the basin, we had come to appreciate the stockman's side of the grazing debate. For one thing, cattle and sheep had signified water. For another, we had been seduced by the openhearted ranchers and their life-style. We had also come to understand the very legitimate concerns they had about environmental purists who wanted not to work with them but to get rid of them. Livestock had come to seem somehow appropriate down there, part of the land and its history, part of a life-style that was honest, out-of-doors, self-reliant. Against this spectacle, this living American legend, the litany of environmental complaints against public lands grazing sounded impotent and mean-spirited.

But here in the mountains, we looked into the murky stream and remembered what we didn't like about sheep and cattle. The high country—grand, remote, and rare—was a place for soaring birds and soaring spirits. This was wilderness, damn it, and the sheep and cattle were a desecration, as appropriate among these great granite walls as they would have been in a church. The Wind River Mountains deserved better than to be used as mere pasture.

Our feelings notwithstanding, we were stuck with our four-footed nemeses. For if the settlers had shunned the high country, the ranchers knew a good summer pasture when they saw it. In the Winds, where grazing is about as old as settlement, the sheep and cattle have squatters' rights.

To its credit, the Forest Service has terminated or redrawn a few grazing allotments to better accommodate recreational use. As usual, the compromise position satisfied neither side. While the Forest Service trumpets the modifications as an example of its sensitivity to recreational needs, wilderness users want the cows and sheep out of wilderness, period. At the same time, the ranchers bitterly complain that the Wilderness Act takes away public land from local interests and turns it into a playground for out-of-state vacationers— a designation that obliquely refers to the ever-suspect group of Californian and East Coast environmentalists.

The argument about grazing allotments has united two longtime foes: cattlemen and sheepmen. The range in the Winds has been a subject of contention between the two since the first woolies took a bite of sweet spring grass, and you can still see the historic tensions flare up when a cattleman confides that it's "sheep that do the real damage, grazing close to the ground, and cutting the soil with their sharp little hooves."

Back in the early days, no one was talking about resource damage or overgrazing or allotments or grazing fees; the fight was over territory, pure and simple. With all the swaggering of a schoolyard bully, cattlemen would trace a line in the dirt: Sheepmen, take note, and keep your herds on this side of a creek or that side of a mountain ridge. The line was, so to speak, crossed when fifteen sheep meandered through the North Fork of the Green River. If we had camped in this high valley in 1903, our peaceful night under a zillion stars would have been rent with the chaos of an all-out western range war. One hundred and fifty men rode in with a single purpose: to rid the range of the cursed sheep. They did, too: More than 1,000 sheep were killed—and one herder, as well. Raid Lake was named in commemoration of the event.

No sign now, of course, of thundering horsemen and bloodstained streams, of panicked animals scattering in all directions. Nor of the hordes of scavengers—the keening coyotes and sharp-eyed ravens—that must have descended upon the carnage. The mountains are as they were; both sheep and cattle graze here in the summers. The cattle run in front of you on the trail—sometimes for miles—galloping a few steps, then turning back with wild-eyed panic to see if you are still there. And you can hear the sheep: huge herds bleating in a chorus that, distorted by distance and reverberations against mountain walls, sounds like a stadium of people cheering.

≈≈≈≈≈≈≈

The end of the Winds comes rather suddenly. At Green River Pass, the trail turns downhill, following the river as it runs temporarily northward, draining the western slope glaciers of Wyoming's highest peaks. This frothy, raging torrent of ice-cold water will never see an ocean: Before it reaches the mouth of the Gulf of California, it will join the mighty Colorado, and the green waters will become rusty red. Like the rest of the Colorado River system, the Green River will be a working river—only in a wet year will any of its water reach the sea.

But here, in the Winds, it is still an unfettered adolescent, blissfully ignorant of the demands of its future. It rushes headlong over boulders until the land becomes gentler and wider lower down, near the base of the mountains; then it slows to a meandering stroll. Downstream, the river passes through two big scenic lakes, complete with dramatic mountain backdrops and rich wildlife: When we walked past, a family of moose were grazing on lake-bottom grasses with their heads under water. The river then makes a turn to the south, but our route went north, to the open country of the Bridger-Teton National Forest.

Here, the land regains its horizontal orientation. The sky-scraping peaks of the Winds give way to softer, rounder mountains. The gray of upcountry granite yields to the green of timbered slopes, punctuated by aspen groves so purely golden that you might fancy for a moment that a patch of sunlight has taken physical form. The creekbeds are choked with willow, and they, too, wear an autumn wardrobe, also golden, but of a much deeper hue.

The Bridger-Teton National Forest is back in the domain of multiple use, and it was immediately clear to us that some uses are more equal than others. Grazing and timbering, for instance, as opposed to recreation. There were plenty of perfectly good logging roads, but the foot trails were in such bad shape that there was barely a trace of them. Our 1988 map assured us that we were on trail, occasional ax blazes on the trees told us that we were in the right place, but there was no sign of a footway under our feet. With wooded, low hills and gentle, open grasslands, the terrain made for time-consuming compass work. We continually revised our route by trying to figure out which trails—or even which jeep roads—might have a prayer of existing. The road we were presently following along Fish Creek had been all but razed by a landslide, and at one point it ended at the head of a lake that didn't even appear on our maps. The lake was only a couple of years old—mere seconds in geologic time—formed when the unstable rocks that line the hills on either side of the creek had slid into the water, forming a dam.

When recreation does figure into the multiple-use equation, it's high-priced outfitter recreation: Heli-skiing and snowmobiling are popular in the winter; river rafting, packhorse trips, llama trips, and mountain bike tours run in the summer months. In early September, the big business is hunting. Forest Service literature claims this region as one of the best hunting grounds in the United States; certainly it is one of the most crowded. We shared the forest with outfitters gearing up for the fall migration of flatlanders willing to pay a couple of thousand dollars for the chance to kill something big.

If you are going to spend a couple of thousand dollars for a week in the backcountry, you are going to expect a few amenities. Not for you a dinner of aluminum-wrapped freeze-dried shrimp creole, or some similar, promisingly named entrée of unidentifiable ingredients—nor are you going to carry it in on your own back. Not to worry: The outfitters are prepared, and if you're looking for comfort in the backcountry, this is definitely the way to do it. On one forest road, we followed a miniature Conestoga wagon laden with supplies, pulled by two mules and driven by a man who appeared to have just walked off the set of "Gunsmoke." For a couple of thousand dollars, you get some local color, too.

In the Teton Wilderness north of Togwotee Pass it was pack trains, not Conestoga wagons, that brought in the iron cookpots and canvas tents and fresh foods for the hunting camps. Here, in contrast to the national forest just to the south, the trails were plenty easy to find and to follow. Early westerners described this country as impenetrable, but today's weekend mountain men have no such problems. The trails are so overused that they have been turned into a series of a dozen or more parallel tracks worn into narrow ruts, a highway-sized swath of hoofprints gouged through the marshy ground.

As we followed the trail—or rather, trails—north, toward Two Ocean Pass, it seemed that the land was doomed to become an eroded eyesore. The land needs a chance to heal, but for that it will need time. The forest issues about 600 special use permits and 200 outfitter licenses, many of them for wilderness areas, where recreation is the primary use permitted. Any attempt to restrict long-established commercial outfitters adds fuel to the fire that already rages against taking land out of the cycle of production, use, and profit. Besides, the ruts don't pose any particular problem to horsemen, who can let the stock worry about which one to follow. There are plenty of choices as you make your way to Two Ocean Pass, up to the place where the Divide parts the waters of Two Ocean Creek, and on north to the high plateau that is America's most beloved landscape.

≈≈≈≈≈

Yellowstone!

For most people, Yellowstone is, sight-unseen, a place of magic, and it has been a place of magic since rumors of its wonders began drifting about in the early nineteenth century. The images of Yellowstone are national icons. People who have never been there know exactly what it looks like: gushing geysers, habituated bears, herds of buffalo, the Grand Canyon of the Yellowstone, mud volcanoes, Mammoth Hot Springs, Old Faithful. The park sits securely on America's collective mental map of great places.

It has not always been so. John Colter, of the Lewis and Clark Expedition, was the first white man to set foot in Yellowstone, and he didn't arrive here until 1807. Nor did his reports generate much interest; they were roundly dismissed as a pack of lies. Mountain man Jim Bridger was next—and his reports did include a pack of lies, as well as a good deal of truth. But who could know which was which? The glass mountains? The bubbling mud pots? The spouting geysers? What about the "peetrified forests," with "peetrified birds singing peetrified songs"? Later, more reports dribbled in from this last unexplored region of the contiguous forty-eight states, but they continued to be disbelieved. One aspiring journalist failed to publish his account of the journey; the magazine to which he submitted his article responded, "Sorry, we don't print fiction."

Not until 1870 was the park explored, and its wonders moved the men of the Washburn Party to propose that it be withdrawn as a park, excluded as a settlement, and protected for all time—a remarkable suggestion from men who could have filed claims and set up businesses that would exploit the region's wonders. In 1872, President Ulysses S. Grant signed the law the made Yellowstone America's first national park.

Today, of course, we believe the unbelievable: We know Yellowstone as a place of geologic wonders and magnificent wildlife. It looms as large in our national iconography as Versailles does to a Frenchman or the Pyramids do to an Egyptian. Indeed, it has been designated a World Heritage Site by UNESCO—along with Versailles, the Pyramids, and a handful of other natural and cultural sites chosen for their outstanding universal value. With its wildlife, its beauty, its diversity, its mountains, its canyons, and all of its thermal spectacles, Yellowstone represents the abundance and the wonder of the American landscape. This is our Versailles.

Yellowstone has also been designated—again, by UNESCO—as a World Biosphere Reserve, along with more than 200 other areas worldwide. World Biosphere Reserves are selected because they are outstanding examples of major ecosystems and their components; the program seeks to maintain as much as possible of the world's genetic diversity by protecting these areas. UNESCO has developed a program that manages ecosystems by surrounding them with a series of concentric circles to act as buffer zones between the critical ecosystem and the pressures of development. The inner circle is the area to be protected. The next circle is a zone where development would be permitted only if it was compatible with the goal of park preservation; examples of compatible uses might include limited grazing, selective logging, hunting, or sustainable agriculture. In the next circle, more intense development would be permitted, until, at the outermost circles, development might include more intrusive, high-impact activities such as mining or residential real estate development. Unfortunately, in Yellowstone's case, administrative boundaries were drawn up long before UNESCO came up with its concentric circles—long before, even, the idea of ecosystems was even partially understood. Today, those trying to protect Yellowstone as a haven for wildlife must compete with proponents of other resource uses, ranging from gold mining to geothermal developments to ski resorts to snowmobile trails. Not everyone, it seems, has the vision of the gentlemen of the 1870 Washburn Party.

That Yellowstone would be chosen a World Biosphere is ironic because Yellowstone, in the early years of exploration and discovery, was not initially a particularly noteworthy area for wildlife. The plateau has some of the coldest winters on earth, and animals find better winter range in the warmer valleys. Early reports are full of complaints about the lack of game. It wasn't until areas surrounding the park became more and more populated and developed that large herds of wildlife retreated to the park.

Over the following years, mistakes were made. Poaching was rampant. To cut costs, employees were fed meat from elk, deer, sheep, and bison that had been killed in the park. Park Service staff—like just about everyone else in the West—systematically trapped and hunted predators, leading to huge increases in ungulate populations. But today, the Park Service pursues a rigorous philosophy of natural management and noninterference in an attempt to allow the ecosystem to run itself according to its own cycles. Meanwhile, some critics charge that years of mismanagement and interference have created a hopelessly unnatural system that desperately does need active management by informed ecologists. And, while scientists and politicians—not to mention local interests, park managers, and environmentalists—argue over the answers, the fate of some of America's threatened species hangs in the balance. Today, we might debate whether Yellowstone was originally a rich wildlife habitat. But we cannot debate that it is and must remain so today: Yellowstone is one of the last places in America that can support some of our rarest and most endangered species.

≈≈≈≈≈≈

With all of this wonder—with the abundance of wildlife, the thermal features, the canyons and mountains—that awaited us in Yellowstone, we should have been excited. Instead, we were worried. Because for long-distance hikers, another feature of Yellowstone comes to mind first: the park's permit system.

At Yellowstone—as in most national parks—a backcountry permit is required to camp or, indeed, to even carry hiking gear in the park. While the national parks along the routes of other National Scenic Trails have developed policies to aid long-distance hikers—by allowing them, for example, to write for permits in advance or to pick up self-issuing permits while on route—no such efforts have been made on the Continental Divide.

Once you get a Yellowstone permit, you are restricted to a specific, numbered backcountry campsite, and if you camp someplace other than your assigned spot—say you're lost, or tired, or hypothermic, or you simply like some other place and want to camp there— you're in violation of the rules, for which you can be both fined and hauled into court. So much for the freedom of the great outdoors.

On a scale of criminal activities, failing to get a backcountry permit ranks, in most hikers' opinions, somewhere below getting a parking ticket. Unfortunately for hikers, this attitude is not shared by the national park bureaucracy, which goes about the business of enforcing its regulations with the high-minded tunnel vision of a fundamentalist missionary. The stories from parks all over the country are legion, and we had heard plenty of them from friends who have been fined, escorted out of parks, and, in one case, threatened with arrest for such offenses as camping with a dog, kayaking a river without a companion, and neglecting to pick up a reserved permit. Not wanting the hassle of being found permitless in the presence of the law, we decided to be good citizens and acquire for ourselves a Yellowstone backcountry camping permit.

Accordingly, we had begun our quest three weeks in advance, back at our Sweetwater Station food drop, from where we called the South Entrance Ranger Station at Yellowstone.

A young ranger took our call. Our conversation went like clockwork: I said the word *permit*; he responded with a memorized spiel. The bottom line: "You have to come in forty-eight hours ahead, and you have to come in person."

"I know that." I had decided to take a we're-all-reasonable-people-and-we-know-you're-going-to-help-us-out attitude. "But we have a problem. We can't come in person."

"You can't come in person," the ranger repeated, instantly wary.

"No. That's why we're calling. See, we're on foot. We're hiking the Continental Divide Trail."

"The what?"

"The Continental Divide National Scenic Trail."

There was a pause.

"I don't know what that is."

That took a while to sink in. Admittedly, the CDT is a pretty arcane undertaking, and we had gotten used to explaining ourselves and our journey to the people we met on the way. But a Yellowstone ranger was something different: Yellowstone is a national park, it is bisected by the Divide, and Congress passed a law designating a national scenic trail along the Continental Divide. We knew that the proposed route cuts across the park, and we knew that park administrators had attended plenty of planning meetings for the trail—we'd seen reports of those meetings in the CDTS newsletter.

I explained what the trail was, and I explained that we had walked up from Mexico—pausing to enjoy the usual disbelief that accompanied the boast—and that we were trying to follow the Divide as closely as possible all the way to Canada. And I described the route through Yellowstone, which follows existing trails up the Snake River, past Heart, Shoshone, and Summit lakes, and then out the west side of the park via the Madison Plateau.

Fortunately, the ranger was an outdoorsperson himself (while this may seem like a truism, it is not), and he seemed genuinely interested in our trip. We chatted a while before getting back to the matter at hand.

"We can't come in person because there are no ranger stations anywhere remotely near our route." I said. "The trailhead near Togwotee Pass is more than fifty miles from the South Entrance. There are no other roads near our route, and from that trailhead, it's a fifty-mile walk to the first campsite in the park. It's not possible for us to come two days in advance in person, because we can't hitchhike one hundred miles and walk fifty miles in two days."

It was also not possible to get a permit after we entered the park. From where our route crossed the park boundary, it was 26 trail miles to a road, then several more miles, on the road, to the nearest ranger station; moreover, hitchhiking was illegal in the park. Assuming you were able to walk the 26 miles and assuming that someone just happened to offer you a ride to and from the ranger station, you'd still have another 5 miles of walking before you reached the first possible campsite in from the road. And that all assumed that, at the very end of a very long day, a campsite remained available in what just happened to be the most popular backcountry spot in the entire park.

We didn't plan to find out. Walking the length of the United States requires a stubborn streak, and ours surfaced here: We weren't going to walk 31 miles, or even 26 miles, to get a park permit. It was just too far.

"We can't do it," I said, and there was no argument from the ranger: He couldn't have done it either.

After trying for a few minutes to alter our hike to fit the Procrustean permit system, the ranger came to the same conclusion that we had: The hike was perfectly legal, and there was no way to get a permit to do it.

"The problem is," he said, in notable understatement, "that you're on foot."

The only possibility was to have the permit issued over the phone.

That, however, was against policy. I started to feel like I was reading a script from a sequel to *Catch-22*.

"Look," I said, "there has to be a way of doing this: This is a national scenic trail, and it passes through a national park. The trail is designed for hikers. There is a trail system in the wilderness, and it connects to Yellowstone's trail system. It has to be possible to hike on it. . . ."

The ranger agreed: It was time to bring in a supervisor.

Fortunately, one was on hand. It took a host of progressively higher level rangers (this permit business is serious stuff) and several phone calls, but an hour or so later I was issued the precious permit, along with ten minutes of instructions on what to do and what not to do in grizzly bear country. I returned in triumph to Dan, who had been trying to place bets on the outcome with Gordon and Sue—a process that was hampered by the fact that no one in the group wanted to wager on our success.

I wrote down the permit number, and told Dan about the grizzly bears—specifically, that the trail we wanted to take was currently closed because a sow with three cubs had charged a ranger.

"Three cubs?" he repeated.

"Yup."

"Great. What are we supposed to do if the trail is still closed when we get there?"

"There's a roughly parallel trail we can take."

"How far away is it?"

"Not too far. It circles around the other side of a ridge, but it goes to about the same place in the same number of miles."

"I wonder who's going to tell the bear which side of the ridge to stay on."

"Maybe she'll read the signs."

That had been back at Sweetwater Station: coyote and jackrabbit country. It takes no great courage to joke about grizzly bears when the nearest one is 100 miles away.

≈≈≈≈≈

Ursus arctos horribilis. Even if you knew nothing about grizzly bears, their name might give you pause. We stopped joking somewhere in the Bridger-Teton National Forest.

Placards hung at the trailheads announcing our entry into "occupied grizzly habitat" and warning that if we didn't hang our food properly, we could be subject to a fine from the rangers (or, presumably, worse from the grizzlies). Grizzlies, the signs said, had the right-of-way—and who would argue with that? A Forest Service ranger told us that despite several years of signs and public education, 90 percent of visitors didn't take appropriate precautions in bear country. And then there were our fellow backcountry travelers—

hunters, pickup truck drivers, outfitters, and such—who may have been among that 90 percent, but couldn't resist the urge to describe the dangers ahead in lurid detail.

The stories were the same kinds of tall tales we had been hearing since the Mexican border. The rattlesnakes in New Mexico; the lightning in Colorado; the heat in the Great Divide Basin. Now, it was the bears. Everyone we met had a bear story, and every bear story was a grizzly bear story.

Dan and I had plenty of our own bear stories, but the bears in our adventures had always been black bears. Only Dan had ever seen a grizzly in the wild, and his grizzly didn't give him much of a story, since all it did was look up from the stream where it had been drinking, sniff the air, and amble away. Still, that was enough for Dan, who expressed the opinion that one grizzly in a lifetime was enough, and he'd just as soon not meet another on this or any future trip.

As for me, I had learned everything I ever wanted to know about grizzly bears from *Reader's Digest*. I had devoured the "Drama in Real Life" stories as a child, and somewhere in the back of my mind that child still lived: Grizzlies—along with sharks—were the terrorizing lords of the wild, eight feet tall, with four-inch claws, too big to fight and as unpredictably merciless as a bolt of lightning. Since reading the gruesome descriptions of innocent campers being ripped from their tents in places like Yellowstone and Glacier national parks, I had wanted nothing to do with grizzly country. How was it, I tried to remember, that I now found myself preparing to walk through what would turn out to be several hundred miles of it?

At first, the stories we heard were reassuringly secondhand. The yarn spinners had not seen the bears themselves; it was a friend, or a cousin, or a neighbor who lived in some vaguely identified place down the road who "seen one following him up the trail."

But as we walked farther north, the stories changed. Sometimes there was a casual "Oh, yeah, I've seen 'em around here"; sometimes there was a step-by-step description of a particular encounter.

"I wouldn't go walking in there," a man told us, just south of the Teton Wilderness. "Horseback, yeah; they usually don't attack a horse. But you wouldn't catch me in there on foot." He was loading firewood into his truck, and our conversation had turned, after the usual introductions, to the bears. Only this story had a different ending: The man had shot the bear. Self-defense, he said. After a pause, he allowed that it might not technically have been self-defense. He didn't sound happy about it, but he didn't sound sorry either. Killing a grizzly was just the way it was.

It happened hunting, he told us, packing out of the woods with a fresh-killed elk. "Had a good rack," he said. "So I was carrying the head. There was me on my horse, then the horse carrying the carcass. I felt something crawling on the back of my neck—you know how you can tell when something is behind you? Hell, I knew it was a grizzly before I even turned around. And there he was, just following behind the second horse, walking down the trail like he belonged with us. I didn't have to wait to find out what that bear had in mind. . . . Didn't report the shooting, though. All that damn paperwork—there's a fine if they say it's not self-defense. On account of the endangered species business. You folks packing a gun?"

We weren't.

He shook his head. "Be careful out there."

Other folks added to our bear lore with advice. Go upwind so the bear knows you're there, or go downwind so he doesn't. Make a lot of noise so he hears you, or be quiet and observant so you see him first. Stand your ground so he retreats or act submissive so he doesn't regard you as a threat. Drop your pack to distract a charging bear, or don't because it will only reward him and make him that much more dangerous to the next hiker. (If you were about to be charged by a bear, would you be thinking about the next hiker?)

Various people—usually middle-aged men in pickup trucks—offered warnings about how menstruation and sexual activity attract bears, but they sounded more matter-of-fact than offensive: Just something you should know, ma'am. While researchers haven't been able to figure out whether or not bears are attracted by either factor, folklore has no doubts on the subject.

The ranger at Yellowstone had given us instructions, too; and on top of that, Gordon and Sue had clipped a revisionist article from an outdoor magazine that purported to set the record straight—and, predictably, contradicted most of the folklore and some of the standard ranger-issued warnings, too.

We had the basics down: Cook and eat well away from the tent area and hang food bags out of reach of ursine curiosity. We knew we were supposed to stay away from sows with cubs or food sources like berry patches or carrion, although how this avoidance was to be accomplished was not clear; hiking trails pass through berry patches and bears camouflage their food caches under piles of leaves and dirt.

And above all, we knew we were not supposed to run, not ever. If a charge appears imminent, the ranger had said to climb a tree. This was not reassuring: The monocultural stands of lodgepole pine were approximately as climbable as your average telephone pole. Unfortunately, we weren't any more enamored of the other option: curling up into a fetal position and letting the bear have its way. (The idea here was that the bear might maul you and scare you, but he probably wouldn't kill you.)

After sorting through all the warnings and the advice on what to do when and if, we weren't much better informed than before, but we were a good deal more nervous. Dan brought up a macabre subject.

"I've been thinking," he said. "This isn't very romantic, but we should really discuss what we're going to do if one of us is attacked by a grizzly."

I stared at him. This hadn't been covered in the marriage vows, but it is the unromantic truth that two people against a bear aren't any more effective than one person against a bear. Sobering, to say the least.

"We both know that a grizzly can kill two people just as easily as one," Dan said. "To be blunt, if I'm attacked, don't get any stupid ideas about trying to fight it with your Swiss army knife. Because if it's you that's attacked . . ." He paused. "I'm not going to be able to do anything. And neither one of us should get ourselves killed doing something romantic and suicidal."

He was right, of course. No sense in suicide. How perfectly rational—and how perfectly awful. I looked around, and the forest seemed, for the first time, evil, malignant. Was there a bear behind those trees? For the first time on the walk, I was afraid. And so was Dan.

As usually rational adults, of course, we knew that we were grossly overreacting. Normal grizzly bears do not prey on humans—to the contrary, they go to great lengths to avoid encounters with people. Also, they are listed as a threatened species, and with a population, in

the contiguous states, of less than 1,000, you have to be very lucky—
or unlucky, depending on your point of view—to see one.

Statistically, you are safer sleeping in a tent in grizzly country
than you are riding the New York subway system or even, to make
the comparison less dramatic, driving a car through the park itself.
In the United States, an average of one person per year dies from a
grizzly bear attack; twelve die from beestings, twelve from snake-
bites, and fifty from lightning. To be honest, I don't know about the
New York subway system, but I'm betting it's better than one per
year. In Yellowstone, more people are injured by moose, or by
buffalo, or by falling into hot springs or off of mountains, than they
are by bears. Between 1959 and 1987, 537 bears died in Yellowstone
as a result of encounters with man—that's an average of 30 per year.
A grizzly bear is more likely to be killed than to die of old age, all
of which puts a different spin on the question of who is a danger to whom.

Still, statistics did not calm the lingering child who dwelt in the
back of my mind. There is something sensational about the grizzly:
sensational power, sensational size, sensational strength. And there
is something terribly, inconsolably vulnerable about being a human
in the face of such awesome, uncompromising wildness. All things
considered, I would rather be stung by a bee.

≋

We reached the park boundary at dusk. Our campsite was a flat spot
in a stand of mature lodgepole a few yards from the park border.
Across a clearing a ranger cabin nestled comfortably among a clump
of trees. The door was open; outside, two horses wearing bells and
hobbles grazed in a large open field.

We hung our food away from our tent and walked over to get
some water and chat with the ranger, whose name was Tom. As it
turned out, he had heard about us and our hike and the permit over
the park radio system. "I've been wondering if I'd meet you two,"
he told us, and invited us in for some hot cocoa.

If local residents have their griz stories and we have our park
bureaucracy stories, the rangers have their visitor stories, most of
which seem to revolve around tourists doing something unutterably
stupid (trying to pat a bison, or getting just one snapshot of Mom

and the kids with that cute baby bear) and then suing the Park Service for not giving adequate warning. (You need to be warned that a 2,000-pound wild animal with horns might hurt you?)

Tom assured us that people did, indeed, need not only to be warned, but also policed. "Because of one of these lawsuits, every driver that enters the park gets a bright yellow flyer saying that buffalo are dangerous," he said. "Still, you see tourists chasing them with their cameras."

Our conversation was interrupted by the radio crackling news of a tourist-bison accident. Tom didn't say anything, but his expression spoke volumes: Chances are, the tourist was doing someting stupid. Chances are he'll sue the Park Service.

It is not only the RV crowd that fits the stereotype of the camera-toting, wildlife-chasing car camper from New Jersey or Iowa or some other flatland state. Tom had a few hiker stories, too. "People still don't hang their food," he told us. "Which gets me really angry, because the bears have enough stacked against their survival to begin with. A bear that becomes habituated to human food is a dead bear. Period."

The permit policy, he told us, at least ensures that one member of each party gets a personal lecture about bears. Whether he or she listens is another story. In any event, the battle to keep grizzlies innocent of human food is an uphill one. In Greater Yellowstone, bears have plenty of opportunity not only to sample freeze-dried delicacies but also to dine on hunting remains, horse pellets, domesticated livestock, grain, orchard fruit, and municipal garbage dumps. Inside the park, Yellowstone's management has attempted to establish policies that let natural processes take their course—a laudable goal, most environmentalists would agree—but in doing so, they may have put further pressures on the vulnerable grizzly population. Possibly the most controversial management decision was the 1967 recommendation to close the park's backcountry garbage dumps, in which garbage-addicted bears had been feeding for years. The rationale sounded good: Wild grizzlies should feed on natural grizzly foods, not human garbage. But many critics, including the highly regarded bear researchers Frank and John Craighead, believe that the ecosystem can no longer support a sustainable bear population without supplemental feeding, and that the elimination of this admittedly artificial food supply would lead to both a reduction in grizzly numbers and an increase in human-grizzly confrontations as the grizzlies roam about looking for other sources of food. More than twenty years later, the argument continues.

Just how common are human-grizzly encounters?

"It depends what you mean," Tom told us. "It's not at all uncommon for people to see a bear on the trail. It's pretty rare for people to get hurt, but it does happen. Last week, a couple of hunters were mauled in the Teton Wilderness—you came through there; you might of heard about it?"

We hadn't.

"One of them got between a sow and her cubs, and the sow attacked. The guy's buddy shot the bear, so now there are two orphaned cubs. The grizzly always ends up losing in an encounter with man. Always. And the grizzly population can't sustain those kinds of losses."

Tom's story reminded us of the bear incident on the Snake River Trail, and we asked about the trail's current status.

"It was reopened yesterday," he said. "In fact, the sign that closed it off is probably still there, but you can go on through it."

"I hope someone told the bears."

"Well, they are out there," Tom said. "But there aren't many of them."

No one knows how many. The estimates of North America's grizzly population vary wildly. Most of the bears live in Canada and Alaska, although historically grizzly bears once roamed through almost the entire West. They became extinct in California during the gold rush, and in the Southwest during the 1920s, aided by the predator control act. Wyoming, Idaho, and Montana populations were decimated in the 1940s. In 1982, the Colorado Wildlife Commission unanimously voted *not* to reintroduce grizzlies or the gray wolf into the state. In the contiguous United States, there are only two areas that have significant populations today, and both of them—Yellowstone and Montana's northern Rockies—were on our route.

The grizzly may be strong, fierce, huge, and fast, but this king of the forest needs a big forest for a kingdom. Like the spotted owl, the grizzly is threatened primarily because it needs land—lots of isolated, quiet, undisturbed wilderness. Without it, the bear doesn't reproduce, or reproduces less frequently. And even when they aren't under stress, grizzlies have one of the lowest reproduction rates of any large mammal, raising a litter of cubs once every three years, at most. We humans may not be able to fight, outrun, or tame the grizzly, but we can conquer him nonetheless with housing subdivisions, shopping malls, clearcuts, ranches, and roads.

And while Yellowstone Park is big—humongous, seen through eastern eyes—it is not big enough. Although it is often referred to as the largest essentially intact temperate zone ecosystem left in the world, it is important to realize that the Greater Yellowstone ecosystem comprises not only Yellowstone National Park but the surrounding national forests, wilderness areas, BLM lands, state lands, and private holdings, all of which are managed with different mandates, philosophies, and priorities, and all of which have an effect on what goes on inside the park. By itself, Yellowstone is not big enough to support its population of grizzlies, many of whom wander outside of the park's boundaries in the course of their day-to-day ranging and feeding. Outside, they are no longer protected by the Park Service. While scientists in Yellowstone worriedly examine every death and fret about every nontransmitting radio collar, Montana actually has a hunting season on grizzlies, and poaching is a continuing problem in the national forests surrounding the park.

But by far the biggest threat to the grizzly bear is loss of habitat through development. The maniacal rate of logging in the adjacent Targhee National Forest has all but destroyed grizzly habitat to the west of the park; a hard-rock mining project in the heart of occupied grizzly habitat in the Absaroka Mountains threatens to pollute the headwaters of three Yellowstone River tributaries, one of which flows into the park; and subdivisions for so-called ranchettes interfere with everyone's winter range and travel corridors.

No one was thinking about ecosystems or wildlife or grizzly bears when Yellowstone first entered the national consciousness: It was the thermal wonders that Yellowstone's national park status was supposed to protect. Even after the park was designated, poaching was rampant, and the park's early attempts at wildlife management reflected utter ignorance of how ecosystems work—not surprising, since the concept hadn't even been properly defined yet. In all, it is somewhat miraculous that, with only one exception, every mammal native to the Yellowstone region still exists there, although not necessarily in stable populations. By comparison, Yosemite has lost 25 percent of its mammals since becoming a national park; Rocky Mountain has lost 31 percent; Mount Rainier 32 percent; and Bryce Canyon 36 percent.

Yellowstone has lost only the wolf.

Or has it? Once in a while there's a wolf report, usually unconfirmed and usually unreliable. We had one ourselves, sort of: as unconfirmed and unreliable as the rest of them, but enough to raise the question, in our minds at least.

We had heard it south of the park, early in the morning, a mournful howling that went on for several minutes. Music, really: deep and full-voiced, and above all melodic. A coyote, you would have to say, since there aren't supposed to be any wolves left. But we'd heard hundreds of coyotes in the last months: wailing, howling, yipping, and calling. This one sounded different. If it was a coyote, it did one hell of a wolf imitation. After it finished, and the last notes died away in the clear morning air, there was silence. Nothing answered the call.

We were reminded of it as we sat talking to Tom about the grizzly bears. A coyote was howling his heart out, and we stopped to listen. "What about wolves?" we asked, as the call was answered in an enthusiastic chorus.

"That's a coyote. Got a pretty deep voice, doesn't he?" Tom replied.

"Not him," I said, and I described the sound that had remained in my ears.

"Could have been a wolf," said Tom. "I know, they say there aren't any left. But I've been in this country for ten years now, and every once in a while, I hear one that doesn't sound like a coyote, and the hair on the back of my neck goes up. I think they're out there, and I think if you hear them, you know it."

≈≈≈≈≈

As we left Fox Creek the next morning, Tom handed us a bag full of fresh vegetables. "I bet you don't get much of this out here," he said. We said our thanks and our good-byes, and followed the trail into the park. The sign closing the Snake River Trail was still there, but—per Tom's instructions—we ignored it.

Heading downstream, the trail crisses and crosses the Snake River a multitude of times, back and forth, and back again, each ford becoming deeper and wider as the river picks up momentum from hundreds of tiny trickles. The river truly snakes its way from its headwaters north toward Heart Lake, wiggling through progressively steeper canyons. But before it gets to the lake, it makes a sharp turn to the southwest, and eventually it flows out of the park toward Jackson, Wyoming. Watching it twist and turn, you might think that you knew the origin of the river's name; you would, however, be wrong. The name does not refer to the river's shape. Early settlers, communicating in sign language with the Indians who lived near the river, mistakenly translated the wiggling hand motion for "water" as "snake."

We walked along armed with bamboo sticks, discarded ski trail markers that we had found in the woods back at Wolf Creek Pass in southern Colorado. The sticks had begun to split with 1,000 or so miles of use, and the broken bamboo made a loud, satisfying *thwack* as we banged it against stones and tree stumps. Tom had told us that most humans who are injured by bears are injured because they surprise the animals. We joked that we planned to make so much noise that we would be the only people to ever walk through Yellowstone without seeing a single animal, but any confidence we had that the noisemaking would clear our path was shattered early on, when we rounded a bend to see a moose staring balefully in our direction. Moose are actually responsible for a lot more injuries to humans than are grizzly bears: They are reputedly shortsighted, nasty tempered, and aggressive, but this one just seemed long-suffering. We waited for him to get out of our way, which he did, moving at an ungainly, leisurely pace on his stiltlike legs and looking vaguely offended. We didn't know whether the moose had heard our noise-making and ignored it, or whether the clattering of the sticks hadn't carried over the wind. What if next time we turned the corner it was a bear sitting in our path?

We were relieved to arrive at our campsite near Heart Lake: Once in camp, we were far less likely to have any accidental encounters with wildlife, since the animals would have to run into us—something their instincts would help them avoid, we hoped.

The first order of business in bear country is hanging the food bags, for which you need a rope, a rock, and a decent tree. The tree is the critical element: With a nice, clear, high branch, bear bagging can be accomplished with a flick of the wrist. But in a lodgepole forest, you can count on an hour of increasing frustration. The branches are twiglike sticks that couldn't hold the weight of a squirrel, let alone a twenty-pound food bag. And why is the alternative always a fir with branches so dense with greenery that your rope gets entangled in the thick brush? Nowhere, it seems, are there trees that resemble the illustrations in the wilderness brochures, which describe how to bear-bag as though every tree has a perfect branch, twelve feet off the ground, sturdy enough to hold the food bag four feet from the trunk, but not sturdy enough to hold the weight of a bear.

There is one advantage to Yellowstone's designated campsite system. To make up for the paucity of suitable trees, they have constructed bear poles: thin logs suspended twelve feet off the ground between two trees. As promised, our campsite was marked by a neat, numbered stake in the ground. Over to one side was the bear pole and cooking area. Some distance away—not far enough, by our reckoning—was a cleared flat place where we were to pitch our tent.

Our campsite was a stone's throw from Heart Lake's outlet stream. A moose tramped past, and later a bull elk splashed through, his black, matted beard dripping light-filled droplets of water as he strode purposefully through the stream. So much for animal instincts to avoid people. Later, at night, we listened for more animals, hard, and of course we heard them—in the slightest rustle of dry branches, the shifting of leaves, the snap of a twig. Our nerves and our attention magnified the night sounds until the rustles became roars and the snapping twigs turned into approaching footsteps. And when something did go *splash* through the stream, we froze, and I felt my pulse, fast, against the back of my ears, and my blood, ice-cold, pounding through my body. What I felt was fear.

"Did you hear that?" I asked Dan, as if it were possible not to. We started listing what it could have been, although a list was hardly necessary. Another elk? A moose? Or was it a black bear . . . or a griz?

"The first three we don't have to worry about," said Dan. "The last, we can't do anything about. Go to sleep."

Which was easier said than done.

Why does the night air carry sound so much farther than the safer air of daylight? Coyotes called back and forth, and, in soprano counterpoint, the bull elks announced the onset of autumn, challenging all comers to contests of strength and virility. Strange that male potency would be heralded by such haunting, ethereal music. Bugling, they call it, although to my ears the sound was more flutelike than brassy as it trilled up and down its unfamiliar scales in a brilliant coloratura—a virtuosic performance to make any wind player jealous.

And then the woods were quiet again, mostly. There were no more splashes, and no bears either. The next morning we continued walking, constantly thwacking our bamboo poles as we made our way toward the South Entrance Road.

There are so many Yellowstones that it's easy to forget about some of them altogether. We had been walking in the Yellowstone of wildlife, although the Yellowstone of fire had intruded as we passed through patches of blackened earth and skeleton trees—scars from the great fires of 1988. On the forest floor, flowers bloomed, and an army of tiny seedlings proclaimed their intent to someday grow up and become a new forest. Across Heart Lake, smoke was rising from a clearing. Fire? Instantly, I pictured the news footage from two years back: flames racing toward the Old Faithful Inn; hysterical reporters; yellow-jacketed crews from as far away as Alaska and Hawaii, from Maine and from California—25,000 of them—fighting the blazes with axes, rakes, and hand-held computers. But surely, Tom would have told us about any forest fires.

Dan didn't think it was a forest fire at all; he thought that it was a group of hikers cooking up morning grub. Early explorers coming upon the same sight might have thought it was an Indian camp, and they, too, would have been mistaken. For what they didn't know, and what we had forgotten, is that Yellowstone is, perhaps first and foremost, a land of geyser basins. And so we walked into our first backcountry geothermal system much the same way that the early explorers would have: completely unprepared.

What we saw was remarkably similar to what the early explorers might have seen. There were no other tourists, no wooden planks to walk on, no signs or railings to keep us away from this or protected from that, no flashing cameras. All there was was a bubbling, steaming, hissing cauldron of geysers, hot springs, and mud pots, connected by a creek where the water ran hot.

"Hell is certainly close to the surface here," wrote an early visitor. He was right: While the hot, liquid magma under the earth's crust is usually some 35 to 40 kilometers underground, in Yellowstone it is only about 3 kilometers beneath the surface, sometimes less. Yellowstone may, in fact, be the hottest place in the world.

About 600,000 years ago, the area we now know as Yellowstone exploded in a volcanic eruption some thousand times as big as the Mount Saint Helens eruption. The Yellowstone volcano collapsed into a huge caldera measuring 140 miles at its perimeter. But this caldera is no dead volcano: 2,000 tremors have been recorded in a single year, some of them earthquakes measuring between 6 and 7 on the Richter scale.

The force that fueled Yellowstone's huge eruption—and still heats its geysers and hot springs—is a "hot spot," a bubble of intense heat that lies in the liquid magma. With heat, water, and an elaborate underground plumbing system of cracks and fissures left over from the volcanic eruption, Yellowstone has the unique geomorphology required for geysers to erupt. There are 10,000 hot springs in the park, and more than 300 geysers—60 percent of the total geysers on the entire planet. By contrast, the next biggest centers of geothermal activity—Iceland, New Zealand, and Chile—have a measly 25 geysers apiece. Yellowstone is where you go to find superlatives: the most, the biggest, the highest, the most regular—make up your own superlative, you'll find it here.

≋≋≋

We made slow progress that morning. Every bubbling mud pot, every colored pool, every hissing geyser was the subject of intense observation as we walked along steaming Witch Creek with its sour, sulfur smell. The very jaws of hell, the early explorers said, looking into the steaming, churning cauldrons, hearing the earth speak in a deep rumbling voice that told of violence and power.

Heart Lake was only a modest beginning.

The next day took us to Shoshone Lake's larger geyser basin, remote and isolated. Again, there were no boardwalks or signs, although a well-worn trail led us through the deep turquoise pools, the bubbling geysers, and the fumaroles that vented steam through cracks in the earth. A cold rain drizzled down, and we had the misty, steamy cauldron all to ourselves. A few miles later, we made our first sighting of other backcountry users: a couple who tried to give us directions to Lone Star Geyser: "Turn left at the buffalo," they babbled, clearly overwhelmed. Lone Star Geyser didn't oblige us by going off as we walked by, but the buffalo, looking stupid and slow, did indeed pose for a photograph. We remembered Tom's warnings, and used the telephoto lens.

And then—what contrast!—we arrived in the frontcountry, right in the middle of the madness of Upper Geyser Basin, home of Old Faithful. Oh, there's no doubt about which is the most spectacular: The basin that surrounds Old Faithful is many times larger than the Heart Lake Basin—larger, too, than the Shoshone Lake Basin. And as for geysers, what can compete with Old Faithful itself, which not only sends up its thousands of gallons of steamy waterworks but does so according to a conveniently posted schedule?

At Upper Geyser Basin, there are buildings, and stores, and restaurants, and the Old Faithful Inn, and a ranger station, and a post office. We went first to the post office, which was holding our next food drop. Or so we thought. The clerk was helpful and attentive, but it soon became clear that no amount of help, or attentiveness, or phone calls to the other post offices in the park, or searching around in the back was going to produce our package. The box, containing the food and maps we needed to get us to our next resupply, was nowhere to be found. As lost food drops go, we told each other that this was probably one of the better places for it to happen: Some of the maps we needed could be repurchased at Yellowstone, and a variety of food was available. But disappointment and frustration clouded our day as we thought about the map work that would have to be redone to prepare for the next leg.

Not that there weren't enough clouds. The drizzly, cold rain continued as we waited for Old Faithful to erupt on schedule, which it did, although after the buffalo and the backcountry basins and the elk and the moose it seemed vaguely anticlimactic. A lady behind me said in a disappointed tone, "That's all there is then?" and wandered off. So did we: We had 3 more miles to walk, which would take us through the Upper Geyser Basin of the Firehole River.

Sue and Mac accompanied us. The rain infused the geysers with a ghostly mist. We began to wonder if we would make it through the maze of boardwalks and trails to the next road crossing, where Gordon would be waiting for us with the van, before darkness fell.

"It looks about normal to me," Sue said, joking about her own blindness. Mac trotted along, similarly unconcerned by the lack of light.

"We can always follow Mac," Dan said.

"He doesn't know where he's going," Sue replied. "But if we get lost, he will be able to take us back the way we came."

We were glad to see Gordon and Sue. The only reason they had come to Yellowstone was to help us through the continuing permit saga. Although the rangers had been cooperative, getting a permit for the last night had proved problematic: The only campsite in the park between Lone Star Geyser (where the buffalo was) and the first water out of the park, 28 miles farther, had been closed because of the damage the 1988 fires had done to the area. So here, too, the permit system, taken at face value, was going to require us to walk a ridiculous distance. Gordon pulled out his maps, and we figured out that if he and Sue met us at Biscuit Basin, the mileage for the last day would be reduced to a still-too-long-but-doable 22 miles. As far as camping that night went, Gordon would drive us to a campground—something we couldn't have managed on our own because of the no-hitching rule, and because all the campgrounds are filled by early afternoon. This convoluted scheme seemed less complicated than trying to convince the park bureaucracy to give us a permit for a closed campsite.

So Sue and Gordon had arrived the previous day to claim a spot in a campground. As she usually does at national parks, Sue stopped in at a ranger station to get information. She also wanted to talk to the rangers about bringing Mac on the trails. Usually, her visit is an attempt to forestall hassles: Seeing-eye dogs are of course exempt from Park Service rules that forbid pets on trails, but Sue has learned from tedious experience that overeager rangers often need to be re-

minded about federal access laws. At Yellowstone, though, it wasn't
access that concerned Sue; it was the bears. Was it safe to take Mac
into grizzly country?

This was not a question the rangers dealt with regularly. The
problem, an earnest young ranger told Sue, was "I don't know what
our policy is about the handicapped." Yellowstone does, in fact,
have a handicapped access coordinator, but as far as Sue could tell,
the person in charge had never considered the possibility that a handicapped person might want to hike into the backcountry. If he had,
that information had not trickled down to the ranger station, where
the rangers carefully examined Sue's ID card certifying that she was
blind, and then fretted over what to do about Mac.

It was a reasonable concern; the scenario is predictable. A dog
catches scent of a bear; the dog finds the bear; the bear growls at
the dog; the dog runs to its owner; the bear follows the dog—causing
what the Park Service officials euphemistically call an "encounter."
But what about a dog that is not only on a leash but in a harness?
Mac wasn't free to go sniffing about in the woods—he wasn't even
free to leave Sue's side. Was he safe? In the end, the rangers tried
to be helpful, but they couldn't offer much in the way of conclusive
advice. As one of them said, "We can tell you where the bears are
more likely to be, but they can show up anywhere. Your dog might
not sniff one out, but you could run into one on the trail." Sue
decided that she would probably be too nervous to get any enjoyment
out of hiking in the backcountry. At Yellowstone, she would be
trapped among the boardwalks and the cement paths.

We reached the next road crossing just at dark, and Gordon
whisked us off to the campground at Grant Village, one of those
monolithic man-made slices of ugliness that you have to see to believe, and even then belief comes hard. More than anything, it is a
giant parking lot on the edge of Yellowstone Lake, with room for
403 units. Winnebagos line up, one larger than the next, each pulled
into its parking space next to a picnic table. It was like one of those
suburban developments where all the houses look exactly alike. I
wondered how the RV owners all ended up in the right vehicles at night.

We had no such problem; ours were the only tents in sight. Gordon
had managed to find a good campsite, as RV park campsites go. We

had neighbors to our side and back, but in front of us there was an unobstructed view of the lake. If you didn't turn around to look at the endless string of RVs, you could fool yourself into thinking this was the great outdoors.

In 1902, the secretary of the interior sent the following message to the acting superintendent of Yellowstone Park: "The Department had been officially advised that there is a likelihood of persons making a tour of the park during the coming season using therein, for transportation purposes, automobiles . . . [would it] be practicable or desireable to permit conveyances of the character indicated to be used in the reservation under your supervision?" The Answer: No.

It took thirteen years before the first automobiles were permitted in Yellowstone. On the first day the park was open to automobiles, fifty cars made the tour, fueling concerns about congestion.

Today, Yellowstone claims some two million visitors per year, most of whom arrive in, and tour the park by, automobile. Not to miss one of America's legendary family vacations, we decided to spend our day off at the park seeing Yellowstone the way the rest of America does: through the windows of an automobile. We polled the rangers for the best way to see Yellowstone's frontcountry in a single day—a ridiculous question, but they were used to answering it—and we set out with Gordon and Sue and the dogs in the white van with the canoe on top. Nobody looked at us twice.

Well, you know what this part of it looks like: more geyser basins, the road jammed with traffic every time a moose or a buffalo shuffles into sight, the burned forests, the mugs and T-shirts and pens and stuffed animals at the concessioner's store, the churning mud pots, the yellow stone of Yellowstone's Grand Canyon. We drove in the van, slowed down for the animals, took photographs as though we owned stock in Kodak, followed the paved trails on five-minute hikes to scenic vistas where helpful signs told us endless facts about when and who and how and why; and we ended the day like everyone else, barbecuing steaks on a picnic table. As we prepared for bed, the RVers next door asked if the tents were for the dogs to sleep in. They sounded serious.

The next morning it took exactly five minutes to leave all of it behind. We started early—we had a long day ahead of us—and walked in solitude through the geysers and colored pools of Biscuit Basin. A wooden boardwalk led us to a trail that leaves the backside of the basin and heads off for Summit Lake, 10 miles away.

Like most trails in national parks, the trails in Yellowstone are generally well marked, gently graded, and well maintained. Most hikers notice trail work in its absence, and so it was with us when we reached Summit Lake. The trail crews that had cleared the debris from the 1988 fires had not yet made it past the lake. It took exactly ten steps beyond the lake before the trail disappeared—*completely*. For 2 miles we followed our compass one degree south of west, and as we fought our way through the debris we learned, very much firsthand, exactly how hard the trail crews had had to work to restore the other paths we had hiked on in the park.

The compass led us to a steaming basin of hot springs, which, according to our maps, was smack on top of the Divide. On the far side, we picked up the remnants of our trail, a shallow rut in the ground. The trail had originally been marked with small, orange metal tags nailed high in the trees. Occasionally—and just often enough to keep us on track—we saw the remnants of one of them in what was left of the trees.

Some of the worst fire damage in the park can be seen on the Madison Plateau. We had already walked through burned areas in other parts of the park: It would have been impossible not to, given that more than half of the park was affected by the fires. But on the Madison Plateau, the damage was different. Elsewhere along our route, the fire had passed through, leaving behind a patchwork quilt of damage. Some parts of the forest were consumed; others were let alone. Most often, the trunks were blackened but the canopies were still green. In the understory, brilliant magenta fireweed had moved in; so too had new seedlings: hundreds and hundreds of baby lodgepole pines, all taking advantage of soil made fertile with nutrients from the fire, and plenty of sunlight let in by the openings in the canopy.

Here, the fire hadn't raced through; it had bogged down, and it had burned, and burned, and burned until there was nothing left.

You can still sense the raw power of the fire, and you can believe the unbelievable statistics—1,500 lightning strikes in one ten-day period; winds that pushed the fire along at a rate of 5 to 10 miles a day and flung it over fire lines 120 feet wide; the driest summer in 112 years; firestorms that were so big that they created their own weather patterns—and you wonder, looking at what is left, whether anything could have stopped the flames.

The forest floor gets plenty of sunlight now. The trees are bare, white and skeletal, and there are no green canopies overhead. Only 1 percent of Yellowstone's earth was burned so badly that its organic matter was destroyed; some of that damage occurred here. As we walked, we saw no fireweed, no little pine trees, no baby forest that the public relations people could show to the news media and the folks back home.

Environmentalists have long been champions of prescribed fires, of letting nature take its course by allowing fires to perform their natural function in wilderness. But even a staunch environmentalist needs a strong stomach to stand among the burned trees of the Madison Plateau and proclaim that what happened here was a good thing.

Is it healthy? Dispassionate scientists say yes; in the long run, nature will take its course. In fifty years, the dead standing timber will have fallen, and it will decompose and replenish the soil. Eventually, the baby lodgepoles will come back to colonize their ancestral home, and in a couple of hundred years no one will be any the wiser. But for our lifetime, a good part of the trail through the Madison Plateau will be a path of desolation.

Those of less dispassionate temperaments, or those with more pragmatic, short-term values, looked for someone to blame after the fires. Well, we could understand that: Fire may be healthy, but everything in moderation. How can a forest that looks like this be a forest that has been properly managed?

It may not have been. For one thing, fires were fought in Yellowstone for most of its history as a national park. Even backcountry fires were eradicated, thanks to airborne firefighting crews. As in the Gila, the buildup of highly flammable fuel resulted in a highly flammable forest. It also may be true that the fires were simply inevitable: Recent research shows that lodgepole forests undergo a major conflagration, on average, every 200 or 300 years, and that Yellowstone was about due.

If the fires were unavoidable, so too were the second-guessing and controversy and recriminations that followed. "They let the fires burn!" critics charged, forgetting, or ignoring, the fact that some of the most damaging fires had been fought from the very beginning. "They let the fires burn," they said, forgetting that total-fire-suppression policies may protect a forest in the short run, but doom it to uncontrollable and unavoidable conflagrations in the future.

Enter the government. Federal agencies are political agencies, not scientific ones: The secretaries of the interior and agriculture departments ordered that all fire plans be reevaluated. It is easy, these days, for Forest Service managers to get funding for wildfire prevention. What is difficult is to get funding for prescribed fire-management programs. At the same time, Yellowstone visitors' centers offer a full-scale apologia for the fires: glossy photos of new forests and healthy wildlife, captions explaining how and why what happened happened, and printed material that explains how fire not only is an inevitable part of nature but a positive one.

"What is Yellowstone's current policy on fire suppression?" I had asked the official behind the information desk. I had a notepad ready, on which I had been scrawling facts from the exhibit.

"Are you with the press?" he asked back, looking at me suspiciously. "If you're with the press, you'll have to go through the public affairs office."

"No, I'm not with the press," I said.

"All fires in Yellowstone are being fought."

Is it human ego, or human folly, or just plain ignorance to think that, if we can only find the right policy, forests will burn only when and how much we want them to?

N

MONTANA

CONTINENTAL DIVIDE

Butte •

Chief Joseph
Pass

Lost Trail Pass

Big Hole

MONTANA

Gibbonsville •

Bitterroot Range

Salmon •

Centennial
Mountains

West
Yellowstone
•

WYOMING

Lima •

Mack's Inn

Monida Pass

OUR ROUTE

TARGHEE
NATIONAL
FOREST

IDAHO

9

THE NORTH COUNTRY

At the Yellowstone boundary the Continental Divide heads northwest, arcs around the Henry's Fork headwaters, and then zigzags
almost due west, forming the border between Idaho and Montana.
The ridge itself is primarily in national forest land, a thin corridor
of wildness between areas of intense multiple use.

We were 2,000 miles into our journey, and at this point, we
thought, we had seen it all. Our trail had led us through everything
from the driest desert basins to the highest snowy mountaintops. We
had walked through Indian reservations and national parks, through
wilderness areas and BLM lands, through ski resorts and ghost
towns. We had seen wilderness protection at work, and we had seen
multiple use, too. We had shared water with cattle, peered into old
mine shafts, and walked through acres of clearcut forests.

But nothing prepared us for the logging in the Targhee National Forest.

For all practical purposes—and here, purposes are very practical—
the Targhee is not a forest; it is a tree farm. One of the most heavily
logged national forests in the country, the Targhee cuts fully half
of the commercial timber logged in the entire Greater Yellowstone
ecosystem. Approximately 1.4 of its 1.8 million acres are classified
as commercial timber. The largest clearcut in the United States (save,
as usual, for Alaska) was a few miles to our south, in the Moose
Creek drainage just west of Yellowstone. Throughout the forest, the
clearcuts are so big that they show up in satellite photos: They look
like arctic tundra or desert.

Clearcuts like these are an act of violence. It's not so much that the
trees are gone as the mess that is left in their wake. A clear-cut hillside
looks as though a giant had had a temper tantrum and hadn't bothered
cleaning up after himself. It looks as though a tornado had cut a huge
swath through the forest, ripping trees from the earth and leaving up-
turned roots and branches lying this way and that. Sometimes the roots
and treetops are left to rot; sometimes they are piled and burned. Either
way, a clear-cut hillside looks violated, ravished—raped.

It's the cheapest way of cutting timber. You don't have to go to
the trouble and expense of selecting trees for harvest; you don't have
to worry about whether or not you damage the trees to be left standing. You go in, you cut, you load up the trucks, and you get out—
driving on roads especially constructed for that purpose.

Behind you, here is what happens:

Because the trees are uprooted, they can no longer hold the soil
in place. Erosion increases as runoff digs trenches in the ground and
washes topsoil downhill, where it collects in streams. Without shade,
the water temperature of streams increases; sediment builds up, disturbing riparian habitat. In the clearcut itself, animals have neither
shade nor shelter; most of them leave, although a few highly adapt-
able species like deer and elk stay for a while.

In winter, there is no tree cover, so all the snow that falls reaches
the ground and forms a dense snowpack, covering animal forage. In
spring, the increased snowpack contributes to more erosion as it
melts. Landslides become more common as the hillsides become
more and more eroded.

The Forest Service and the lumber companies defend clear-cutting, particularly in stands of tree species that are fire-adapted. They tell us that clear-cutting duplicates natural processes like fire and insect infestations, and that new seedlings will grow up to be a healthy future forest.

But natural processes don't look like this, and the new seedlings will never become a natural forest—they will always look like a timber farm, intersected with roads that cut through the forests, disturbing wildlife. In the Targhee, clear-cutting has all but annihilated grizzly habitat. In fact, the development and land use in the Targhee and the Beaverhead national forests—cattle and sheep grazing, tourist facilities, and logging—have virtually closed wildlife travel routes between Yellowstone and areas to the west of the park.

Our first night in Idaho, we set up our tent on a closed-off road. To either side of us were stands of seedling conifers, planted in anticipation of more clearcuts some years down the road. We looked for a tree big enough to hang our food, but there weren't any. Dan walked down the road, and a quarter of a mile farther, he found a lonely sapling, four feet tall. He stashed our food in its branches: If we couldn't hang the food properly, at least we could store it far away from the tent. Any bear that chanced along would have had a good laugh at this attempt to put food out of his reach, but we weren't terribly concerned. This was not bear habitat; it was a logged and roaded mess, and any grizzly was likely to turn tail and run at the first sight of it. So would the average backpacker.

The next day, we followed the logging roads past more clearcuts and reseeded timber farms to Mack's Inn, Idaho, a pretty town on the Henry's Fork of the Snake River. They call it the Henry's Fork here—in the West, it's a matter of faith that you know what river drainage you're standing in. The Henry's Fork is one of those places that shows up in ''hunting and fishing in the great outdoors'' sorts of magazines, in articles about ''my favorite secret spot'' or ''how an old-timer showed me the ropes in an old-time fishing hole.'' There's blue-ribbon trout fishing here, and it brings in anglers from all over the world. As we crossed the bridge between the motel (also called Mack's Inn) and the town's only restaurant (a chicken-fried-steak-and-home-made-mashed-potatoes kind of place) we saw people standing in the middle of the river, wearing waders and casting flies.

We had another reason, besides our food boxes, to go to Mack's

Inn; Sue and Gordon were waiting for us to say good-bye. For the last couple of weeks, Sue had been in increasing pain due to the cold nights. She had been fighting it as long as possible in order to stay with us, but now, with nightly temperatures routinely below freezing, her circulation was simply unable to cope with the cold. She and Gordon were headed home to southern Missouri for the winter. Since meeting us in New Mexico, Sue had walked well over 1,000 miles, most of them with Mac; Gordon had walked a few hundred miles of his own, in addition to logging more than 5,000 miles of driving. Gordon and Sue had been supportive in so many ways: interested in every detail of the trip, always encouraging, and willing to do anything they could to make our journey more pleasant and more fun. They had showed up at road crossings with fresh fruit, or special cakes to celebrate crossing a state line. They had given us rides into town to resupply, and they had come to the rescue with needles and threads, tools to fix zippers, extra tent stakes, and maps. But most of all, they had been our friends. Sue's determination and perseverance had been an example to us—and a reminder of how lucky we were to be able to make this trip. We would miss them.

There was another personnel change at Mack's Inn: Our friend Sandy was joining us to hike for a few days. Her boyfriend, John, had driven up with her from Colorado. John, however, wanted nothing to do with our walk. He was, he said, going to spend a few days at nearby Chico Hot Springs. "I've finally figured out this backpacking business," he told us, as he watched us going through our gear. John is a gourmet cook, and we could tell that he was aghast at the prospect of actually eating the freeze-dried dinners we stuffed into our food bags. "You hike all day till you don't care what you eat, and when you go to bed, you're so tired that you don't care that you're sleeping on the ground. And then you wake up so sore from a miserable night's sleep that you can't wait to start walking again. Do I have it right?"

Well, in a way. He forgot the part about getting lost.

≈≈≈≈≈≈

Entering the Targhee meant that we had entered the Idaho-Montana segment of the Continental Divide National Scenic Trail. In the entire state of Wyoming, we had not seen a single CDT marker. Act of

Congress or not, there had been no trail, no signs—and, as far as we had been able to learn, no plans to do anything. One BLM manager had told us that a trail didn't really have to exist to be a trail, and that they were thinking of letting the Great Divide Basin section of the CDT exist as "an idea, or a suggestion." This was novel: a low-impact, cost-efficient rationale for letting backpackers follow an idea across 200 miles of Wyoming desert!

In contrast, in Idaho and Montana, the Forest Service had announced that the trail had been designated from Yellowstone National Park to the Canadian border. Indications were good as we started out: Even our Targhee travel plan map had a tiny CDT logo superimposed over the Divide. Did this mean that the trail existed?

It was an important question for us, because the answer would help determine our route. This new official trail was different, in places, from the older guidebook route. In our initial planning, we had used the guidebook, because it was the most complete source of information about the Continental Divide. We had also used it because of its aesthetic: The author of the guidebook had spent years scouting and evaluating possible routes for the trail, and his route reflected a commitment to find the most scenic, environmentally sound, historically and culturally interesting path. In contrast, where the guidebook route diverged from the Forest Service route, the discrepancy often reflected the multiple use values of the Forest Service: The Continental Divide Trail was, after all, only one of many projects for that agency, and sometimes the Forest Service's recommendations—for instance, to follow the Colorado Trail, or to bypass the Mount Zirkel Wilderness in Colorado—reflected compromise and convenience rather than strict adherence to a higher standard.

So, again we were faced with the decision: Where the routes diverged, should we allow ourselves to be lured off our maps by the promise of a trail? Would the new, official trail be a better route than the one we had planned? If we did follow a newly marked path into the unknown, would it last long enough to take us back onto our maps? Or would it end without warning in the middle of nowhere?

The route through the Targhee, according to the Forest Service maps, was a combination of a preferred official route and an interim route, which was to be used until the preferred route was in place.

These designations were a good sign; they indicated that provisions had been made for places where the trail was not yet in place.

The system worked only in theory, as we learned when we tried to follow one of these interim routes up to the Divide. The path had been annihilated by a massive clearcut. The rules require loggers to mark a path through clearcuts that disrupt a trail system, but this hadn't been done, perhaps because here, the route of the CDT was supposed to only be temporary. Regardless of the reason, we were stuck: Even with a detailed topographical map, we couldn't make head or tail of where we were. Remains of uprooted trees, bulldozed earth, and tree stumps littered the ground, and the roads switch-backed up and down, so altering the landscape that we couldn't even figure out where we were supposed to be trying to get to.

Above the clearcut, the forest was dense. If we couldn't find a trail to lead us through it, we would be in for the worst kind of bushwhacking: through thick timber and deadfall, heading uphill to the wooded ridge of the Continental Divide.

We detoured around the drainage on a dirt road, hoping to find another trail that would lead us up to the Divide. A couple of locals stopped to offer us first rides and then advice. They had hunted this country, they said, and they knew it well. When we asked them about the trail we were hoping to take, they looked dubious. We walked on. A retired Forest Service employee stopped, and when he asked where we were headed, we dispensed with our usual "Canada" response, and instead got right down to business. "Table Mountain; do you know how we can get there?"

He knew the trail, he said—like the others, he was a hunter. But the trail hadn't been maintained; we'd be lucky to even find it. We could try looking for some of the old blazes back in the woods, behind a bulldozed pile of earth that blocked an old road. We might be able to follow them up the mountain.

We arrived where the trailhead should have been in early evening. Sandy volunteered to find us a campsite while Dan and I went off to find the trail. There were a few bulldozed piles closing off roads, and finding the right one, and then the trail blazes, took about an hour. After we were satisfied that we had found the trail, we set up camp.

The next morning, our spirits soared as we began the 1,000-foot climb, following a neat, easily discernible path. This wasn't so bad, we told each other, as though our optimism could affect the outcome of our climb. Once in a while, the blazes disappeared, or the footway disintegrated into a labyrinth of game trails. But we always found the blazes again—until we were about halfway up the mountain, and the trail disappeared in a mostly open hillside meadow.

We weren't lost: The last blaze was right there at the bottom of the meadow, two big ax cuts on both sides of a tree. We split up, confident that we could find the next one. There was no path, no tread, no indication at all which way the trail might have gone. We searched through the meadow, around it, over the top of it, into the woods on either side. We looked for the trail for an hour or more, knowing that if we found it, the hour would have been well spent.

But we didn't find it, and we were in store for the very same kind of cross-country bushwhack that we had tried to avoid the previous day. Worse yet, this time, all we had to guide us was a Forest Service map, since our detour had taken us off our planned route, and hence off our detailed topographical maps. We were on our way to the navigational twilight zone.

Being lost—whether intentionally or otherwise—was a condition with which we were well familiar by now. We had been lost in the desert; we had been lost without water. We had gotten lost coming down off mountaintops; we had become lost in valleys. We had gotten lost on trails that ended in swamps, at reservoirs, in cow paths, at passes. Sometimes it was our fault; sometimes the maps had been inaccurate.

Almost always, we had managed to find our way out of whatever mess we had gotten into quickly, without walking too many extra miles. It would seem that at this point in our trip, being off-trail with a lousy map would be old hat for us—that we would just set our compasses and keep walking.

But hiking is an activity that occurs, intensely, in the here and now. The successes of yesterday's navigation mattered as little to us as yesterday's dinner; the fact that, if we kept walking, we would eventually get somewhere was of absolutely no comfort. Being lost was one of the few things that could completely upset our balance. Being lost meant that we couldn't count on water. It meant walking additional miles. It meant not knowing how far we'd have to go before we could set up camp, find water, eat, sleep. The only thing that mattered to us when we were lost was getting back on route as soon as possible.

This present-tense orientation defines hiking. Everything is of the moment; the things we had to think about were reduced to a few simple ideas. Water. A campsite. Mileage. Elevation gain. Route finding. Food. That's about it. Everything else was intensely of-the-moment. Where are we now? What are we seeing now? How much does this climb hurt now?

Climbing is perhaps the best example. You climb—hurting, tired, swearing, wondering why you're doing this in the first place—and once at the top, rewarded with a view and a rest, you immediately forget the pain and discomfort it took to get you there. It is said that women forget the pain of childbirth, which explains why they are willing to go through it again. I don't know about that. I do know that every time I swore I would never climb another mountain, I forgot my oath the second I reached the top. Then, it was the view and the wind and the magic of the high country that defined my present-tense world, and the climbing that was forgotten.

Now, being lost dominated our here and now. Being lost—and going uphill. We fought our way over the thick deadfall, spreading out to try to find the easiest way through the woods. But there was no easy way, and every time I consulted my compass, it seemed to lead through precisely the worst, thickest, prickliest vegetation. The only thing that intruded onto this present-tense misery was the prospect of more of it in the immediate future. There was no room for common sense—no room to tell ourselves that this too would pass. Our entire world was circumscribed by the ridge, the map, the thick trees, and the fact that we didn't know where we were.

Sandy and I were the navigators. Sandy, new to the trail, cheerfully attacked each new route-finding problem as though it was a particularly interesting puzzle. Having done this more times than I could count in the last few months, I was more jaded. The charms of this particular puzzle had long since worn off; besides, I could anticipate, as Sandy could not, some of the problems we were likely to confront as the day wore on. So I swore like a sailor.

Despite our different attitudes, we both—intensely—wanted to figure out the easiest, most direct way out of the mess we had gotten ourselves into. We continued through the woods, fighting our way over the underbrush and looking for clues that would tell us where we were. Finally, four hours after we had begun walking, we stopped to reassess what we were doing—and came to exactly opposite conclusions.

I thought that we had arrived at the point where the map told us we needed to change direction, and that meant descending slightly into a drainage and then climbing back up the other side. Sandy concluded that we needed to stay high so we could see where we were. I countered that if we continued in the same direction we were going in, all we'd see was that we had gone the wrong way. Sandy said that there had to be a way to stay high and go around the top of the drainage to the ridge we were looking for.

This was not a theoretical discussion; it was an argument that reflected the immediate physical repercussions of what we were doing. We were tired and frustrated now; if we went the wrong way, we would become even more tired and frustrated. We were hurting, and if we were wrong, we would hurt even more.

Unfortunately, there was no way to resolve the discussion other than by force of will: We were in such dense forest that our visibility was limited to the trees in front of us. And, since both of us were convinced that to cede to the other meant more of the same painful walking, our conversation took on tones of increasing frustration and recalcitrance.

Fortunately, while we were debating, Dan had wandered off, as usual, abandoning the maps in favor of visual surveillance. Twenty yards in front of us, he literally stumbled on the blazed trail. Both Sandy and I felt instantly vindicated: Just like I said, the trail turned north. Just like Sandy said, it stayed high.

We couldn't help but appreciate how ridiculous the whole situation had been—the three of us stumbling and arguing and running around in circles on this huge mountainside, while the trail was just off to one side. Was some omniscient being watching us, laughing, as we bumbled around, the trail so close to us but so completely hidden and out of our reach? And if so, why hadn't he or she just plucked us up and put us where we belonged?

We continued on, the climb and the lost trail immediately forgotten. We were, already, in a new present tense, which was a decided improvement. This trail led us past a clear, cold spring directly to the Divide, where, unbelievably, it suddenly sported blazes on every tree. Every meadow now had huge markers at either end; every turnoff was heralded with double blazes. It was, probably, the best-marked section of trail we had yet seen, so well marked that a New York City scout troop with blindfolds could follow it. It ended in a couple of miles, but by that time the Divide had opened into a huge, clear, grassy ridge with a two-track jeep trail along its crest.

The forests gave way to grasslands the color of copper in the evening sun. Clouds rolled in, threatening rain, but instead delivering a brilliantly variegated sunset. To either side of us, we had clear, wide views of the surrounding country. Below us was open, remote terrain, ranchland with more cows than people. We found a grove of trees for our campsite, grateful for the end of the day, for a rest, for knowing where we were. Grateful for this new, perfect present tense.

By the time we were approaching our food drop, at Lima, Montana, Sandy was tired, moving with the wooden stiffness of muscles that had been pushed past any reasonable expectation. I didn't blame her—I was tired, too, after this tough stretch. Like Dave's first few days with us, with long mileages imposed by water shortages, Sandy's hike had been lengthened by route-finding problems. Now, as we walked the last few miles along a dirt road that paralleled an interstate, she was about ready to stop—and, to be honest, so was I. A car honk interrupted our conversation, and we turned to see John's blue Chevy Suburban pulling up on the interstate shoulder.

Of course, Dan and I couldn't take the ride. That was the only inviolable rule on our walk, and we never, ever broke it. We didn't even give John our packs. But Sandy had no such self-imposed limitations—I've never seen anyone get self and pack so quickly over a fence. Within seconds, she was ensconced in the car. Dan and I walked on.

A mile farther, we had one more offer for a ride from a disreputable-looking duo who were sitting in front of a salvage yard. Their pile of scrap metal appeared to be at the very end of any conceivably useful life, and the vehicle they pointed to looked like starting it would be a minor miracle.

As it turned out, the salvage yard matched the town of Monida, where John and Sandy waited for us in the Suburban. Monida is named for the two states straddled by a nearby pass in the Divide. It is a modern-day ghost town, an exit off the interstate where you'll find a few free-ranging domestic goats, the salvage yard, and, rather surprisingly, a working telephone. Sandy was talking on it by the time we got there: With her backpack and boots, she might have looked like a hiker, but her glasses, notepad, and address book gave her away as a working woman, linked to the world of calling cards, voice mail, and modems by high technology in this most unlikely place for any technology at all. Behind her, a handwritten scrawl on the wall of an old store proclaimed "Cheap stuff"; in front of us, a settler's cabin was slowly disintegrating.

We resupplied in Lima, 16 miles from Monida on the Montana side. Sandy and John drove off, back to Chico Hot Springs—were we sure we didn't want to come? Instead, we rented a hotel room and took a day off to rest and to go over our route for the next section. We had our work cut out for us.

The next stretch was a problematic segment, through the remote Italian Peaks of southwestern Montana, and then along the rugged Bitterroot Mountains. We had not been able to obtain some of the necessary topographic maps from the USGS; they had been either out of print or back-ordered, so we were stuck hoping that the Forest Service maps were up to date and the trails clear. The new official route and the guidebook route differed here, so no trail maintenance was likely to have been done on the guidebook route. And after our experience during the last few days, we were afraid of following the Forest Service route without the necessary maps. Added to all that was the fact that this was a long section—thirteen days—over difficult terrain: The guidebook had warnings about tricky cross-country segments and rock scrambles on steep scree. And no less a duo than Lewis and Clark had had trouble finding and getting to Lost Trail Pass—our destination—when they explored the region in 1805. According to Clark's journal, their journey took them "over rocky hill Sides where our horses were in pitial danger of Slipping to Ther certain distruction & up & Down Steep hills, where Several horses fell, Some turned over, and others Slipped down Steep hill Sides.''

We also had the weather to worry about. So far, it had been sunny and warm, with clear, brilliant colors, and bright blue skies. Dan wrote a batch of postcards describing the golden Indian summer. It certainly didn't look like winter was imminent, we said to the locals. Don't you believe it, they told us. Don't believe it for a moment.

Dan and I had absolutely no illusions that we were a match for a Montana winter—even the beginning of one—but now that winter seemed just around the corner, at least as far as the locals were concerned, we needed to figure out what to do about it. We didn't intend to try to snowshoe through the high country to the Canadian border; that would have been beyond my strength, and a miserable, dangerous ordeal for both of us. Even the old-time mountain men had better sense than to go trudging into Montana's high country when winter had set in. But we did intend to hike for as long as we could.

Until Mack's Inn, Gordon and Sue had been carrying two pairs of snowshoes in their van for us; we had intended to start carrying them on the trail when the weather looked like it could turn on us. The snowshoes would be a safety precaution: If we needed to hike out of a big storm from a remote area, we wouldn't be stuck. At Mack's Inn, the snowshoes had moved to John's Suburban. In Lima, we eyed them again—a couple of pounds per pair. Our packs were already bulging with a thirteen-day supply of food, cold weather gear like warmer sleeping bags and extra layers of clothing, an additional two days' worth of food in case of emergency, and so on. The sky was all innocence, the weather pleasant. We would be starting out in shorts and T-shirts; we decided that we could wait another week, at least, for the snowshoes. Before Sandy had left for the hot springs, we asked her to take the snowshoes; we'd call her at our next food drop and tell her where to send them. ''Are you sure you won't need them before then?'' she had asked.

No, we weren't sure. We weren't sure at all.

≈≈≈≈≈≈

Winter in the north country had replaced the grizzly bears as the subject of dire warnings. You couldn't do anything about snow, just like you couldn't do anything about grizzly bears, and it could kill you just as dead—hypothermia kills a lot more backcountry recreationists than grizzlies ever did. Still, I'd take snow over a grizzly bear any day. You can fight snow with clothes and gear and fire and hot drinks. Snow was something we could be philosophical about: Winter was going to come when it did, and thinking about it wasn't going to change its arrival date.

But we couldn't avoid the subject. Everyone we talked to had an opinion on how far we would get. We were told about bodies that had been found frozen to death, warned about how fast the storms came in. When did it usually get bad around here? we asked. But folks couldn't say for sure about that; it changes every year. Sometime about now, they figured, we'd start seeing some snow.

Guessing the arrival day of real snow is something of an art in the north country. That's not surprising, since winter defines the north country life. But the weather here defies predictions: It is irascible, changeable, moody; at times playful, at times vicious. No two years are alike. In one winter, the snowfall can be as little as 50 percent of normal; in another, 170 percent as much snow might fall. In one town in the state, the temperature might be −20; nearby, the thermometer might read 40. Sometimes, cold arctic air and warm maritime air will collide and, unable to merge because of their differing densities, they will simply fight it out. Then, the temperature in the same place will swing back and forth like an out-of-control pendulum—sometimes changing by an astonishing sixty degrees. The chinook wind—the Indians call it the *snoweater*—can work the same extreme changes, warming the air by as much as forty degrees in as little as fifteen minutes.

Like any other mountain system, the Continental Divide creates its own weather. But in Montana, the Divide is high, and largely unbroken, and it is the last barrier to the western movement of the moist Pacific air mass that blows in from the Northwest. It is also cold; winter, they say, is to be avoided or endured. Snowfall varies— dramatically—from place to place and from year to year; in some sheltered cirques in the Bitterroot Mountains, the snow can be as much as 800 inches deep, almost 70 feet, the height of an eight-story building. On exposed ridges, no snow may accumulate at all. Often, there are avalanches, roaring down mountain slopes at speeds of up to 100 miles per hour. Such speed can rip a tree out by its roots as though it were a pickup stick; you don't have to have much of an imagination to know what it can do to a person.

And when it's not snowing, the wind creates its own blizzards, although it's impossible to know just how hard the wind blows around here; most of the wind-measuring equipment simply ices up on the Divide. At the passes, the wind is strong enough to rip tree tops off—that would put it at hurricane force, between 60 and 100 miles an hour. Even in less extreme moods, the wind is strong enough to stop a person from walking forward. That's all we needed to know about the wind.

As far as temperature goes, no one can say. The coldest temperature ever recorded was −70 degrees, on Marias Pass on northern Montana's Divide. But that was as low as the thermometer could measure, and the reading occurred at 2:00 A.M.—when the temperature was still dropping.

As we walked on from Monida, the temperatures we were facing were quite pleasant, in the fifties mostly, dropping colder only at night when we were safely ensconced in our sleeping bags. The Divide changes dramatically on Montana's southwestern border with Idaho. Just north of Yellowstone, we had been bashing our way through thick forest. Now, the mountains were dry and open. There wasn't much moisture, not enough to grow trees. A few clumps of golden-leaved aspens, brilliant in their full fall finery, grew in the drainage gullies, where they could take advantage of the wet soil. There wasn't much water for us humans, either, and what water there was was usually fouled by cattle.

Our route continued to be a combination of official trail and seat-of-the-pants navigating, and it led us through a series of dirt roads, where folks stopped to see if we needed help, offer us water—and warn us about the winter. So far, the only sign of winter had been the increasing shortness of the days. We noticed it suddenly: It seemed that we had all the daylight we ever needed until one day, when we were walking later than usual and just barely managed to set up our tents by the time it got dark at 7:30. The weather, however, continued to be pleasantly mild. But the locals took no comfort from the blue sky and comfortable temperatures. They knew for sure that winter was coming.

We had our first hint of trouble on Elk Mountain, the last peak of more than 10,000 feet on our route. It's a tough climb up an exposed knife-edge, and we made it in a biting wind that was blowing a steadily building bank of clouds toward us. Snow clouds.

Snow clouds don't look anything at all like rain clouds. They ride higher in the sky, flat and steely, with a calm determination. They have none of the temperament of a thunderhead, none of the oppression of a daylong downpour. They take longer to build than the mercurial storms of summer; they don't so much fly across the sky as they settle in it, gathering, building up.

These clouds were our single warning shot. They dribbled a fraction of an inch of fat, lazy flakes, and the next morning they were gone. They were not quite ready to invade the north country. Not yet. But they were a warning.

We went on.

There were other signs of winter. The cattle were being moved downcountry, out of the mountains and into the valleys. We passed a ranch where a roundup was in progress: several hundred cattle were being sorted by men working on horses, with dogs to help. The noise was incredible, as calves, newly separated from their mothers, bellowed their confusion and were answered by a chorus of mournful moms. As we passed the huge corral, the road led us only a few yards away from the skittish calves, and to these range-raised calves with no mothers to protect them, that was too close by far. We could see the panic building as wild eyes turned on us and little feet started a nervous dance. The shifting and dancing was contagious: First one, then another of the high-strung animals began the edgy, agitated fidgeting that precedes a stampede. All it would take was one panicked calf to send them all scattering through the line of men and dogs. One of the cowboys had picked up on the activity back in our corner, and he started riding over, slow and tense, watching us, obviously concerned. The roundup of that many cattle must have been a whole morning's work. Dan and I slowly backed away from the calves, circling wide around them and going off the road until the calves seemed to calm down. Even though we were still a good fifty yards away from the cowboy, we could see him relax as the calves went back to their aimless meandering and mooing. As we walked on, we saw the cowboy briefly raise his hand in thanks before he turned his horse around and rode back into the line.

At the next ranch, we had more animal encounters: A dog raced out, barking energetically. We slowed down, hoping that a person would show up, too. It was late afternoon now, and for the last hour we had been walking against an evil wind. The wind made everything hard: walking, talking, even thinking. It was time to stop for the night, but we were in a patchwork of private land, where every single creek was dotted with a ranch house.

We needed to find a place to camp. In front of us, there was a creek, edged by willows that might hide our tent. We didn't want to camp so near the house without permission, but the next water was several miles farther, and the map told us there was a house there, too. In between, the land was wide and open.

Since no one came out at the ranch, we walked on. Twenty yards later, some sort of sixth sense made us turn around to see a man standing at the side of the road, watching us. We retraced our steps, back to the ranch.

"Can you show us where we are on the map?" we asked him, by way of a conversation opener. We didn't need our location confirmed any more than if we had been sitting on our front porch at home, but since we had had to backtrack to the man, we figured that we better have some sort of a reason, and asking for help with the map was a better way to open a conversation than "Can I camp on your land?"

The wind made the map flail around so much that it was impossible to point to what county we were in, let alone what road we were on. We followed Pat Murphy into a huge, spotless building; once a barn, it was now used as a workshop. With our location on the map suitably confirmed—no surprises there—we got into a conversation about what we were doing.

"You might get some snow," Pat said.

"We got some yesterday," we told him.

"There's more on the way."

While we talked, Dan and I glanced around at the workshop. It was a huge building, sheltered from the god-awful wind. We were both thinking the same thing: if only the rancher would let us camp in the barn. The last thing either one of us wanted to do was go back out into that wind.

"You can get some water here," Pat offered, when we told him we were looking for water so we could camp. He led us to a small cabin and opened the door.

"There's a shower in here. You can use it if you like."

We accepted gratefully: It had been something like five days since we'd had one.

"Matter of fact, you can just camp in here. My wife's got the place all fixed up, and there's a bed and a wood-burning stove."

Dan and I were dumbfounded. We had walked back to the ranch, hoping for clean water and a place to put our tent. Here we were being given a whole cabin for ourselves.

"And there's wood out back," Pat added, pointing to a barn, where cords of split firewood had been neatly stacked.

There was dinner, too, as it turned out. Pat's wife came in to meet us a little while later, and when she saw our packages of freeze-dried dinners sitting on the table, she invited us over for a real meal. Their son even chimed in with an invitation to his school soccer game the next day, but that we had to decline. We had, it turned out, a date with a snowstorm.

We left the ranch after breakfast, fortified with an entire apple pie and a half gallon of milk, which the Murphys had given us the night before. We walked up the road, climbing back into the Bitterroot Mountains as we passed a herd of cattle being trailed the other way— down, to their winter pasture. A Forest Service truck pulled up, and the ranger looked at us in alarm. "Storm coming in," she said. "It's going to snow above five thousand feet."

We could feel it coming. The air pressure dropped suddenly, there was an uplift to the wind, a moist weight to the air. The clouds were collecting over the Divide, and once they got in place, they stayed, like an army amassing for battle, one regiment at a time. By afternoon the snow began to fall. It was winter.

Two days before, we had flurries. But this snow was the real thing: the kind of snow, in our other lives, that causes traffic jams and closes airports and gives schoolchildren reason to celebrate. Here, it just accumulates. We put on our rain gear and hats and gloves and covered our packs, and trudged on, upward. No more flirting with cold. No maybes about it. The clouds meant business. This, now, was winter.

We walked on until evening. The snow was still falling: It had accumulated a few inches. We had reached a campground, but, looking at the map, Dan informed me that there was a ranger cabin a half mile away.

"It's probably locked," I said.

"It might have a porch. I'll go see."

A porch would be a treat: We could set up camp without getting snow all over everything, and sit on a wood floor instead of the cold ground. We left our packs on the roadside, and while Dan walked over to investigate the ranger cabin, I checked out the campground. There wasn't much there, just a latrine, but it had an overhanging roof under which we could cook, if the cabin didn't work out.

Dan returned shortly.

"The cabin's locked tight as a drum," he announced.

I picked up my pack to start walking down to the campground, but Dan didn't follow.

"But!" he said, grinning from ear to ear. "There's a trailer. And it's open."

The trailer was apparently used for Forest Service work crews during the summer. There were two doors: One was locked tight, but the other door was open. Inside, the trailer was completely clean and completely empty save for two sets of bunk beds, a wood-burning stove, and a couple of chairs. Hardware for fixing the lock was laid out on the kitchen counter.

We took one look at the beds, the stove, and the snow outside and dived into the trailer. On our walk, we had so far passed several cabins that were open to the public. We didn't know if this was one of them, but no one was going to be patrolling this remote road at night in the middle of the first big snow, and even if an unexpected ranger did show up, no one in Montana was going to kick us out in weather like this.

We set up house and fixed our dinner, and then tackled the question we had been avoiding: What were we going to do now that snow was here? Ahead of us was a section described by our guidebook as particularly difficult, with a tricky high-mountain cross-country segment—the section with the missing map, the section of William Clark's "steep rocky hillsides." With the snow, the alpine cross-country segment would be foolhardy to attempt. We studied the maps, linking together alternate roads and trails, trying to find a way to Chief Joseph Pass; after a couple of hours, we sketched out a possible route.

The next day, there was more snow. We walked on, following easy jeep roads through a winter wonderland. Snow paints the woods magic, somehow. A hush descends; if I were to describe the word *quiet* to a deaf person, I would point to snow falling in a forest. The sun comes out, and the snow turns into a blanket of sparkling diamonds, playing with the magic of multicolored light.

There weren't any ranger cabins at Van Houten Lake; we put up our tent, instead, at a Forest Service campground. Setting up camp took much longer than usual; everything is different in the snow. Chores that used to take fifteen minutes now take forty-five. The stove is more stubborn, or your fingers are more clumsy, or the matches are wet. Metal stove parts and fuel bottles are so cold they almost burn when you touch them, and they can stick to your fingers. So can tent stakes. You have to be careful what you touch.

Setting up house takes more time, and if you rush it, you find that along with your down sleeping bags—which won't keep you warm if they are wet—and your clothing bags, you have dragged too much snow into the tent. You sweep it out, and then try to remember each time you go in and out to brush off the snow that clings to your pile clothing as though attracted there by a magnet. There are more clothes to take on and off, of course, but the cold makes you loathe to change, and you delay and delay until the last possible minute, and oh, why not sleep in the same clothes anyway? It's not possible to get any dirtier.

In the tent, winter rules apply. Boots go into a garbage bag at the bottom of your sleeping bag so that the sweat in them doesn't turn the boot into a chunk of ice. Water bottles join the boots in the sleeping bag—but check that the lids are on tight first. The camera goes in, too—to keep the batteries warm. Loose gear gets dragged into the tent vestibule so it won't get covered and hidden with a new layer of snow. At Van Houten Lake we were lucky; we could stash our gear in the outhouse.

The walking is different, too, especially if the trails are only occasionally marked and hard to find. You have to work hard to lift your feet, and daily mileage can take a nosedive to single digits. And there's less time to do all of this: The sun rises late to trace its low lazy arc in the southern sky, and it quits early.

We reached Chief Joseph Pass, three days later, at dusk. It was time for a day off, and our first order of business was to get ourselves to Gibbonsville, Idaho, some 15 miles down from the pass. But for the first time ever, all of the nice, generous, concerned people of the West had disappeared. We stood at the pass till dark, holding out our thumbs to the few passing vehicles. No luck. We had carried water with us, in case we'd have to camp, and we put up our tent in the woods at the side of the road, near a sign that announced that the Montana-Idaho segment of the Continental Divide Trail had been dedicated, whatever that means—it certainly didn't mean it was finished—in 1989.

The next morning, our hitchhiking success was exactly the same. We walked 3 miles down to Lost Trail Pass, where a road junction promised better traffic. Still no luck. My feet were turning into blocks of ice, and I was starting to shiver; if we didn't get a ride soon, I would have to start walking, or put up the tent and crawl inside my sleeping bag.

There's a rest area at the junction, and two ladies stopped to use the facilities, but they declined our request for a ride. A Forest Service official stopped, but he was going the wrong way. Finally, two pickup trucks towing campers stopped at the rest area, and they agreed to let us ride in the bed of one of the pickups.

"It's going to be cold back there," the man warned, but we answered that nothing would be worse than standing at the pass for another couple of hours.

Both predictions were right: It was cold, but no worse than the pass. Down in Gibbonsville, we found that there were thirteen boxes waiting for us in the pint-sized post office. Two of them were our food drops; the rest were gifts. Fortunately, the driver had agreed to wait for us and drive us all the way to Salmon, Idaho, for a rest day. Among other things, I had worn a hole clear through the sole of my boots, and I needed to get them repaired.

In town, with one eye on the weather and another on the weight of our packs, we again talked about the winter gear: What about the snowshoes? We had done fine without them so far. What about the winter tent? It was another throw of the die in what had become one big crapshoot.

In retrospect, I can't really explain the decision we made. Maybe we didn't want to admit to ourselves that the snow really and truly was going to chase us out of the high country—soon. Maybe it was that down in the valley, the snow seemed so far away. Or maybe we just didn't want to carry the extra weight. The weather forecast was good. If we wanted the snowshoes, we'd have to wait for Sandy to send them to us—and if we were racing with winter, did it make sense to wait? Maybe we should take advantage of the good weather and keep going. We settled for putting some extra emergency food in our packs. If a storm came while we were on the trail, we agreed, we'd just have to wait it out.

To get back up to the pass, we planned to take something called the Bitterroot Stage, which, we thought, was some sort of bus. It wasn't a bus—it was a small truck, with room for one or two passengers. When we showed up at the hardware store, where the truck stopped to take on its cargo and passengers, there was already a woman seated in the front.

The driver's name was Mike Riley, and he offered to let us ride in the back, at no charge, which was a decided improvement over the alternative: hitchhiking. After the trouble we had had getting a ride down from Lost Trail Pass, we had no desire to try our luck again with passing motorists.

"You sure you'll be all right?" Mike asked, as he showed us into the back of the truck, where we each took up a position on a tire well. We nodded, and he slammed the doors shut. We heard the metallic clang of a latch being fixed into place outside, and then the rumble of the engine. We rearranged ourselves against our packs and waited for our eyes to get used to the dark.

Dan's voice came out of the gloom. "I stayed awake most of last night thinking,'' he said, ''and I think that we might have made the wrong decision about the winter gear. It might be time to start our road walk.''

I was, to say the least, surprised. We were all packed to go back into the wilderness. I was surprised, too, that it was Dan who brought the subject up; usually, I was the one who came down on the side of caution.

''I think we should take the last snow as a warning,'' Dan continued. ''This next section is in a wilderness. If we get dumped on, it won't be easy to drop down to a road. We don't have snowshoes, and we don't know how well the trail is marked.''

We sat in the dark, chewing on the decision. If we continued, we might be able to beat the weather for another week or two, but maybe not. I remembered how badly my hands had hurt from the cold at Van Houten Lake, and the waxy white color of my fingers.

''What about going back and asking Sandy to send us the snowshoes?'' I asked.

''Look,'' Dan said. ''We can do that. And it might buy us another week. But that week could cost one of us a finger or a toe. The bottom line is that we can't get to Canada on trail. There's already snow in the Bob Marshall; Glacier has closed the Going-to-the-Sun Highway. We're going to have to leave the trail at some point soon.''

We had agreed that when the snow came for real, we would make a clean break. Dan was adamant about that: He didn't want to dance on and off the ridges, here a road, now a trail. If the snow was bad enough to force us out of the high country, then that's where we would leave the Divide. Next year, we'd come back to the mountains to finish on the trail itself.

Finally, we decided. We would leave the high country and take roads north. By road, we were less than 300 miles from the border. Canada suddenly became so much closer: We could walk 300 miles in less than three weeks. A valley walk would take us out of the snowbound high country. We pulled out maps and a flashlight and started planning.

At Lost Trail Pass, the van pulled over, and with more clanking and rattling, the driver opened the back door to let us out.

Our eyes were immediately blinded by the light—but it was not sunlight. We had not known, as we were being driven up to the pass, what the weather was like outside. We had not been able to see the gathering clouds that obscured the high peaks. So it was a complete surprise, as we climbed out of the van, to find ourselves stepping into the total whiteout of a full-fledged blizzard.

"You sure you want to do this?" the driver said. "I can take you into Missoula."

"We'll be all right," we told him. "While we were riding up here, we decided that we'd walk the roads from here on. Looks like we made the right decision."

The cars skidded around us and our eyes hurt from the shards of snow that the wind was driving toward us. The mountains were fogged in, hidden behind the clouds, and visibility was next to nothing. We put our packs on and started walking downhill, on the road, to Canada.

CANADA

UNITED STATES

GLACIER NATIONAL PARK

Polebridge ●

Kalispell ●

● **Bigfork**

Flathead Lake

Polson ●

FLATHEAD
INDIAN
RESERVATION

Mission Mountains

CONTINENTAL DIVIDE

● **Missoula**

Bitterroot Valley

Anaconda Range

Butte ●

OUR ROUTE

Lost Trail Pass   *Chief Joseph Pass*

N

10

≈≈≈≈≈

HITTING THE ROAD

≈≈≈≈≈

The rhythms of road walking are different than the rhythms of hiking. You take long, even strides. You don't watch where you put your feet; you watch for cars. There is no compass work to do; there are no steep hills to climb; there is no chance that the road will end in the middle of a clearcut or a meadow.

In a snowstorm, the walking is different still: unfamiliar hard pavement under slippery snow; cars sliding past, trying to control the curves.

Just then, the snow was swirling around us, blowing hard, silently accumulating. Needlelike shards blew into our faces, stinging our eyes, our cheeks. We squinted into the wind, but we could barely see. Glacier glasses didn't help, either, since we would have needed windshield wipers to keep them clear. Above us, the sky was a dead serious gray.

Cars stopped to offer us rides at regular intervals—if only they had been around a couple of days ago, when we were hitchhiking so unsuccessfully. But we declined the rides. Today, we were walking. To Canada. It didn't seem that far anymore.

But now that the end was so suddenly and so unexpectedly near, something happened that completely stunned me: My defenses fell with a thud. My feet began to ache with a persistent soreness that seemed to have moved into the very center of my bones and muscles. My legs stiffened until every step became an ordeal.

I was astounded by this betrayal by my body. My legs had carried me 2,300 miles, my back had hauled anywhere from thirty to fifty pounds, my feet had taken close to five million—that's right, *million*—steps. How dare they give up now?

Back at home, before the trip, I had worried about whether or not I would have the strength to tough it out through the breaking-in phase. I had expected blisters and backaches and sore muscles at the beginning of the journey. It had never even occurred to me that I might have a problem near the end. Ironically, the breaking-in had been easy for us, because of the training we had done before the hike, and because New Mexico had been gentle in its demands. By the time we came up against Colorado's mountains, we were ready for them. I had expected to get stronger and stronger the more I walked. It had never even occurred to me that my body might say "Enough."

As the days went by, my feet got worse. The walking was fast: 3 miles an hour, at least, sometimes more. But the hard surfaces were punishing, and we had to agree to limit our distance to 15 miles a day. Three miles, then a break; 3 more miles; another break. My traitorous feet screamed with every step, and after each break it became a little harder to start walking again. At the end of most days I was limping.

But we had to finish. It wasn't even a question. It wasn't an issue of heart or guts or toughing it out or wanting it badly enough. It just was.

We remembered, too many times, having answered the question:
"Where ya headed?"
"Canada."

We remembered the guard at the border station:

"That's a long way to drive."

And the feeling: slightly proud, slightly ridiculous, slightly uncertain. Well, we owned this trip now—the deserts of New Mexico, the peaks of Colorado, the ranches of Wyoming. We wanted to own the boast, too. We had said we were going to walk to Canada. We could no more stop and go home than we could fly to the moon.

Canada, Canada, Canada. . . . It beat a rhythm into my brain.

≈≈≈≈≈

If the rhythms of road walking are different, so are the logistics. Finding a place to spend the night was the biggest problem. Montana's Bitterroot Valley is no metropolis, but it is settled, with ranches, private property, and towns. We couldn't sleep just anywhere; we had to look for campgrounds, or motels, or places where we could hide. The highway signs were not particularly helpful: They are spaced at distances that make sense if you happen to be traveling in an automobile. A motel or a campground is 2 or 3 or 10 miles away; in a car, the difference between 2 and 10 miles is a couple of songs on the radio. On foot, that same 8 miles translates to half a day of walking.

In a car, if you are ready to stop for the night, you can drive a few miles farther to see what there is. If you're on foot, you choose the best place you can, knowing that there is no way to tell whether the next bend will reveal a perfect jewel of a campground—or a vast tract of posted ranchland.

In the backcountry, we had become accustomed to throwing up our tent anywhere we liked, but we couldn't do that here on the roadside. As we descended farther into civilization, we felt less like wilderness backpackers and more like transient bums. Our criteria for a campsite changed. Choosing a tent site in the woods, we had had the luxury of considering the view we might have of the world; now, we worried about the view the world might have of us. "Are we hobos or hikers?" Dan wondered, as we hid our gear in a clump of trees and walked back to the road to make sure our tent wouldn't be visible. Sometimes, we found public campgrounds, all but abandoned this time of year; sometimes, we stayed in motels.

If sleeping logistics were more complicated, eating logistics were much easier. We were carrying plenty of food: We had, after all, packed for the wilderness. But we soon found ourselves taking advantage of roadside amenities. What backpacker wouldn't have traded in freeze-dried shrimp-chicken-turkey tetrazzini-creole-florentine for your basic western hamburger with "everything-on-it-and-an-order-of-fries-make-that-a-double"? We could count on filling up our canteens with fresh tap water—no problem with *Giardia* here—or better yet, some fruit juice. The camping food sank deeper and deeper into our backpacks as we made our way north, resting our aching feet at the occasional restaurants, cafés, diners, and two-aisle quick-marts. If my feet hadn't been so sore, this homestretch would have been nothing more than what hikers call "slackpacking." As it was, for me this was some of the most difficult walking of the entire journey.

From Lost Trail Pass, the Bitterroot Mountains continue due north, and the Continental Divide makes an abrupt swing to the east. The valley itself is long, and low, drained by the Bitterroot River, which feeds into the Clark's Fork, and then the Columbia. This is country that was originally explored by Lewis and Clark, in 1805, en route to the Pacific Ocean. They had crossed the Divide to the south, at Lemhi Pass, and then followed the Lemhi River through the area that is now the city of Salmon, Idaho, hoping to find that the Salmon River was a navigable route to the ocean. It wasn't.

Instead, they climbed back to the Divide, near Lost Trail Pass, and descended north from there, into the Bitterroot Valley, without, of course, the benefit of the road we were now following.

The Bitterroot's waters are bound for the Pacific Northwest, so it is appropriate that this is timber country, filled with thick forests of dark evergreens like lodgepole, ponderosa, and western white pine; as well as Douglas fir, western larch, and red cedar. On our way downvalley, the logging trucks roared past us, splattering us with snow and slush. Some of the trucks unloaded their cargoes at one of the several log-home businesses that dot the valley, where piles and piles of long, straight tree trunks are turned into contemporary log houses. The houses are built twice: first erected here so that the logs can be fitted together and numbered; then taken apart and shipped to the homesite, where they are reassembled. It seemed an awfully labor-intensive process, but jobs are scarce in Montana, and labor is cheap.

As we descended, we began to notice the green signs. First one on a gate, another on a mailbox. A third in a window, a fourth on a door. On homes, on stores, on motels, on fences; the signs popped up, some faded by weather, but all bearing the same message.

"This family supported by timber dollars."

"We support the timber industry."

"This business supported by timber dollars."

We stopped in a homey roadside diner, with just such a green sign taped to the window by the front door. What, we asked the waitress, had happened in the valley to cause such an outpouring of support for the timber industry?

"The environmentalists are trying to shut down the whole logging business in this valley," she explained. "They've just about done it, too. What, don't those people from California use wood products? They build fancy log homes here, and then they say no one else can use the forests. They use paper, don't they? They use toilet paper? I don't mean to be rude, but where do they think it comes from?"

Logging has virtually been shut down in the valley, she told us, thanks to an environmental organization called Friends of the Bitterroot, which, according to those who sympathize with the logging industry, has a reputation of appealing every timber sale that the Forest Service opens for bidding.

"It's not people from around here who are causing all the trouble," the waitress continued. "It's the ones from California. They sell their houses there and make a lot of money, and then they come here where land is cheap. A lot of them are retired; most of them don't have to work. They just want to come in here and have things the way they want. They don't care about the local people. We have to work for a living."

The controversy began in the mid-1960s, when environmentalists noticed the terracing and bulldozing that had occurred on steep hillsides. The Bitterroot, along with Pennsylvania's Monongahela National Forest, was thrust into the forefront of a public outcry about poor management and clear-cutting of the national forests. The issue was one of those emphasized in the first Earth Day celebration in 1970, and the uproar over clear-cutting led to the National Forest Management Act of 1976. Nonetheless, here in the Bitterroot, the Forest Service has continued to offer more timber for sale than environmentalists think is appropriate, and both the environmental and logging advocates have become organized and vocal. The process of litigating and appealing timber sales has become so polarized and bitter that, before the bidding process even begins, the Forest Service advises loggers on the likelihood that a timber sale will be appealed. Sometimes, there are no bids.

Logging began here back in the gold rush days, and later supplied Montana's huge copper industry, providing lumber for housing and fuel, and supplying the voracious appetites of the smelters. When the railroads came through, Montana became a timber-exporting state, and the railroads made use of their land grants by cutting timber on them—and on adjoining federal land as well. The laws were inadequate, and failed to prevent years of timber trespass on public lands as the railroad and timber industries took advantage of the state's rich lumber resources. Montana's first mechanical sawmill was built right here in the Bitterroot Valley, near present-day Stevensville, by a missionary. Father Ravalli's contribution to the local economy was so important that the entire county, as well as a town farther north, bears his name.

Timber jobs have always been a hard way to make a living. They promise hard work and low pay, and the early logging camps featured accommodations that could best be described as primitive. Nonetheless, timber is an important industry in Montana, and Montanans are fighting hard to keep these jobs. For the first time since New Mexico, we started seeing signs about spotted owls. The spotted owl in question here was the Oregon variety, which doesn't even live this far east. But the loggers and their supporters aren't taking any chances.

It's fairly obvious where the Forest Service's sympathies lie. This is traditional logging country, and regardless of multiple use, logging is the Forest Service's favorite son. According to environmentalists, the timber industry has liquidated its own lumber assets and is looking for public timber to cut down, a process supported by the Forest Service. When the Forest Service was directed to evaluate roadless areas for possible wilderness designation, its response was to build as many roads as possible as quickly as it could, thus making the areas in question ineligible for wilderness protection.

But even if more wilderness areas were declared here, it would take more than federal protection to return these forests to their natural state. Old photographs of the region show massive, old-growth trees—the Forest Service calls them, in its peculiar lexicon, "overmature." The trees, some of them 400 years old, are so big that it takes two or three people to reach around their girth. Grainy old photographs show what the trees used to look like—and what happened to them. Pictures of logjams on rivers show thousands and thousands of huge trees floating downstream. They don't make forests like that anymore, at least not around here. We hadn't seen a single "overmature" tree—not in the woods, not on the roads, not even in the piles of logs waiting to become part of a log-home kit. The trees that grow here now, you can put your arms around all by yourself.

≈≈≈≈≈≈

As we continued walking north, a bright red car stopped and a big voice boomed: "Hey! Are you guys the people who are hiking the Continental Divide?" Before we had a chance to respond, the man answered his own question with a series of exclamations: "You are! You have to be! Who else would you be?"

Dan and I looked at each other in some confusion: Who was this screaming lunatic, and how did he know about us?

"This is great," he was saying. "Listen, I have to talk to you. . . . Tell you what, can I buy you breakfast? There's a place just down the road."

We started to explain about not accepting rides, but it seemed that our visitor knew all about that. "I'll drive you back here afterward," he promised. Now there was an offer we couldn't refuse. We climbed into the car.

Our new acquaintance, it turned out, knew a great deal about long-distance hiking and the Continental Divide. In 1980, he told us, he had started his own trek, down in Antelope Wells, New Mexico, and in October of that year, he had gotten snowed off the Divide at Chief Joseph Pass. The next year, he had returned to continue to Canada.

But he didn't stop at the border. At Waterton Lakes, the Canadian border seemed just an insignificant clearcut compared to the vast scope of the Rocky Mountains. The Continental Divide, after all, continued. Dan Cooper continued, too. He had gotten hooked on the hiking and the mountains, and by the time it was over, five years later, he had walked from Antelope Wells, on the Mexican border, clear to the Bering Strait.

The Bering Strait?

Dan and I kept exchanging glances, both of us alternating between astonishment and disbelief. The Arctic Circle? Polar bears? Frozen oceans? Igloos? By contrast, we had been on an extended Sunday picnic.

Dan Cooper had recently moved to the Bitterroot Valley, and he had been driving up to Chief Joseph Pass for old times' sake, he said, when he stopped for a snack at the Sula store and learned that we had stopped there the day before. After breakfast, Dan drove us back to the place where he had picked us up and wished us well. But three days later, the red car pulled up again: Did we want to stay with him for the night?

Dan Cooper's house could only belong to an outdoorsman. Strewn about were various pieces of used equipment: a stove on the kitchen counter; a mattress pad behind a chair. Every once in a while, he would pull out a cardboard tube and unroll a couple of maps to point something out. We pulled out some maps of our own, to show him how we planned to get to Canada—a direct route to the border station on a backcountry road that parallels the North Fork of the Flathead River on the western boundary of Glacier National Park.

But we were worried about arriving at the Canadian border on the North Fork Road. The road is remote: It runs through national forest on the U.S. side, provincial forest on the Canadian side, and there are no nearby towns in any direction. If we arrived at the border station after it was closed for the winter, we would have to turn around and start walking back—you can't hitchhike if there is no traffic. And let me go on the record as saying that there was nothing in the world that I wanted to do less than, after having walked from Mexico to Canada, turn around and start walking back. We were also concerned about getting caught in the middle of nowhere in an early winter storm: We didn't know whether or not the road was plowed, but we were guessing that it wasn't.

Dan Cooper offered to drive up to the border and pick us up—he was pretty sure, he said, that his car could get through anything that the North Fork Road would throw at it in late October. We added up the miles between us and the Canadian border, divided by fifteen and estimated an arrival date of October 30.

"I'll come and get you," Dan promised, with the typical western-er's combination of generosity and total nonchalance regarding dis-tances. Or maybe after you've walked from Mexico to the Bering Strait, a 400-mile round-trip in a car doesn't seem like much.

⁓⁓⁓⁓

The next few days took us around the Missoula commuter belt—boring walking under drizzly gray weather. Missoula is a small town by East Coast standards, but it is big for Montana: with 35,000 people, it is one of the largest cities in the state, and it sports a busy business district of franchises and shopping malls, a couple of inter-state exits, and an airport. Its biggest tourist attraction is the Forest Service smokejumpers' school, where young men and women train to parachute into the backcountry to fight forest fires.

The walking was dispiriting here: Cars roaring past us splattered us with wet mud; the weather was never better than dreary; and my legs and feet maintained a running litany of complaints. We were just putting in the miles, one day at a time. But even here, motorists stopped to offer us rides, and people promised us that the Flathead Reservation up ahead was beautiful. All we had to do was get out of the city sprawl.

By contrast to Missoula, the Flathead Indian Reservation to the north is quiet and rural. The Flathead have traditionally lived on the west-ern side of the Divide, crossing it only to hunt buffalo on the eastern plains. Today, of course, the buffalo no longer roam the plains, but there is a national buffalo refuge on the western side of Divide, within the boundaries of the Flathead reservation. Its 19,000 acres support a herd of between 300 and 500 animals, which makes this herd one of the most important remaining populations of American bison.

The terrain here was much improved as we walked past the Mission Mountains—a dramatic range just west of the Continental Divide that is managed by the Flathead as an official wilderness area. We passed the Saint Ignatius Mission, among the oldest buildings in the valley, and, a couple of days later, we walked around the east side of beautiful Flathead Lake, the largest freshwater lake west of the Great Lakes. The weather, too, had improved, although clouds still clung to the high country, sometimes clearing to reveal the shining white of new snow. Occasionally we would meet someone—a hunter, usually—coming down from the mountains, talking about drifts so deep the horses couldn't get through them. Even counting for exaggeration, it was clear that winter had come to the mountains. We hoped to reach Canada before it arrived in the valleys, too.

Telling folks we were walking to Canada didn't elicit much of a reaction anymore: The reaction came when we mentioned where we had started our walk. There was plenty of trail magic here on the road. A tribal fish and game warden stopped to offer help; a store clerk slipped some candy bars and chips in with our Cokes. A motel clerk offered us the use of her car. We ate lunch with a trucker who confided that he wanted to take a horse and ride the Divide himself one day.

But despite the trail magic, our biggest difficulty continued to be finding places to stay the night. Campgrounds were closing for the season; so were motels. Sometimes, we threw up our tent in a closed campground and hoped no one would come poking around. One evening, we found ourselves stuck: 15 miles from the next town, in open developed farmland, with not so much as a tree to hide behind.

We had been eyeing a gully rather too near a garbage heap: not much for aesthetics, but somewhat back from the road. There was a store nearby—a big, modern building that seemed to cater mostly to tourist traffic. We stopped in to buy some sodas and ask the women behind the counter if they knew anywhere where we might be able to stay. There was, we learned, a motel a couple of miles off our route, but when we called, the owners told us that it was closed for the season.

"Nonsense," said a woman who had been behind us on line at the cash register. She called the motel and identified herself (Mary), and where she lived (up the road), and who we were (a nice young couple who have walked here all the way from Mexico). Dan declared himself willing to be called young.

"There," she said, after she got off the phone. "You can camp at the motel."

By that time, we had had other offers: from both of the women who worked in the store, and from Mary herself, who lived up in Columbia Falls. A few minutes later, the phone in the store rang: It was the owners of the motel calling to say that we could have a room in their house, if we liked.

We decided to accept the offer that was nearest our route and stay with a woman named Julie, whose apartment was only a mile from the road we were following. Julie said to go on ahead; she would be back after work, around ten or so.

When we got to the house, we were surprised to find someone there waiting for us: Julie's fiancé, who was supposed to be on his way out to go hunting. We chatted for a while, and a few minutes later Jim left, telling us to make ourselves at home.

"I think we should put up the tent outside," said Dan. "I get the feeling that Julie reconsidered having strangers staying in the house and was too polite to back out of the offer."

"Why?" I asked.

"I saw her on the phone, just before we left the store, and it sounded like she was having a serious discussion. My bet is that she called home to tell Jim we were on our way, and he said, 'You did *what*?' That's probably why he was here when we arrived: to check us out. Anyway, she's probably wondering if she did something nice or something stupid, so why don't we just eliminate any doubt and put the tent up."

Julie arrived home just after ten o'clock and came outside to talk. Ten o'clock is way past a backpacker's bedtime, but we struggled a while to stay awake and make conversation. Jim had, she told us, indeed thought it was a bad idea to invite strangers over—especially since he was going away. But she didn't seem worried anymore, particularly since we were outside and nearly comatose. Dan had read that situation right.

⁓⁓⁓

We were behind schedule by the time we saw the first signs for Glacier National Park. Some days we had covered less miles than we had intended because of my feet. Now my knees had started to ache, too—and swell. I needed a day off, in a motel with an ice machine, to give the swelling a chance to go down. We tried to call Dan Cooper to tell him that we were running late, but he was in the process of moving and setting up a new business, so all we got was his answering machine. We hoped he would get the message.

The North Fork Road was the homestretch, but when we reached it, a couple of days later, the first thing we learned was that we had underestimated the distance.

"About sixty miles," a clerk at the Forest Service ranger station told us, when we stopped in for information about the road and the border station.

"Sixty miles!" I exclaimed to Dan. "We figured it to be less than fifty."

"Don't take it seriously," Dan advised. "We're usually better at estimating mileage than the Forest Service."

I devoutly hoped so. Strange that at the end of a 2,600-mile journey, a discrepancy of 10 or 12 miles should loom so large. But there is a huge difference between walking 16 miles a day and walking 20 miles a day, and this new information told us that instead of three relatively easy days, we were in for three very long days. And I had completely run out of energy. I could only hope that our estimate was the right one.

It wasn't. A couple of miles later, we saw our first sign for the Canadian border—"58 MILES." The curves and bends in the road hadn't shown up on our map. So that was the way it was going to end, I thought: This trek was going to challenge our endurance right until the last.

We didn't really have a choice, though: We had to be at the border station by October 31. We had left several messages for Dan Cooper giving him this new date, and we had no way to contact him and tell him otherwise. Not only that: We had just learned that the border station closed for the winter on October 31. If Dan Cooper hadn't gotten our messages and wasn't there to take us out, we would have a better chance of hitching a ride if we arrived when the border was still open.

We walked on, following the North Fork Road as it entered the quiet forests of the Flathead National Forest, hoping that the miles would be easy, that the weather would be good. Hoping that my legs would outlast the road.

According to writer Thomas McNamee, "The wretched gravel road that ascends the North Fork of the Flathead River fosters the inescapable sense that one is very near the tip-tale-end-of-nowhere." McNamee is right about the "tip-tale-end-of-nowhere" part, but we wouldn't have called the road wretched. Of course, we weren't trying to drive over and around its ruts and bumps and gulleys and potholes. For us, the road was quite lovely, and the farther up we went, the lovelier it became, as the gravel turned to softer dirt (no doubt this was the "wretched" part). The surrounding forests were tall and cool: larch, mostly, a deciduous conifer that sheds its needles each fall. Some of the trees were bare; others were dressed, as if for Halloween, in a deep, orangey gold.

The remoteness of the North Fork Road is somewhat deceptive. Although the road runs along the wild and scenic North Fork of the Flathead River, which forms the western border of Glacier National Park, the surrounding area is a bit more settled than it appears. There is a community of people living here, mostly in summer homes, but a few brave the winters to stay year-round. About once an hour, a car drove past us.

The hub of the North Fork community is the town of Polebridge, a place that looks like it belongs on the Alaskan frontier. It consists of a few log cabins, a youth hostel, and a single store: the Polebridge Mercantile. Behind the store, outside, is a row of outhouses. Among the amenities offered by the Polebridge Mercantile is the only public telephone for a good 30 miles, and we tried one last time to contact Dan Cooper—to no avail.

There was a surprising amount of traffic in and out of the store, and to and from the telephone. One of the people who came to use the phone was a young mother, Cindy, holding a little girl who, although not yet old enough to talk, was old enough to offer us animal crackers with a big, wide smile. Western hospitality begins at an early age, it seemed.

Cindy told us that north of Polebridge most of the land was privately owned and posted: We'd have trouble finding a place to stay, although it would be possible to hide in the trees. She lived, she said, 7 miles up the road; if we could get that far, we could stay with her. That would make for a 24-mile day, but it would solve the problem of finding a place to sleep. We shouldered our packs and kept walking, 7 miles, in a light rain. On the surrounding mountainsides, we could see a thin dusting of new snow.

The miles were erratically marked on the North Fork Road by numbers posted to the trees. We were closing in on the last mile marker, just before the turnoff to Cindy's house, when a pickup truck stopped and a rugged-looking man said, "I've been sent to see if you're coming for dinner."

So, for our last night on the trail, we enjoyed a last night of trail magic. Instead of the spaghetti sauce we had purchased at Polebridge, we had a homemade turkey dinner with mashed potatoes, stuffing, and vegetables. And instead of huddling in our tent, we were treated to the comforts of a wood-burning stove and a pull-out sofa.

Steve and Cindy's house was still under construction. They didn't yet have running water: They were saving money for a well, they told us, and in the meantime they hauled water in from a spring down the road. They had just installed a bathtub, however, and we took turns in the shower. Water was heated in a huge pot on the stove, poured into a large plastic-lined canvas container that looked like an oversized hot water bottle with a spigot attached, and hung from the ceiling in the bathroom. The toilet, however, was still outside.

Steve worked on the house when he wasn't working at his job. Right now, he told us, he was on a crew that was clear-cutting a few acres up the road near the border. The logging controversy went to the hearts of these people, who had moved here because they loved the land, yet knew firsthand how hard life can be in a rural, resource-dependent economy. Jobs are scarce, and they don't pay much, Cindy had told us, echoing what we had heard throughout Montana. It's a beautiful place to live, but you have to bring your work—or your money—with you.

There is, however, local resentment of people who do resettle in Montana, bringing enough money with them to exempt them from its economic hardships. On the North Fork Road, property values have skyrocketed in the last few years as Hollywood actors and the attendant beau monde have discovered the rural West and bought up huge tracts for fantasy ranches and rural retreats.

As elsewhere in rural Montana, there is tension between the newcomers and the old-timers. The green signs supporting the timber industry pop up on gates and mailboxes, and one property owner had put out a notice declaring that his land was managed for multiple values, including wildlife, water quality, timber, ranching, and several others. People—like Cindy and Steve, who love the region and have made sacrifices to live here—are stuck right in the middle of the debates.

Meanwhile, other threats loom on the horizon. There is a coal mine up in Canada that threatens to pollute the North Fork, and the Forest Service has opened part of the area near Polebridge for oil and gas exploration. Any development at all is opposed by wildlife researchers, who have several study teams at work up the road, near the border, studying the area's small wolf population and its grizzly bears. And in turn, the wildlife biologists are belittled by local timber and grazing advocates, who see all this research as a big waste of time.

From Steve and Cindy's house, it was 16 miles to the border. The road was muddy and slippery as we walked those last miles, eagerly looking around every bend: Could we see the border station yet? And then we finally did: flags and signs and two wooden buildings.

Canada. It was right in front of us. Strange, somehow, that the Canadian side of the border didn't look any different from the United States side. The same road; the same trees; the same rain. Between the two sides, a thin clearcut through the trees marks what is known as the friendliest international frontier in the world.

We didn't see anyone as we started walking over to the Canadian side. But two men, wearing the different uniforms of the American and Canadian immigration services, started jogging toward us from the Canadian building as we approached the clearcut.

"We're closing!" the Canadian guard said.

Dan and I looked at each other. Closing? We had walked here all the way from Mexico, and Canada was closed?

"You won't be able to come back across this way," the border guard explained when he got closer to us. "We're shutting down for the season."

We assured him that we had no intention of violating any international treaties, but could he please take a picture of us at the sign that said "CANADA."

The guards warmed up when we told them about our trip, and the American customs officials invited us in for a soda. This was, we learned, one of the quietest stations on the entire border between the United States and Canada. Even in the summer tourist season, it doesn't get much traffic: no more than thirty cars a week. We watched the customs officers board up the windows and shut off the water and the power for the winter. The snow, they told us, would completely cover the buildings.

We sat in the customs station, trying to absorb our new reality: Our long journey was over. At least, this part of it was over. Here we were, at the tip-tale-end-of-nowhere, having just walked up the length of the country. From Mexico. The trip was ground into our feet, into our bodies, into our very beings; still we couldn't quite grasp the enormity of what we had done, and the even greater enormity of the fact that it was over.

But not quite over. We had achieved one of our goals: We had walked from border to border, and we had done it in a single continuous journey. But we had one more piece of unfinished business. There was still the high country between Chief Joseph Pass and the Canadian border to be walked—the actual route of the Continental Divide itself, now snowbound and inaccessible. What adventures waited for us there, in the Anaconda Pintlar Wilderness, the Bob Marshall, the Scapegoat? In Glacier National Park? More mountains, more wildlife, more climbing. More navigational problems, no doubt. Next year, we would come back again. To the high country of the Continental Divide.

But for now, we could rest—and wonder about the next logistical problem. How were we going to get out of here? Dan Cooper hadn't come up to the border, at least not yet, since the guards told us that no one had come looking for us. Would he be here? And if not, what would we do? We decided to wait until dark, assuming that, if Dan had gotten our message, he would arrive before then.

If Dan Cooper didn't come, we would have to start walking back. Seven miles back to Cindy and Steve's place, and then maybe even more miles if we had difficulty hitchhiking out.

Or, said the American guard, we could ride with him; he'd be leaving at five.

We chewed on that possibility for a while. But what if Dan had gotten our message and was on his way?

The guards told us that it takes at least three hours to drive the 60 miles of the North Fork Road—especially in the wet, rutted condition it was in. If Dan Cooper was driving up on the road, we would be certain to see him as we rode out; there was no other road to the border station. By the time we would reach the end of the road, it would be about eight o'clock—well past dark. If Dan was indeed coming to get us, he would have to be on his way along the North Fork Road by then. If he wasn't on the North Fork Road by eight o'clock, he wouldn't be at the border station until after eleven at night—and it seemed unlikely that he would be planning to show up at the border in the middle of the night. So we concluded that if Dan wasn't on the road by eight o'clock, he hadn't gotten our message and wasn't coming. And if he was on his way, we would see him. We decided to go out with the border guards. It wasn't until several days later that we learned, to our chagrin and embarrassment, that Dan Cooper had indeed come up to get us—and he had arrived at the border just after eleven o'clock that night. We must have missed him by minutes.

Riding out on the dark road, we could feel the temperature dropping. The drizzle had become sleet, and then a heavy, wet snow. The truck navigated through the potholes, bouncing along slowly. It was well past dark when we reached the beginning of the pavement. A short while later, we arrived at the sign that announced we were 58 miles from the Canadian border. Joe pulled the truck over to the side of the road and turned his siren lights on. The revolving orange light lit up the darkness as Joe climbed on top of the truck and reached over to pull out the bottom section of the sign—the part that told motorists that the border station was open from nine to five. He turned it over, and slid it back into place, as snow continued to drift down.

In the orange light, we could read the sign now: "CLOSED FOR THE WINTER," it said.

Time for the border to close. And time, for now, for us to stop walking.

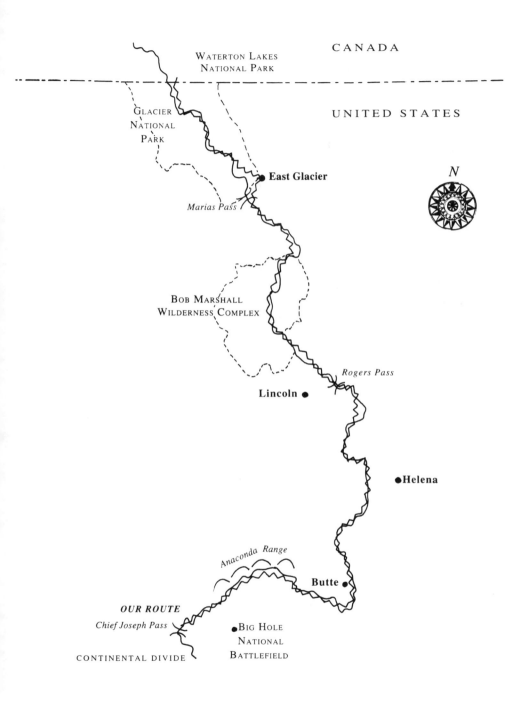

CANADA

WATERTON LAKES
NATIONAL PARK

UNITED STATES

GLACIER
NATIONAL
PARK

East Glacier

Marias Pass

BOB MARSHALL
WILDERNESS COMPLEX

Rogers Pass

Lincoln

Helena

Anaconda Range

Butte

OUR ROUTE

Chief Joseph Pass

Big Hole
NATIONAL
BATTLEFIELD

CONTINENTAL DIVIDE

N

11

≈≈≈≈≈

O CANADA!

≈≈≈≈≈

Chief Joseph Pass was a very different place the next July. There was no snow on the ground, no threat in the air. The temperature was a balmy 70 degrees. Farther north, snow still clung to some of Montana's high places, but here it only existed in our memories.

We had returned to Montana the long way, on a cross-country car trip that began in New York and took us to Montana via New Mexico. We had gone all the way back to the border station at Columbus, and then, for six weeks, we had driven north, following a meandering course that roughly paralleled the Divide. Our purpose: to return to the communities we had visited the previous year to collect information about things we had seen and learned and questioned. When we told the New Mexican border guard that we were going to Canada, there was no coy surprise lying in wait for his response. Yes, we agreed, it was a long way to drive.

Driving north from Columbus in our pint-sized red hatchback, we had marveled at the miles: 100 miles, 200 miles, covered with barely a break. The car was stuffed not only with backpacking gear but with car-camping necessities: a two-burner Coleman stove, an ice chest, pots and pans, a case of beer, several changes of clothing, a box of laundry detergent. There were two boxes of notes, books, pamphlets, reports, and scraps of paper with scribbles telling us to "talk to Joe at the district office" or to "call Bob about grazing." It was amazing how much stuff we had; amazing how many things became necessities the minute we used a car, and not our backs, to haul them around.

Six weeks later, Gordon and Sue met us in Stevensville, Montana, 60 miles north of Chief Joseph Pass, where we had been visiting with Dan Cooper. He had forgiven us for last season's wild-goose chase, and now he agreed to do us yet another favor by keeping our car for the summer.

In addition to Gordon and Sue, the van personnel included Mac and Muggsie, of course, as well as Cameron, a friend Gordon and Sue had met on the Pacific Crest Trail. Cameron had driven out from the Northwest to say hello to them and see us on our way.

The canoe was once again lashed to the top of the van. Sue blew up balloons for us to tie to our walking sticks, and produced a chocolate cake as a send-off treat. We took our pictures at the pass: Dan and me with balloons. *Click.* Dan and me with the cake. *Click.* Dan and me and Gordon and Sue with the cake and the balloons. *Click.* We looked every bit as ridiculous as we had the previous year, setting out to walk across the New Mexican desert accompanied by a canoe. Within minutes of regrouping, it was as though none of us had ever been apart from each other—or the Divide. We were home again.

We couldn't help comparing the beginning of this part of our journey to our first days in New Mexico a year earlier. A year ago, I had never met Gordon and Sue; now they were old friends. A year ago, we had been nervous and uncertain about what lay ahead and how we would handle it. Now, we were old hands: confident of our abilities and our strength, and confident, too, that we could work together to get through the hard parts. There was no question about whether or not we could walk almost 600 miles on trail: With the entire summer ahead of us, we could average an easy 12 or 13 miles a day and be finished walking by midafternoon, if not earlier. Last year, Dan had egged us on to do as many miles as possible. This year, we wanted to linger, to savor the end of our journey. We would have plenty of time to sit out at glacial tarns, read books, and watch the mountains change from gray to pink to purple as the stars came out for their nightly performance.

One thing that had changed was our planning. After leaving the trail the previous year, we had learned that a new guidebook, describing Montana's Continental Divide Trail, had been published by a local commercial publisher. The foreword informed us that the "portion in Montana and parts of Idaho has been completed, signed, and dedicated." We responded to that news suspiciously: We had purchased the book immediately after leaving the trail the previous October, and we keenly remembered plenty of places north of Yellowstone where the trail didn't qualify as "completed, signed, and dedicated." We remembered, in fact, plenty of stretches of trail that didn't even exist. Still, with a guidebook that laid out the new, official route for us, we could at least obtain the appropriate maps and attempt to find the trail.

Armed with the new guidebook, we requested information from the supervisor's office at the Bitterroot National Forest. What was the condition of the trail immediately north of Chief Joseph Pass? Gordon and Sue did the same at the ranger station, and Sue asked additional questions of a ranger she had met in the woods. All three gave us different information about the status and condition of the trail. The new guidebook's claims notwithstanding, nothing had changed.

At Chief Joseph Pass itself, however, there are actually signs for the Continental Divide Trail. On the highway, there are the large blue-and-white national scenic trail markers. And a few yards into the woods, along a thin footpath, there is a large, handsome wooden plaque declaring the dedication of the trail in Montana. We had camped there the previous year, when we hadn't been able to hitchhike to Gibbonsville.

The footpath continues, past the plaque, to a high-grade Forest

Service road. Despite the business about the "completed, signed, and dedicated" trail, despite even the big plaque, there were no blazes to show us which way to turn, no CDT markers. Nothing. This was the same kind of "now you see it, now you don't" trail that we had encountered last season—regardless of claims to the contrary. On the spot, we decided to do the same thing we had done the previous year: select each stretch of trail on a case-by-case basis, and always make sure we had the necessary maps.

THUMP-thump-thump-thump, THUMP-thump-thump, thump.

The night magnified the noise.

"Do you hear that?"

THUMP-thump-thump-thump.

"What do you think it is?"

"I don't know. What do you think it is?"

"I don't know. But it sounds like something human. Too regular for an animal."

"There aren't any humans here."

"What about the horse packers?"

"They're half a mile away. And it's two in the morning. What did they do? Bring recordings of tom-toms with them?"

"Go to sleep."

THUMP-thump-thump-thump.

Sure.

We lay awake, both of us quiet, not wanting the other to know that we were straining our ears, listening.

A few minutes later: "Are you asleep?"

"No."

"Me neither."

Finally: "I'm going out to see what it is."

Pause.

"Do you want to come?"

Was he out of his mind? Besides, I had already figured out what was making the noise. I just didn't want to talk about it.

Dan left the tent, flashlight slicing through the night. I stayed in my sleeping bag, listening, but the noise stopped. Then it started again, fainter this time.

I heard Dan rummaging around in the bush, and then I heard his footsteps as he returned to the tent.

"It's down by the stream," he announced. "It sounds like water flowing through a pipe. Maybe it goes underground through some rocks."

I didn't tell him that that didn't make sense: If the noise was caused by some regular, physical phenomenon, it wouldn't stop when Dan started investigating. But like I said, I already knew what was making the noise, and I didn't press the issue. Dan went to sleep, convinced that the noise was caused by water flowing under some rocks. I stayed awake a while longer, listening to the ghosts of Chief Joseph and the Nez Perce Indians.

≈≈≈≈≈≈≈≈

They had camped here, back in August 1877. They were a day or so ahead of the United States Army, trying to flee a war that had begun in the usual way: a fight between settlers and Indians over land. The land was to the west, in Idaho, and, as usual, the fact that the Nez Perce had lived on it for generations did not influence the outcome of the argument.

War had broken out between the nontreaty Nez Perce—those who had refused to move from their homelands to a crowded and inadequate reservation—and the United States Army. It was a war that the Nez Perce did not want, and they had been running away from it for two months now, hoping to find a new home among the Crow people.

As the Nez Perce slept here, they had no way of knowing that a new army contingent, led by Colonel John Gibbon, had been sent from Missoula. The Nez Perce thought they were several days ahead of their pursuers; in fact, Gibbon and his men trailed them by only a day. The next morning, they moved down Trail Creek to a campsite on the edge of the Big Hole Valley, where they hoped to take a few days' rest. They did not know that army scouts could see them as they went about the business of setting up their camp. They did not know that before dawn the next morning, soldiers would aim low at the tepees, in an ambush that was to kill between sixty and ninety Indians—as many as two thirds of whom are thought to have been women and children.

It was an effective ambush, so flawlessly executed that even the Nez Perce horses and dogs were unaware of the intruders until it was long past too late. But the Indians rallied, and, in a bitter, bloody fight, they killed twenty-nine of Gibbon's soldiers and volunteers. Twenty-four hours later, the Battle of the Big Hole ended in a standoff: the Nez Perce continued their flight, leaving Gibbon's men behind to nurse their wounds.

The Nez Perce continued their escape for two more months as Chief Joseph led them farther east. They fled when possible and fought when necessary. Having realized that the U.S. government would not let them flee in peace, they had changed their destination, and were headed for Canada, where they would be welcomed by the sympathetic Sioux and, more important, where they would be safe from the American army. The Nez Perce's escape route took them first southeast through the Yellowstone country and then north to the Bear Paw Mountains, where they were engaged in battle for the last time. Here, just short of the Canadian border, Chief Joseph of the Nez Perce surrendered, in words that contain the heartbreak of his people's history: "I am tired of fighting. He who led the young men is dead. It is cold and we have no blankets. The little children are freezing to death. Hear me, my chiefs. I am tired; my heart is sick and sad. From where the sun now stands, I will fight no more forever."

It was not, of course, Indian tom-toms I heard as I drifted off to sleep. In the bright light of morning, Cameron asked whether we had heard the sage chickens during the night.

"What do they sound like?" I asked.

"Sort of like a drum," he said, and he made the noise. *THUMP-thump-thump-thump*.

I still prefer my explanation.

It felt familiar to be walking again—not surprising, since we had spent most of the last year walking. Two miles into the hike, I got a blister from letting my feet sweat under a pair of Gore-Tex gaiters. We stopped, and I took care of the problem, immediately, but without the sense of dread that had accompanied last year's blisters. My first aid kit would take care of this one. It always did.

The walking might have been familiar, but the change in seasons was remarkable. This far north, it stayed light until 10:30, and it seemed that the sun had no sooner retired for the night than it was creeping back over the horizon. One account of the Battle of the Big Hole remarks that the battle began with the first gray streaks of dawn—at 3:30 in the morning. I devoutly hoped that Dan would not realize just how early the sun did rise: A morning person, he is deservedly notorious for his "dawn patrols."

There were other, less pleasant reminders of the change of season. This was snowmelt time, and the saturated, soggy earth was a breeding ground for insects. There were hordes and hordes of mosquitos, buzzing their high-pitched chain saw whine, and equivalent armies of flies: the slow fat ones that merely annoy you by walking on your arms and legs, and the agile fast ones that bite, and bite hard. In camp, we stood over a fire, hoping that the smoke would deter the insects, and we doused ourselves in insect repellent, more of it, during our first two weeks in Montana, than we had used in last year's entire six-month trek. But, no matter what the advertisements say, the repellent works only on mosquitos, who respect it enough to avoid biting you but not enough to go away. As far as the flies are concerned, the repellent might just as well be chum.

Trails in wilderness areas tend to be well marked; as a rule, you don't need much more than a Forest Service map to find them. The Anaconda Pintlar Wilderness was no exception, as we followed neat paths up and over a series of 9,000-foot passes. Snow still clung to the high slopes, and it occurred to us that some of it might have been left over from the storm that had chased us away the year before. Now, the snow was meekly melting into the frigid waters of jewellike alpine lakes.

It was early in the season, and we had the wilderness to ourselves, except for one or two horseback riders. It wasn't until we were on our way out, a few days later, that we saw any other backpackers— a couple, trudging up the switchbacks to the high country. Farther down, we ran into a lone day-hiker: To our surprise, it was Jim Wolf, the head of the CDTS and author of the guidebook that we had used the previous year, here to check out the new trail for a revision of his Montana guidebook. It was sorely needed; the old CDTS book was out of date, and the new, commercially published book we had been using was incomplete and rife with errors. Jim told us that he had met Gordon and Sue the previous evening: They were on their way up the trail to meet us. He also told us that we had just missed meeting a couple who were trying to hike the Continental Divide southbound. Joe and Carol McVeigh had stayed at the Forest Service campground the previous evening, but they had decided to road-walk around the wilderness. The snow farther north had put them behind schedule, and they were worried about running into more of it in the Pintlar Mountains.

North of the Anaconda Pintlar Wilderness, the mountains become modest again, staying largely below tree line. The Divide makes another of its huge meandering arcs, this time to the east. As we approached the city of Butte, the trail became frankly boring, following networks of logging roads. Even the Forest Service man told us that we wouldn't miss much if we just skipped this part. The trail goes through logged areas, old mines, and ranches, following high-grade gravel roads. Still, we were here to see the Divide, and if the Divide was an unspectacular wooded ridge crisscrossed with logging roads, then that was what we would see. Every once in a while, a pickup truck stopped, and a curious face emerged to find out just what we were doing there.

"Where you from?" demanded one, whose truck looked like it was hauling some sort of contraption for cleaning out septic tanks.

"New York," we told him.

"Different there."

"Oh yeah."

There was a long silence, and I felt obliged to fill it in. An eastern habit: You see space, you build on it. You hear silence, you talk through it. I started babbling inanities about New York: how crowded it was, how many people seemed to live on top of each other.

The man nodded. "Know just what you mean," he said. He pointed, an expansive gesture that took in the entire gray-green hillocks of the virtually uninhabited valley. "It's gettin' to be just like that around here."

Dan and I followed his gesture down the broad sweep of the valley—miles of sagebrush and forest. But the man was dead serious.

"I'll tell you," he said. "Everyone's taking up their forty-acre parcels. There's gettin' to be a building on every drainage. How are the elk supposed to get down into their winter range with all these people here? Used to have huge herds. Not anymore. Overpopulation is going to ruin this valley.''

≋

The gravel roads might have been unattractive and utilitarian, but they did make for easy walking and easy navigating. The grades were gentle enough that I could keep up with Dan for most of the day, and when I got tired, we could each walk at our own pace without worrying about losing the route.

We were hiking apart, inevitably, before our midday lunch break. The walking wasn't particularly strenuous, but the heat of the sun was enervating: It reflected off the roads, and there was little shade in the open sagebrush and the heavily logged forests. Dan was ahead of me, a quarter mile or so, but when the road curved on a long, tight turn, we found that we were separated by only a hundred yards of wide, vegetation-choked streambed. We shouted back and forth across the gully, mostly about stopping for lunch, and we followed up our lunch stop negotiations with a series of silly noises and endearments. Most couples generally reserve this sort of thing for private, but this was the luxury of western space: We could scream them at the top of our lungs in the great outdoors. The last thing we expected to see on this dusty, unremarkable Forest Service road was a trio of backpackers walking around the bend.

We responded to them with the same surprise that the pickup truck drivers and ranchers usually bestowed on us. This was not recreation country, it was multiple use country; it was not (CDT notwithstanding) a hiking trail, but a dirt road—and a rather unattractive one at that. There was only one reason that anyone would be carrying a backpack here: These three had to be trying to hike the Continental Divide.

And so they were. Steve and Bill had started in Canada in early June; Sam had run into them a couple of weeks later. Dan and Steve compared backpacking dossiers and learned not only that they had both hiked the AT and the PCT, but that they had once shared a night in a lean-to in Virginia. This semiremembrance of a passing acquaintance made them blood brothers, at least for the moment.

Fortunately, it was noon, none of us had had lunch, and we were right near a stream. With a small patch of shade, all the necessities were in place for a break. We pulled over on the side of the road and spread out our maps, trading information on what lay ahead.

What lay ahead for us was many more miles of these Forest Service roads. Steve complained about blisters from the sharp gravel, and all three of the guys were starting to wonder if hiking the Continental Divide was such a good idea after all. We assured them that they were near the end of this stretch of road-walking; they told us that our next week or so was going to be pretty dull.

It was. The Divide is low and wooded around Butte. More than anything, this is mining country: The tourist brochures call it the "Gold West," and the state motto is *Oro y plata*—"Gold and silver." That, however, is misleading. It is true that Montana was a gold rush state, but as in Colorado, the drama of Montana's mining boom emerged from the exploitation of another metal. In Colorado it was silver that built the opera houses and the Victorian mansions and the legends; in Montana, it was copper. Butte, Montana, located just at the base of the Continental Divide, was the home of the Copper Kings—and yet another of the West's "most fabulous mining camps in the world."

The Divide here is highly mineralized, and there are abandoned mines and tailings and prospect holes anywhere you look. There are ghost towns, ranging from the rotten remains of a few shacks to carefully restored towns like Bannack, Montana's first territorial capital, founded when gold was discovered in 1862 in nearby Grasshopper Creek.

Butte, however, is no ghost town. It began as a modest gold rush town in the 1860s, grew with a boom in silver, and by the 1880s had become the world's greatest copper producer, supplying a full 18 percent of the copper mined in the United States. Marcus Daly, one of the legendary wheeler-dealers of the Old West, built the world's largest copper smelter in nearby Anaconda—named after his copper company. In his spare time, he amused himself with horseracing, owning a baseball and a football team, and getting into price-fixing wars with other industrialists.

The mining industry still dominates Butte, pulling copper and molybdenum from an area known, with typical western understatement, as the "richest hill on earth." In the center of town is Montana's deepest body of water: not a lake, nor even a reservoir, but an open-pit copper mine, 7,000 feet long, 5,600 feet wide (that is, about a mile and a quarter by a mile), and 1,800 feet deep, 700 feet of which is filled with water.

Like so many other western towns, Butte has had to turn to tourism to keep its economy strong. Many of the mines have closed, and in one six-year period this city of some 40,000 people lost 1,500 jobs. We resupplied in Butte, staying long enough to take a tour of its major tourist attraction, so-called Hellroarin' Gulch. Like Butte's giant mines, its ornate Victorian mansions, and its dignified downtown buildings, Hellroarin' Gulch was built in grand style, with everything from old railroad equipment to cobblestone streets to the display items in an apothecary shop.

North of Butte, the trail continued to follow networks of roads, and occasionally trails that posed an interesting assortment of navigational problems, worst among them getting lost in a swamp so infested with mosquitos that we couldn't stand still for long enough to consult our maps to find a way out of it. The southbounders we had met had told us that once we reached the Helena National Forest we would find that the quality of both trail and terrain was much improved. They were right. Where the trail had been completed, the trail crews had done an outstanding job, marking the route as though they intended hikers to follow it without constantly referring to maps and guidebooks. In a few places, the trail passed through large clearcuts, and the land was scarred with the usual debris of roads and slash. But even in the clearcuts, the route was clearly marked—something we had not seen anywhere else on the Continental Divide.

In Helena, Dan's friends Deb and Mardell joined us. Dan had met Deb and Mardell on the PCT in 1986, and had hiked with them for 1,000 miles. But I had never met them before.

One of the most interesting things about hiking with new people is seeing how different people cope with wilderness challenges. Hiking with new people brings habits into focus, spotlighting both differences and similarities in the ways we humans learn to deal with environmental stress.

In the animal kingdom, the same thing happens. Species evolve—or perish—as a result of how well they respond to the stresses they face. As always, water is a good example. In the desert, one animal may minimize how much water evaporates through its sweat; another may tolerate going thirsty for long periods of time; a third may simply store water in its body.

Backpackers, too, adapt to environmental stress. Just as different animals evolve different ways to tolerate a lack of water, the four of us responded to the water shortage north of Helena in four different ways.

Dan is a planner: He studied the maps to identify water sources and to figure out how we could plan our day to use them to best advantage. We would arrive at water in mid-afternoon; did anyone object to eating dinner then, so we wouldn't have to carry ten pounds of cooking water 5 miles uphill? I was a rationer: I didn't want to carry an ounce more than necessary, but I didn't want to run out, either. I knew how much water I needed to get through a dry stretch, and I kept an eye on the contents of my canteen, careful to always have a little left for the end. Deb did not want to be thirsty, period, and she didn't care how much she had to carry. She filled her canteens, and when a passing pickup truck driver gave us an old plastic jug, she tied that to the back of her pack, and filled it, as well. Mardell did exactly the opposite: She would drink as much as possible at each spring as though she could carry the water inside her like a camel. Then she would suspiciously eye her canteen as though some extra water might have snuck inside, and try to decide if she really and truly did need all of it to get her to the next spring.

North of Helena, our route stayed largely on the waterless crest of the Divide, giving us plenty of time to see how our various systems worked. In the end, we all had what we needed.

The trail varied from well-marked footway to the black hole of new construction. Sometimes we found ourselves either going cross-country through difficult, tangled terrain, or following dirt roads; more often, we were on trail, or on the open highlands of the Divide itself. This was dry country, high country, rocky country—mountain goat country.

And also, grizzly country. Again. This year, however, we were carrying a new piece of equipment: a can of bear repellent, which we had found in a sporting goods store in Great Falls.

For years, we had read that grizzly bears didn't like cayenne pepper. How this was learned, and how it could be helpful, had always seemed uncertain to me—one couldn't, for instance, defend oneself against a charging bear with a heavily spiced freeze-dried dinner. Now, someone had developed a bear repellent using capsicin, which is the active ingredient in cayenne pepper. It comes in a can, about the size of a can of hairspray, and I wore it in a pouch that hung from the belt of my backpack.

We can't vouch for how well the repellent does or doesn't work, or whether it will stop the express-train charge of a grizzly sow who thinks her cubs are endangered. But believing that there was something we could do other than roll over and play dead completely changed how we felt about walking through grizzly country.

The terrain improved dramatically as we approached Rogers Pass, a highway crossing of the Divide in northern Montana. The Divide here is a high open ridge, and for the past three days we were almost entirely on top of it. The crest was treeless, windswept and rocky, and devoid of all but the hardiest vegetation. There were short, wiry grasses, and rocks colored by multihued lichen. Occasionally, we would see the delicate deep pink flowers of the bitterroot, Montana's state flower, growing among the rocky rubble of the alpine zone. The ridge rose and fell as it led us closer and closer to the high country of Montana's northern wildernesses. We were near the end now, the 275-mile grand finale of the Scapegoat Wilderness, the Bob Marshall Wilderness, and Glacier National Park.

But first we had to resupply in the town of Lincoln, where we learned that our maps for the next section had been lost somewhere in the postal system. But here we were lucky: Lincoln was one of the only towns on our entire route where a general store actually had a complete selection of local USGS maps.

Almost everyone who has ever attempted the Continental Divide trail has resupplied in Lincoln, and, since the 1970s, the post office there has maintained a register of long-distance hikers. We borrowed the two battered notebooks for the evening and browsed through them, noting familiar names of hikers we had met on other trails.

Because Lincoln is so close to the northern terminus of the CDT, the register included notes from almost everyone who had ever tried to hike the trail southbound; there was no way of knowing who had actually completed the trip. They had left rave reviews about the scenery, along with the typical litany of complaints about food, horseback riders, blisters, trail conditions, Glacier's park rangers, and grizzly bears. We added our comments, along with a brief notation about our trip.

〜〜〜〜〜〜

From Rogers Pass, a steep climb took us back to the crest of the Divide. The open uplands continued to Lewis and Clark Pass, an ancient crossing of the mountains. It is a windy pass, so much so that the trees that do grow on it have actually been bent clear to the ground by the wind; they grow horizontally, toward the east, cowering in the face of the pass's hurricane-strength winds.

On this isolated, weather-battered pass, we felt a strong sense of walking in the footsteps of history. By the time Meriwether Lewis showed up to ''discover'' it, the pass had already been in use for centuries: It was a route used by western slope Indians to travel to and from the buffalo that lived on the plains to the east. When Lewis came through (the expedition had split, and Clark was exploring the southern portion of the state), he found a herd of 10,000 buffalo just 2 miles to the east. On the pass itself, there are gouge marks in the earth—not the recent ruts of pickup trucks or off-road vehicles, but older cuts, made by generations of Indians, who dragged buffalo meat and skins over the Divide in wooden travois.

We left the Divide at the pass and descended into the Alice Creek drainage. Water was scarce on this stretch of trail, and we would be able to cook our dinner at Alice Creek—where, incidentally, Lewis had camped in 1806—and then climb back up to the Divide to camp.

The climb was not steep, but long, and it seemed even longer because the day had been a tough one. But a reward awaited us at the top: a panoramic view and a sunset to match. The mountains were higher now, and more rugged. To the north, we could see steep pinnacles, and patches of snow, and long escarpments of upthrust rock formations. At some point soon, we would look to the north and the view would extend into Canada.

We had carried some fruit from town, and since we had eaten dinner at midday, we still had our lunch food: crackers and cheese—as usual—and some sausage. We spread it out, and somehow it seemed a princely feast, as we watched the sun go down over waves of mountains from our perch on top of the world.

≈≈≈≈

The Scapegoat Wilderness is named after Scapegoat Mountain, so called because it was blamed for problems encountered by the USGS team that surveyed the area at the turn of the century. We had no such problems: Our route was clear, following obvious trails and open ridges from where we could see miles and miles of wilderness. Most of it was scarred by fire.

The Canyon Creek fire had roared through here in 1988. Fanned by wind and steep upslopes, it had even managed to cross the Divide in a few places. This had been a violent, uncontrollable wildfire; as in Yellowstone, its aftereffects will alter the landscape for years to come. Everywhere we looked, there were signs of the fire: the familiar blackened earth, whitened tree trunks stark as skeletons, entire slopes of matchstick forests.

And flowers. Thousands upon thousands of acres were covered with more flowers than our eyes could comprehend, flowers as brilliant as rainbows, as countless as stars. I don't think that anyone, in an entire lifetime—not a florist, not a funeral director, not anyone—would see as many flowers as there were in front of us at any one place in that one day.

The Scapegoat Wilderness was blanketed with flowers. There were miniature forests of brilliant magenta fireweed; there were deep purple lupine in a hue that perfectly complemented the verdant, heathy grasses. Golden aster covered the ground like a solid blanket of sunlight, and still there was more: yellow and purple daisies, crimson Indian paintbrush, lilies and yarrow and violets and thistle that sprang up among the ashy trunks of dead trees. Entire hillsides were covered, euphoric, in a wash of color.

This was a forest celebrating itself. The fire here had been an agent not only of change but also of brilliant, exultant creation; a wild, uncontrollable artist who, in a fit of frenzy, had created an overwhelming and wondrous beauty.

We walked slowly that day, stopping to take photographs that never really could capture the brilliance and the scope and the color and the numbers and the variety of flowers. We walked through shoulder-high fireweed, sat in fields of aster so thick that we were hidden among the flowers, and followed trails that cut through this most abundant of wilderness gardens. When we reached the end of the burned area, and walked back into the deep green woods, it was as though we had stepped out of a kaleidoscope into a black-and-white film.

The Scapegoat Wilderness is separated from the Bob Marshall Wilderness by a high-grade dirt road. Roads are prohibited in wilderness areas, but this one is there because the Bob Marshall and Scapegoat wildernesses are managed as two separate entities within the larger Bob Marshall Wilderness Complex. There is also an airstrip and a guest ranch and a Forest Service campground and a parking lot—none of which would be allowed if the wildernesses were managed as a single unit. But this way, the Forest Service gets to indulge in its road-building addiction, and the outfitters gain access to this most remote part of Montana's Continental Divide; the road is permitted here by the letter of the Wilderness Act, if not—one could argue—its spirit.

The road also allowed Sue and Gordon to drive in and meet us for the last time. Usually, Sue and Gordon would not have been able to come in on the dusty, bumpy road. Fortunately, Deb's van was available, and, after a complicated logistical shuttle, Sue and Gordon arrived to greet us at the Forest Service campground with a finish line made of toilet paper, streamers, and balloons. This was not, obviously, Canada, and we were not finished walking, but Sue and Gordon were finished traveling with us: They had decided to spend the fall with the southbound Continental Divide hikers whom we had met earlier in the month. We were disappointed that they wouldn't be at Waterton Lakes to meet us when we finally came to the end of our odyssey; we had always assumed they would be there to share the finish with us. But we understood their reasons. From here north, there were only a few more road crossings where Sue would be able to meet us and hike for a while, and all of them were in grizzly country.

So, we dug into a cake with "Congratulations" and "Canada" written in icing, draped ourselves in toilet paper, and tied balloons to our packs. Gordon and Sue headed south toward Wyoming; Deb and Mardell had come to the end of their hike with us, and they left, too. Dan and I were alone again as we repacked our food and supplies for the next leg of our journey into the Bob Marshall Wilderness.

The Bob, as it's known, is one of the nation's better known wilderness areas, perhaps in part because of the beloved conservationist after whom it was named—a man, incidentally, who was reputed to think nothing of walking 30 or even 40 miles in a day. It is large, and remote, and wild, and it provides a haven for those animals that simply cannot or will not share their habitat with humans. Almost every big game species in the United States can be found in the Bob, including elk, bighorn sheep, and mountain goats, as well as black bears, grizzlies, and wolves.

It is wild country, with soaring peaks and deep canyons, and lush, thick forests. Our route through it generally stayed low, following river bottoms and wooded trails—pretty enough, if you forget that you have been routed off the nearby high peaks and ridges. Still, there was drama: The most spectacular geologic component of the Bob Marshall Wilderness is on the Divide itself—the 18-mile-long, 1,000-foot-high Chinese wall, an escarpment of overthrust limestone that is indeed the natural equivalent of its namesake. For a day, we walked along the base of the gigantic cliffs, looking up in awe at one of nature's geologic extravagances.

The area is heavily used, particularly by people on horseback, and the trails reflected that use: well graded, but damaged from poor drainage and constant traffic. It didn't help our morale that it rained the entire time we were in the Bob, nor that the rain turned the trails into slippery rivers of mud.

These were the days the ads for outdoor gear don't mention: the days that make you wonder what you're doing out here in the first place. The rain was interrupted occasionally by marble-sized hailstones that seemed frankly vicious, and it was impossible to stay dry, regardless of our high-tech fabrics. When the rain did stop, out came the mosquitos.

The rain kept our minds off the grizzly bears, who, we hoped, would show better sense than we did and stay holed up somewhere. But there was plenty of evidence to the contrary: claw marks carved into trees; tracks on the ground; scat deposited in neat, new piles on the trail. We kept the bear repellent handy, and plowed on ahead, through thick forest and big patches of bright red thimbleberries, just coming into season. The thimbleberries were a delicious trailside treat, like raspberries, but sweeter—and they had no thorns to snag greedy fingers. But the bears liked them too—that much was obvious from the thimbleberry content of the bear scat on the trail. We didn't much relish the possibility of an argument about who had dibs on a berry patch, so our berry picking was furtive and quick—we grabbed at the fruit closest to the trail and kept on walking.

Montana has a hunting season on grizzly bears, which seems a ludicrous contradiction, given that the animals are officially classified as a threatened species. The Forest Service and the state of Montana defend the policy, saying that it keeps the bears wild, and that hunted bears, unlike park bears, are more afraid of humans. But that night we woke up to something sniffing and rooting about our tent—whatever it was clearly wasn't alarmed at our human scent. Dan silently reached over for the bear repellent, released the safety lock, and waited for whatever was out there to make the next move. A few moments later, the noise stopped.

The southern boundary of Glacier National Park runs along a road and a parallel railroad track, and on the map the lines run together unless you look at them closely. We hadn't, which is why we were surprised to find out that the place we had intended to camp when we left the wilderness was actually inside Glacier National Park.

Signs on the gates that led into the park reminded us of the regulations: We needed a permit, and we needed to stay in a designated backcountry campsite. The nearest ranger station was in East Glacier, 6 miles away.

We looked for a place to camp along the road, but this was open country, and we would have had to go a good bit off route to find a place to hide. We decided to continue on the highway for a while and see if we could find a place to put up the tent. We found, instead, a roadside diner, and, as usual, after we had some fresh food in our stomachs, the road ahead looked suddenly much shorter and easier. East Glacier was now only 3 miles away—why not go all the way in and be done with it? The next day we'd be able to take some time off while waiting for our friend Tom Carlin to join us for the last part of our walk—a trek through Glacier National Park.

Our first inkling of problems ahead came from the motel manager, who told us that the ranger station at East Glacier had been closed all summer due to budget cuts. How then, were we supposed to get the permit to start our hike into the park?

We called ahead to the ranger station at Two Medicine Lake, which was 10 miles into the park via our route. To our surprise, the man who answered the phone absolutely refused to even talk to me about the permit over the phone. I explained what we were doing, and that, since we were on foot, we were concerned that by the time we could walk to the ranger station, some of the sites on our route might be filled up.

"Look," I pleaded. "The rules say we can get a permit twenty-four hours before we start our hike. It's not our fault that your office in East Glacier is closed. It's not like we can just walk to another one. Can't you reserve the spots for us over the phone, and we'll pick up the permit when we get to Two Medicine Lake on Friday?"

The official didn't budge. "Now you're bringing up the issue of whether the rules make sense," he told me in a scolding voice. "And that is inappropriate. This may be a bugaboo, but it's a bugaboo we all have to live with."

He sounded quite pleased with himself.

That night, Tom surprised us by showing up in a rental car. A stroke of fortune! We could drive around to the ranger station and get this permit business over and done with.

So the next morning, we piled into the car and headed off to Two Medicine Lake, a sacred place to the Blackfoot Indians. Two Medicine Lake is one of those picture postcard places that shows up on calendars and outdoor magazines, one of those places you can't quite believe even when it's right in front of you. It was in front of us now: deep blue, surrounded by huge glacial sculptures and the impossibly narrow vertical tower of euphonically named Pumpelly Pillar. I ignored the scenery and went straight to the ranger station. The man I had talked to the previous day—a volunteer, I learned—wasn't there. No harm in that—it wasn't as if he had been helpful. Another volunteer was in his place, an elderly gentleman whose primary job was taking care of the car campground at the foot of the lake. He looked up in confusion when I said "backcountry permit."

"You should have come earlier," he told me. "I already gave out a permit this morning. I don't know if there will be any left."

I didn't know whether to laugh or put my fist through the wall, but I restrained myself from doing either and asked, "Do you think you could find out?"

"Well, I'll tell you one thing," he said, shaking his head. "You can't hike on the trail to Grizzly Medicine Lake. It's closed. I can't give you a permit for Grizzly Medicine Lake."

"Grizzly Medicine Lake isn't on our route," I said, pointing to the map.

The review of our schedule occurred at a glacial pace. First, he checked each campsite against a map. "That's a long way to walk," he told me, referring to one 10- or 12-mile stretch between sites. I assured him that we could walk the 12 miles, and he went on to weigh the pros and cons of our next planned site while my neurotic imagination heard the central backcountry office assigning away all the permits.

"There's a problem with this one," he told me. "I can't issue this. You see there?" He pointed to a listing of campsites; the one we wanted had an asterisk next to it. "It says you can only camp at Reynold's Creek with subdistrict ranger approval."

"I think that's because that particular site is reserved for long-distance hikers," I said.

"Well, I wouldn't know anything about that," the volunteer replied.

"Is there a subdistrict ranger we can talk to?"

"No, he's off right now."

"Maybe there's someone else who could help?"

"The assistant subdistrict ranger is out on the lake," he said doubtfully. "She should be back soon."

A half hour went by. I got up to use the rest room, but another volunteer had come in, and informed me that the rest room was for rangers and staff only. I could use the one outside. I was afraid of missing the ranger when she returned, so I sat back down.

Finally, the volunteer tried to reach the ranger by radio. He paged her twice before an irritated voice crackled over the air. "What?"

"There's a young lady who needs to see you."

"What does she want?" the voice snapped back.

"It's about a backcountry permit."

"I'll be back in a while. The boat's out of gas." I could hear an exasperated sigh, and it didn't take much imagination to gauge her mood.

An hour went by. Finally, the campground host allowed that I could use the rest room. The assistant subdistrict ranger came in, all business, and studied my permit application. She couldn't approve the campsite, either: It was in another district. There were yet other problems with our hike, we proceeded to learn.

You can only get a permit for a maximum of six nights at Glacier. Our trip required eight campsites. We would have to, we were told, reapply for a permit midway through our hike. Could we extend the permit while out on the trail? Technically, yes—except that there were no ranger stations on our route, and we probably wouldn't run into a ranger until at least the fifth day. We were worried, we said, that by the fifth day, the rest of the campsites we needed would be booked. That was likely, she told us: The campsites we needed to complete our trip were the most popular in the entire park. Was there some way she could help us? There wasn't.

There were other problems: We were expecting two additional friends, Anne and Steve Emry, to join us at the Many Glacier campground. They were driving all the way from San Francisco in order to hike the last four days with us. Therefore, we needed a permit for three people for the first four nights, and five people for the remainder of our hike. Not possible: You can't add someone to your permit in the middle of your hike.

What about booking two campsites for the entire hike? That way, Dan and I could use one site and Tom the other for the first few days; when Anne and Steve joined us, we could double up in one of the sites. No, we were told, that wouldn't work: There is room for only two tents at the Reynold's Creek site.

That was no problem, we said; we only needed room for two tents at Reynold's Creek—Anne and Steve wouldn't be with us until the following day. Could we book two campsites everywhere else, and just one at Reynold's Creek? No, because the permit can only be written for one site or two sites—you can't change mid-course.

That wasn't all. Our route took us through the Many Glacier campground, a car campground where the park reserves a site for hikers who are on a backcountry trip. The site, however, was already fully booked, so our permit would have to end there.

That didn't have to be a problem, we said: Since we were meeting Anne and Steve at Many Glacier, we could stay in their car campsite with them.

No again, the ranger told us: If we stayed in a car campsite, we would be officially in the front country, and that would invalidate the permit. But wasn't the backcountry site only a few yards away? we asked. Wasn't the only thing that differentiated it from a car campsite the sign in front of it? Yes, she said. Then what was the problem? Without a permit for the one, we were not eligible to get a permit for the following night. My head began to spin. I tried to see the positive side. I was, after all, a writer; maybe this was how Kafka got his start.

When I finally left the ranger station, somewhere after noon, I was muttering incoherently—something about trying to walk through the park, not build a nuclear reactor in it. In my hand, I held a permit for three people for the first six nights. But we were not yet finished with the Glacier permit system.

We had spent so much energy on the permits that as we started walking, we barely noticed our surroundings. Glacier is not named glacier for nothing: It is a classically scoured landscape of classically scoured mountains. Gentle national park trails lead up to spectacular passes, and the walking is so easy that you might forget how steep the slopes are—unless something falls off the trail. Tom set his backpack down; it toppled over, and two bounces and ten seconds later it was 300 feet down the mountain. It took him an hour to retrieve it.

Like Yellowstone, Glacier has a policy of clustering backcountry users together in group campsites. The campsites were bound to disappoint us: After camping wherever and whenever we wanted to for so long, we didn't care for the regimentation and regulation of group sites in the backcountry. The clustering does minimize the risk of grizzly bear problems in camp; it was the trail that we were most worried about. We were far more likely to surprise a bear feeding in a thimbleberry patch, which is exactly where we had been seeing a disconcerting amount of fresh bear scat.

At the campsites, the most frequent topic of conversation is the permit system, and by the end of our first day, we had learned why so many of the park's campsites were booked up.

"What you have to do," another hiker explained, "is make up a couple of fake itineraries that end up putting you where you want to go. See . . ." He pulled out his permit. "You just make up one or two extra days at the beginning so that you can book the permit a couple of days ahead." He showed us how he had reserved two sites he never intended to use in advance, which made it possible for his group to book the sites they did want earlier in the week.

Sometimes people canceled the fictitious part of the trips, sometimes not. One group we met had three permits, which, linked together, gave them the hike they wanted to do. How many people had been told by park personnel that sites were all filled when they were, in fact, booked up because of phony itineraries? And whose fault was that? The hikers' or the administration's?

At the Many Glacier ranger station, we learned that our instincts had indeed been correct: We were headed for trouble, the trouble being that it was technically impossible for us to complete our hike on the route that we intended to take.

This was because of park policy, which is that hikers can only book a hike one day in advance, but once they start reserving campsites, they can book six days in a row. One of the most popular hikes in Glacier begins on the northern side of the park; several days later it passes through the 50-Mountain site, which therefore can be—and usually is—booked several days ahead of time. 50-Mountain was the only possible site on our route for miles in either direction.

From where we stood, it was a two-day walk to 50-Mountain (it's impossible to go any slower—there was only one campsite between us and 50-Mountain, and hikers are limited to a one-night stay at that site). Thus, on our route, it was only possible to book 50-Mountain three days in advance. But—Catch-22—the hordes on the Highline Trail, who are coming from the opposite direction, are able to book 50-Mountain four or five days in advance; thus, no matter how long we were willing to wait, someone coming south on the Highline Trail would always be ahead of us in line. Unless the park made an exception or we broke the rules, it would be—literally—impossible for us to complete our walk. Or, looked at another way (the way I preferred to see it), the Park Service had spent thousands of dollars on a trail that their rules made it impossible to hike on.

Of course, there was never any question that we were going to complete our walk, and that we were going to complete it on the route we intended. If Dan and I had been alone, we might have simply given up on the bureaucracy and hidden in the woods. But we had five people and three tents, and it would have been difficult to keep a group that large out of sight. Too, we didn't want to end our walk worrying about being caught illegally camped in the park—the last thing we wanted was to be escorted out of Glacier within shouting distance of the Canadian border. We decided to give the Park Service another opportunity to let us do our walk legally.

We were, however, running out of patience. We had walked 600 miles this summer to get here, and 3,200 miles in all. Our friends had driven across the country to be with us at the end of our walk. We had done everything we could to get a permit. We had written months in advance. We had driven 40 miles to and from a ranger station in a rented car. We had been willing to change the dates of our hike. We had spent several hours—so far—fussing over the permits. We had walked here from goddamned Mexico, and we were going to walk into Canada at Waterton Lakes.

It took a direct appeal to the supervisor's office. Finally, after telling our story for the umpteenth time, navigating—one more time—through the tortuous regulations of the permit system, and then waiting another half hour or so while various layers of bureaucracy were involved in the momentous question of where and how we could camp, we received the news, and the ranger who wrote out our permit was as surprised as anyone to hear it: We had received special permission to camp in a so-called undesignated site in Glacier National Park.

We couldn't help but reflect on the ironies of the National Park Service. The Park Service, more than the Forest Service, is the nation's real playground. Park Service staff have no timber or mining or—generally—grazing to worry about; their mission is much more clearly slanted toward recreation. Yet it was much more difficult to recreate in the national parks than in the forests. As far as Glacier went, it seemed odd that we would have the most problems here, where park staff had worked long, hard hours to put the CDT in place. In Yellowstone, exactly the opposite had happened: The Yellowstone trail staff had made it clear to us that they didn't intend to do anything at all about the CDT until they had to; yet, when it came down to dealing with individual hikers, they had been willing to help us out and make exceptions. All of the national parks on the Appalachian Trail and the Pacific Crest Trail have managed to find ways to accommodate long-distance hikers. Despite their legitimate concerns about grizzly bears and overcrowding, it seems ludicrous that the parks on the Continental Divide would not be able to do the same. After all, the Bob Marshall Wilderness has plenty of grizzly bears; Yosemite has both black bears and overcrowding, yet in neither of those places must hikers jump through a ridiculous series of impossible hoops to receive permits to hike on a hiking trail and camp in a campsite.

With permits in hand, we heaved a sigh of relief and got down to the business of enjoying the last few days of what had been, for us, an epic journey. Our friends Anne and Steve were waiting for us at the Many Glacier campground, and two other friends had showed up to visit. The campground was equipped with showers, laundry, and a restaurant—this was, after all, the front country—so we took the opportunity to get cleaned up and then sat long into the night talking.

The next morning, we started up to Swiftcurrent Pass, a 2,400-foot elevation gain from the campground. No matter how you grade it, 2,400 feet is a long haul, especially for people on their first day out. But there was no way to avoid it: The mountains are just that big. Anne had never done any hiking before, and it had been a long time since Steve had carried a backpack. They were in good spirits, though, as the climb went up and up and up, leaving the strings of lakes for the rocky slopes of Swiftcurrent Mountain. By the time we reached camp, Anne and Steve declared that it was time for a nap.

As if on schedule, a ranger showed up to check our permits. He also warned us to watch out for the deer: They frequented the campsite, he told us, and were especially fond of the sweat-soaked clothes that hikers often leave hanging out to dry. Yeah, right, we said, and ignored the ranger and his advice until dusk, when three deer did indeed show up, intent on finding something salty to chew on. One was carrying an old, long-stolen T-shirt in his teeth.

We were acutely aware, now, how near the end we were. At the beginning of the hike, we had been slow to accumulate the mental trophies that marked our progress: the first 100 miles, the first 10,000-foot peak, the first time on the Continental Divide, the first town stop. But now that process was reversed. The elevations had been decreasing for almost half the trip. The last 13,000-foot peak was on Colorado's Front Range. The last 12,000 footer—again in Colorado, at Parkview Mountain. The last 11,000-foot peak was in Wyoming; the last 10,000-foot peak in southwestern Montana. This summer, we had dispensed with 9,000-foot elevations back in the Anaconda Pintlar Wilderness, and 8,000 feet a few days earlier. Now, the countdown was progressing with dizzying speed: In the next four days we would go from 7,000 feet all the way down to 4,000 feet—lower, even, than the elevation at Columbus, New Mexico.

This counting down could get ridiculous: The last town stop—at East Glacier. The last resupply—at Many Glacier campground. And the mileage, so quickly decreasing now that we were in double digits: less than 50 miles left, less than 40. The last pass, the last snowfield, the last big climb (how I loved that one!), the last campsite, river ford, campfire.

Finally, the last steps. Dan and I walked them alone. Steve and Tom and Anne had gone on ahead, with our cameras, to the monuments that mark the border. Dan and I sat down—to give them a head start; to take in, finally, that this, really, was the end. In a week, we'd be home. Mowing a lawn. Taking out the trash. Moving furniture. Putting pictures back on walls.

All together, road walk and all, it had been 3,200 miles, give or take. Of that, 2,900 miles had been on the Divide itself, 285 on the roads last fall. Six million steps, near as we could figure; 233 days. Perhaps 300,000 feet of climbing.

We tried to take it all in: the end, the real, final end of this journey. What we had seen, and felt, and experienced all came back in a sort of jumble of images that we would need time to sort out, time to understand.

What had we learned from this?

For me, some of the lessons were simple ones. How far a mile is, and how far a mile can be. That no matter how tired I was, I could always walk a little more. That Dan and I could work together to solve tough problems.

We had both learned new skills out here, walking where the waters divide. We learned to read a landscape, to understand the lay of the drainages and rivers and passes and peaks. We got very, very good with our maps and our compasses. We learned to pace ourselves, to compromise. We learned how to feel the weather change.

And some of the lessons were more complex. We learned about the beauty of wide open landscapes, and we learned how rare they are becoming. We learned that issues that seem cut and dried from far away become much less so up close. We learned that there are few villains and few heroes in the fight over our wild places— and that there are few easy answers, too. We learned to hear the other side of the story, and we learned a respect for life-styles far different from our own. We learned that, no, the Divide has not been conquered, but that it is threatened by forces we cannot afford to ignore.

But most of all, we learned how much we loved this country, this land that had been our first home together. From the driest deserts to the snowiest mountaintops, our walk had led us through some of the remotest, highest, driest, coldest, hottest, windiest, harshest, kindest terrain in the United States. Someday, we decided, we would come back to the Rocky Mountains, to the place where the waters divide. Someday, we will call this land our home.

≈≈≈≈≈≈

The clearcut that serves to mark the border between the United States and Canada runs right down to Waterton Lakes, and then straight up, on the other side of the lake, to the Wilson mountain range. We arrived there on the twenty-fifth of August at 9:00 A.M.

At the border crossing at the northern terminus of the Pacific Crest Trail, the monument is hollow, and hikers traditionally drop in a note—announcing their intentions, or their triumph, as they leave from or arrive at, the Canadian border. Hoping that he could do the same here, Dan had composed a note for the monument.

"Arrived at the border today with my wife, Karen Berger," he wrote. "This site marks the completion of our hike of the Continental Divide National Scenic Trail. Last year, we started our hike on May 2 at Columbus, New Mexico, and finished it at the Flathead Port of Entry on October 31. Heavy snow forced us to road walk from Chief Joseph Pass to Canada. Our trip was 182 days and 2,580 miles in length. This year, we returned to Chief Joseph Pass on July 6 and hiked the official trail route to here. We were on the trail for 51 days and 571 miles. Three friends accompanied us on the last leg of our journey. Tom Carlin, an old hiking partner from the Appalachian Trail and Pacific Crest Trail, hiked with us from East Glacier. Anne and Steve Emry joined us from Swiftcurrent to here. It has been a long and wonderful journey. Often beautiful, often difficult, always worth every step. Even Odysseus returned home, and now our journey must end. Thank you to all the strangers, now friends, who helped us along the way. And thank you, Tom, Anne, and Steve, for being part of the grand finale."

I tried to think of something to add, a few well-chosen words that would sum up the experience for me. But Dan's note said what needed to be said. We had walked a long way, and now our walk was over. I signed my name. Unfortunately, there was no way to leave the note; the monument was shut tight.

We weren't completely finished: We still had to walk from the border to the township of Waterton Lakes, 4 miles farther. But it was just regular walking now. If someone had shown up in a motorboat, we'd have accepted a ride to the end of the lake. Our trip was over.

"Just think," Dan said, looking north. "If we come back to hike the Canadian Continental Divide, we'll have already done the first 4 miles."

If, indeed.

HIKER'S COMPANION:
An Update on the Continental Divide Trail

If your life span is measured in aeons, seven years isn't even the blink of an eye. But while the Continental Divide hasn't changed much, the Continental Divide National Scenic Trail has undergone a surprising amount of growth and development since we took those first steps away from the Mexican border in May 1990.

The trail is still not finished, but it is farther along than it was—by some estimates, the CDT is now about 70 percent complete. But the definition of "complete" is one of those squirmy little details that needs to be captured and pinned down. Does it mean the trail is cut, marked, and on the ground? Described in a guidebook? Marked on maps? Or does it mean that there's a jeep path you can follow? No one seems to be able to say for sure. We are, however, quite certain about what "complete" doesn't mean: It doesn't mean you can buy a guidebook, hop on the trail, and follow it without a map. Using that definition, it may be decades before the trail is complete.

But work is afoot. In 1995, a new nonprofit organization, the Continental Divide Trail Alliance, was formed. This Colorado-based group has assumed the role of collecting information about trail status, organizing volunteer trail work, publicizing the trail, coordinating corporate support, and collaborating with land management agency staff. Meanwhile, the venerable Continental Divide Trail Society continues to lobby for the most aesthetically pleasing, environmentally sound hiking route—a "quiet trail" in the words of the Continental Divide Trail's founder and visionary, Jim Wolf. The similar names of the two organizations and the overlap in some of their activities has, inevitably, led to confusion. In the future, perhaps these two groups will be able to build upon their common ground and bring one of the finest long trails in the world to completion.

To do so, they—and other trail advocates—have to work together. The land-use conflicts that we described are no less intense today than they were when we walked through clear-cuts and grazing lands in 1990. Timber, mining, water resource management, grazing, spotted owls, the embattled Endangered Species Act (up for reauthorization), and motorized trail use are all as timely and controversial today as when we first wrote about them.

Recreation use is growing, even as federal and state recreation budgets are shrinking. In 1996, Congress authorized the national parks and forests to experiment with fee-collection programs. Previously, national parks charged fees only for admission and for the use of developed campsites. Now, you'll pay a higher entrance fee. And in some national parks, not only will you have to stand in line for a backcountry camping permit, you'll have to pay for it, too. In the national forests, a few proposals are being tested, including implementation of yearly visitors' passes and parking fees at trailheads. Some wilderness advocates say it's about time recreationists paid to recreate. Others see the kernel of a dangerous juggernaut—one that might make our public lands off-limits to the very members of the public who need them most.

Trail use has not only increased, it has diversified. Mountain bikes, virtually unknown when the Continental Divide Trail's Comprehensive Plan was written, are a growing presence with increasing environmental impact on backcountry trails. Motorized off-trail vehicles are also on the rise, and the Forest Service has submitted a few horribly misguided proposals to allow them on sections of the CDT that have thus far been open only to nonmotorized use. Horsepackers, bicyclists, hikers, snowmobilers, and advocates for the handicapped have all expressed an interest in the trail. But can a single path meet the sometimes disparate needs of all these groups? Can one trail satisfy a long-distance backpacker's desire for a challenging climb on a talus slope, a handicapped trail user's need for paved access, and a horseman's need for an easily graded trail? Clearly, the trail can't be all things to all users. The decisions that are made will continue to shape the Continental Divide Trail—and the experiences of those who travel along it.

The following state-by-state information describes how some of the decisions made in the past several years have affected the trail. It also describes how the trail has changed since we hiked it.

NEW MEXICO

The border guard who waved us through on our way to Canada won't be seeing too many other CDT thru-hikers at the Columbus, New Mexico, border station. The Forest Service has since decided that the trail will officially start at the Antelope Wells station, which is closer to the Divide. This route will follow the border west for 12 miles until it intersects the Divide, then head north. As yet, there is no cut trail. Hikers who start at Antelope Wells either hike cross-country or follow high-grade gravel roads. Until a trail is actually cut, the Columbus route we described offers an attractive alternative, following a sequence of virtually unused jeep paths, with the occasional cross-country scramble up a dry creekbed or across a plain. It also offers some fine desert hiking through an area of historic significance.

In some parts of New Mexico's national forests, significant trail work has been done since 1990. New Mexico's Continental Divide includes large checkerboard parcels of BLM and private land, and these are the major stumbling blocks to acquiring a protected corridor. Issues such as whether to use back roads or to construct new trails and how to resolve conflicts with other land uses continue to bedevil the trail-planning process. In southern New Mexico, the folks we met at Uncle Bill's Bar—and their counterparts in other small ranching communities—have little use for federal presence on what they feel should be state lands, and no use for federal projects (like a hiking trail) perceived to benefit outsiders. In northern New Mexico, the debate is conducted with a Spanish accent: The problems surrounding the issue of old grant lands and local autonomy affect any use of contested public lands, including their use for something so innocuous as a hiking trail. Unfortunately, in some cases authorities have opted for the easy way out, and have simply suggested putting the "trail" on high-grade—even paved—roads.

Because so much of the trail's route is undecided, long-distance hikers continue to have enormous difficulties planning a route through these sagebrush drylands of cactus and endless sun. Many hikers road-walk mile after mile, and report, not surprisingly, that New Mexico is "boring." In fact, New Mexico offers some stunning landscapes: the vast horizons of its mesas, the brilliance of its redrock country, the endless skies of the southern desert. But in between the designated sections of the CDT, you'll need to plan your own route, using USGS topographic maps to help you find water and guide you on bushwhacks.

A final New Mexico note: The wonderful Ghost Ranch has had to give up its claim as the home of the oldest dinosaur ever found. Since we visited, a specimen that predates the New Mexican *Coelophysis* has been unearthed in South America.

Mail drops: We resupplied in Deming, Silver City, Reserve, Quemado, Continental Divide, Cuba, Abiquiu (at Ghost Ranch), and Tres Piedras. Deming is on the route if you start at Columbus, but not if you start at Antelope Wells. The official routing of the trail will take it closer to Pie Town than Reserve. In addition, some hikers resupply in Chama.

COLORADO

In Colorado, the trail is in much better shape, with a route designated nearly from one end of the state to the other. Guidebooks are also available, which make planning much easier. But take statements that "the trail is completed through Colorado" with a grain of salt. While a trail does indeed exist through much of Colorado, it is not always clearly marked. You still need good maps and the ability to use them.

A few sections in Colorado remain undesignated, and even when designated, will remain controversial. One of them is the spectacular high-country route between Copper Mountain and Rollins Pass—the site of our rugged and difficult windswept traverse. Like so many trail decisions, the final routing will be a matter of consensus. Almost by definition, that means it can't plummet down the difficult and frightening talus slope, teeter across the treacherous ledge over Ice Lake, and then scramble up the other side. Consensus never leads to routes like that. The "liability people" worry about the thunderstorms and the footway, user groups representing horsepackers and mountain bikers complain about accessibility, environmentalists talk about the fragile arctic-alpine vegetation, and nearby property owners say "not in my backyard." The route we took atop the Divide is anything but easy, and in bad weather it can be dangerous. But the experience to be had along those 20 or 30 miles, swinging from high peak to high peak 13,000 feet up in the barren tundra, is unforgettable—like seeing the Grand Canyon, the Himalayas, or Machu Picchu for the first time. My advice to hikers: In good weather, if you're feeling strong, buy a map and take the high road. It is, after all, the Continental Divide Trail. And that— being up there in the clouds—*that* is the Divide.

Mail drops: Pagosa Springs, Creede (both require long hitches), Garfield, Twin Lakes, Winter Park, Copper Mountain, Silverthorne (no longer on the trail), Grand Lake, and Steamboat Springs. Some hikers use Lake City instead of Creede.

WYOMING

In 1990, we saw no sign of a national scenic trail: not one trailhead, not one CDT signpost, nothing. That's not quite true any more, but much work remains to be done, especially in the region in and surrounding the Great Divide Basin in southern Wyoming. Here, the routing will follow the eastern alignment of the Great Divide Basin, although the exact route has not been established. But even without a cut trail, this area offers good dry-country hiking, including infrequently used jeep trails and a sufficient, if not abundant, amount of water. Many long-distance hikers walk the main road straight through the middle of the Great Divide Basin, perhaps in an effort to make up time lost in the mountains of Colorado or the snows of Montana. But the long way is worth the effort. It remains, however, map-and-compass country.

In Yellowstone National Park, thanks are due to trail authorities, who have become markedly more cooperative and sensitive to the needs of long-distance hikers. It is now much easier for people arriving on foot to get the necessary permits to camp in the park. Another change in Yellowstone concerns the wolf song we thought we heard: Back in 1990, it was thought that no wolves lived in the park. But since our trip, a small population of wolves has been reintroduced to Yellowstone, and appears to be thriving, despite ongoing controversy between conservationists and ranchers.

Mail drops: Wyoming was the most challenging state of all in which to resupply because Rawlins was the only actual town near the trail. We also resupplied at a service station near Muddy Gap, the Sweetwater Station General Store, two backcountry lodges, and Yellowstone National Park's Old Faithful Post Office (which lost one of our boxes). Once you plan your route, write to the chambers of commerce for Lander, Rawlins, and Jackson Hole for information about any businesses near your route. Some people have supplied in the near ghost town of Jeffrey City or hitched to Lander.

IDAHO AND MONTANA

Idaho and Montana, like Colorado, boast large sections of completed trail, but (again, like Colorado) the statement that the trail is "completed" should, when encountered, be regarded with skepticism. The Southwest Montana Interagency Map (available from any of the Forest Service offices in southwestern Montana) shows the routing of the Continental Divide Trail; however, a few minor sections are either inaccurate or out-of-date, so hikers need to verify information with individual ranger stations. There is now a good route through southern Montana's Centennial Mountains, and newly constructed trail also runs through the Bitterroots (the "steep hillsides" section described in the Lewis and Clark diaries) south of Lost Trail Pass. Heading north, the section of trail between the Anaconda Pintlar Wilderness and the Helena National Forest is probably in need of the most work; much of the route still follows old logging roads. North of Rogers Pass, the trail is generally in good shape, especially in the Scapegoat and Bob Marshall wilderness areas.

Glacier National Park remains problematic for long-distance hikers. We had hoped that our experience with the permit-issuing bureaucracy was (or would become) atypical, but reports in the Continental Divide Trail Society newsletter continue to describe battles with the permit system and a procedure that makes it difficult to hike the length of the park.

The official terminus of the Continental Divide Trail, it should be noted, is the American-Canadian border station on the main road east of Glacier National Park. However, a more dramatic route—preferred by hikers, trail advocates, and members of the park's trails staff— enters Canada at Waterton Lakes. It's a much more pleasing way to end a 3,000-mile odyssey, but if that's how you decide to enter Canada, you will need to check in at the police station when you get there.

Mail drops (unless noted, they're in Montana): We used Mack's Inn (Idaho), Lima, Gibbonsville (Idaho), Butte, Helena, Lincoln, the Benchmark Wilderness Ranch (on the road between the Scapegoat and Bob Marshall wildernesses), and East Glacier. Anaconda and Basin are two other possibilities.

RESOURCES AND GUIDEBOOKS

Continental Divide Trail Society
3704 North Charles Street #601
Baltimore, MD 21218
(410) 235-9610

It is extremely difficult to describe in a guidebook a trail that is not fully in place on the ground. A person hiking on a blazed trail uses a guidebook for reference: "At 4.2, come to a spring and turn left" tells the hiker that he's walked 4.2 miles when he comes to the spring. But if the trail is blazed, he doesn't really need the guidebook for instructions about what to do at the spring; he just follows the blazes. Most hikers use guidebooks to plan their days (campsites, springs, climbs, and the like) and to keep track of where they are—not to tell them where to go. But on the CDT, it's the "where to go" that is desperately needed. The simple instruction to turn left often isn't enough: If the hiker is relying on a guidebook for directions (as opposed to map and compass), she needs, "At 4.2, come to a spring, turn left, crawl under the barbed-wire fence, then follow a 270-degree bearing for 100 yards." If you consider for a moment how badly most people give directions, you'll understand how difficult it is to describe actual routes.

Jim Wolf's guidebooks, published by the Continental Divide Trail Society, are a model of coherent guidebook writing. There is more information, word for word, in these guidebooks than in any others we've ever seen. The sensible small format is perfect for weight-conscious backpackers. Jim has been working on the CDT for more than twenty years, and sometimes disagrees with the Forest Service over where the route should go. So occasionally, he offers his own alternatives in addition to the most current "official" route. Most of the guidebooks are written southbound, so if at all possible, follow them that way—you'll find it easier.

In addition to the guidebooks, the CDTS sells map sets (including maps by Trails Illustrated) and guidebook supplements (which bring the older guidebooks up-to-date). It also publishes a biannual membership newsletter to keep hikers current on routing changes, trail controversies, and environmental issues.

The Continental Divide Trail Alliance
P.O. Box 628
Pine, CO 80470
(303) 838-3760

Formed in 1995, the Continental Divide Trail Alliance is a nonprofit organization that aims to coordinate the general public, corporations, and government agencies in order to "promote, construct, and manage" a primitive trail along the Divide. To this end, it has sponsored several summits devoted to strategic planning. It is also in the process of publishing a manual for trail users.

In 1997, the CDTA sponsored a project called Uniting Along the Divide. Thirty-one teams, each comprising a hiker, a corporate sponsor, and an agency partner (in English, that means someone from the Forest Service, Park Service, or Bureau of Land Management), were assigned to collect information about 100-mile segments, including trail status and improvements needed. The results will be published by Westcliffe Publishers in a book by photographer and trail activist John Fielder.

Westcliffe Publishers
P.O. Box 1261
Englewood, CO 80150
(800) 523-3692

A new series of CDT books is being published by Westcliffe Publishers, including illustrated guides for the four states (for guidebook purposes, Montana and Idaho count as one, because the trail most often follows their common border). Westcliffe will also be publishing photo narratives about the trail.

Sitting at our desks seven years after our great adventure began, we look back on an experience that was the first of a series of great adventures. Our hearts often return to the Divide. It was the first home we ever had together, and the place we still hope to call home someday. This land and the experience it offers remains one of America's great wilderness adventures. We urge hikers to show their support by planting boot on trail, volunteering for a trail maintenance project, lobbying for the protection of primitive trails, and joining the organizations that are trying to protect and complete this enormous, inimitable national resource.

Finally, on a personal note: Our hiking companions Sue Lockwood and Gordon Smith are once again able to backpack. In 1996, Gordon donated one of his kidneys to Sue, freeing her from the tyranny of the dialysis machine. On a sad note, Sue's seeing-eye dog Mac died in 1995 at the age of fifteen. Mac worked (and for Mac, working meant walking anywhere from 1,000 to 3,000 miles a year) until age fourteen, well beyond the average retirement age (about ten years) for a guide dog. More proof, if you need it, of the relationship between hiking and health. If you see Sue on the trail these days, her new dog's name is Buddy.

—Karen Berger and Daniel R. Smith
Bronxville, New York
May 1997

Index